WINDOWS HOME NETWORKING MADE EASY

Home & Small Office Connectivity

By James Bernstein

Copyright © 2019 by James Bernstein. All rights reserved.

All rights reserved. This book or any portion thereof
may not be reproduced or used in any manner whatsoever
without the express written permission of the publisher
except for the use of brief quotations in a book review.

Printed in the United States of America

Bernstein, James
Windows Home Networking Made Easy
Book 8 in the Computers Made Easy series

For more information on reproducing sections of this book or sales of this book,
go to www.onlinecomputertips.com

Contents

Introduction 5

Chapter 1 – Installing Windows 6
    Clean Installation vs. Upgrade Installation 6
    How to Install Windows 7
    Windows Update 14

Chapter 2 – Networking Basics 16
    IP Addresses and Configuration 16
    Dynamic and Static IP Addresses 19
    Manually Configuring an IP Address 20
    DHCP 23
    DNS 24
    Wireless Setup 24
    LAN vs. WAN 28
    Network Adapter 28
    Hub 29
    Router 31
    Making Physical Network Connections 32

Chapter 3 – Setting up Workgroups 36
    Peer to Peer vs. Client-Server Networks 36
    Workgroups 39
    Domains 39
    Computer Names 40
    Setting Up Your Workgroup 47
    Hosts File 49

Chapter 4 – User Accounts 54

    User Account Types 54

    Local Accounts vs. Microsoft Accounts 55

    Creating User Accounts 57

    Groups 68

Chapter 5 – Sharing Resources 72

    Resource Sharing and Permissions 72

    UNC Paths 74

    Windows Firewall 76

    Sharing Files and Folders 82

    Mapping a Network Drive 116

    Administrative Shares 120

    Sharing Printers 131

    Networked Printers 138

    Remote Connections 141

Chapter 6 - Troubleshooting 151

    Hardware Issues 151

    Cabling Issues 154

    Network Configuration 155

    Permission Issues 158

    Wireless and Internet Troubleshooting 164

What's Next? 170

About the Author 172

Index 173

Introduction

With technology growing at an ever increasingly faster rate, we find that more and more of our devices are connected to each other, and now we are at the point where we can control our entire home from our smartphone or computer. With this in mind, there is still a need to keep things as simple as possible for those who might not be as tech savvy as others so everyone has a chance to be "connected".

Microsoft has done a pretty good job making things easy for PC users at home and even at the office with its Windows operating system. That's most likely why it's the most popular and widely used OS in the world. (Good luck going to your local electronics store and buying a new computer with anything else but Windows!)

With that in mind, there is a need to get our Windows based computers communicating with each other so we can do things such as share files and printers. This is where networking comes into play, and it is the technology used to connect not only our computers, but many other devices as well.

The goal of this book is to teach you how to network your Windows-based computers together so they can talk to each other and share information. This process is done differently at home and at small offices in comparison to larger corporations. Sure you can do it the way they do at work on your home network, but that gets much more complicated, and a lot more expensive. You will learn how to set up Workgroups, user accounts, file shares, printer shares, and even do a bit of network troubleshooting just for some added fun.

I will be using computers running Windows 10 for this book and all of the examples, but if you still have Windows 7 or 8, then things will be very similar. Since Microsoft is always updating Windows 10, (unfortunately) they like to change how things are done from time to time (sometimes for no good reason), so if you find something is not exactly how I said it should be, then you might want to see if Microsoft has released a major update to mess us all up again!

So, on that note, let's start getting some computers connected!

Chapter 1 – Installing Windows

When you buy a new PC from the store or online, it will come with the operating system installed, so, for the most part, you won't need to worry about doing something like that yourself. But, if you are the type that likes to build your own computers so you have the components you want inside your PC, then you will need to install Windows manually afterward.

If your computers are already configured with Windows, then you can skip this chapter (unless you want to learn how to install Windows for future reference or are planning on upgrading to Windows 10 from Windows 7 or 8). Installing Windows is a fairly simple process, and once you do it a few times, you can pretty much do it in your sleep. It's actually pretty hard to mess up a Windows installation unless you do something like install it on the wrong hard drive!

The key thing to remember before you begin the installation process is to make sure you don't have any files on your hard drive that you want to keep because they will most likely be erased depending on if you are doing a clean (new) installation or an upgrade. If you do have files you want to keep, make sure to back them up onto something like an external hard drive, USB flash drive, or burn them to a DVD.

Clean Installation vs. Upgrade Installation
There are two main ways to install Windows on your computer, and which one you choose will depend on what you are trying to accomplish. A clean installation will wipe out any existing copy of Windows you have installed on your hard drive and install a new copy of Windows with the default settings. This is your only option when you have a blank hard drive, or have built your own computer with new parts.

During a clean installation, you will tell Windows what drive to install itself on (if you have more than one), otherwise you will install it on the one drive installed in your computer. You can decide if you want Windows to use the entire drive for the installation, or if you want some space left over for a second partition that you can use later. This is common if you want to have a separate drive with its own drive letter that you can use for things such as file storage etc. (I will go over the installation process later in this chapter.)

Chapter 1 – Installing Windows

An upgrade installation will replace your older version of Windows, such as Windows 7 or Windows 8, with Windows 10 and keep all of your files, programs, installed printers, and other settings intact. It's still a good idea to back up your important files before doing an upgrade installation because there is always the chance that something can go wrong. You may end up with a corrupt version of Windows, and then end up having to do a clean installation regardless.

> **Tip**
> I prefer clean installations of Windows compared to doing upgrades, because when you do an upgrade there is a chance you may keep any existing problems you might have had with your previous version of Windows.

How to Install Windows
Like I mentioned before, the process for installing Windows is pretty simple, and I will now go over the steps to perform a clean installation of Windows 10. You can perform an upgrade from within Windows or from booting to the Windows DVD, but for a clean installation, you will want to boot from the Windows DVD to start the installation process. If your computer is not set to read from your CD\DVD drive first, then you will need to either go into the BIOS and change the boot order, or look for the key that needs to be pressed on startup that will let you choose the boot device. Some computers make it obvious while others don't give you that information. (Many times it's the F12 key.) For information on how to change your boot order, check out the link below.

https://www.onlinecomputertips.com/support-categories/pc-troubleshooting/238-changing-your-computer-s-boot-order

Once you have booted to the Windows DVD, you will be asked to choose your language, time and currency format, and keyboard input (figure 1.1). Normally the defaults will be correct and you can then click on *Next* and then on the *Install now* button.

Chapter 1 – Installing Windows

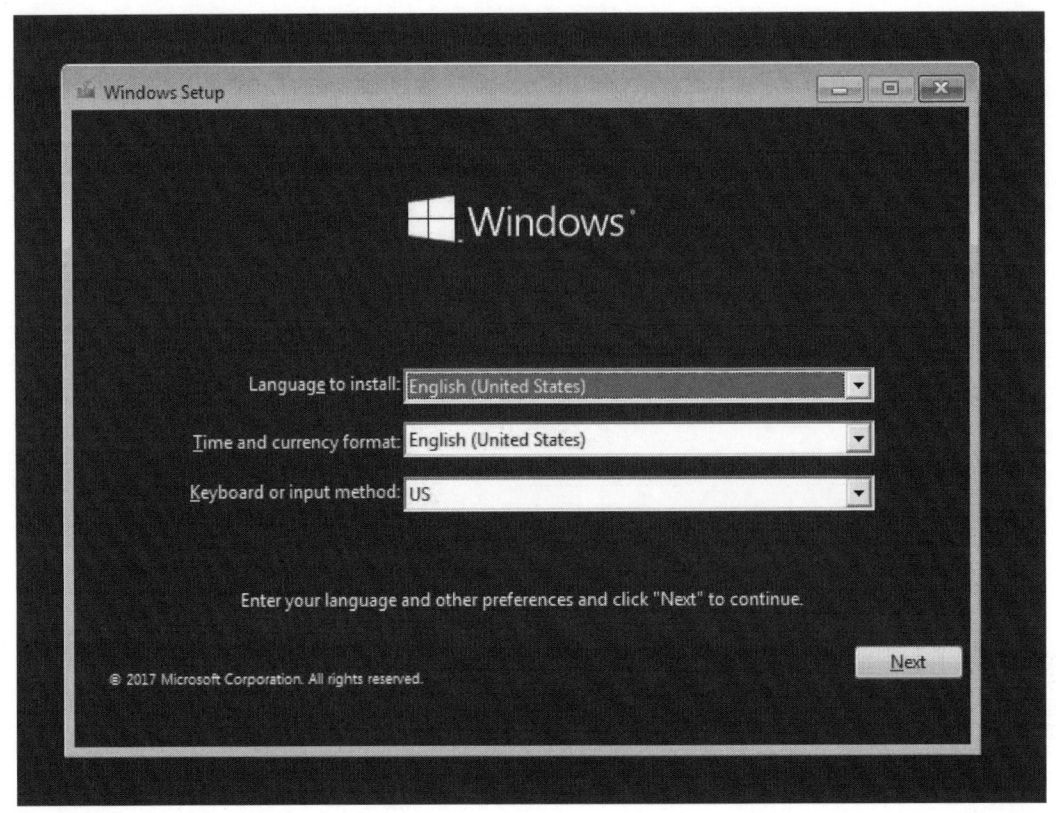

Figure 1.1

On the next screen you will be asked to type in your Windows product key, which will be included with the Windows 10 DVD (figure 1.2). If you are using a DVD that you borrowed from someone and your computer originally came with Windows 10, then you can enter the product key from the sticker that should be someplace on your computer's case. If you don't have a key, you can still install Windows and then enter one later, or use it in trial mode for a limited period of time.

Chapter 1 – Installing Windows

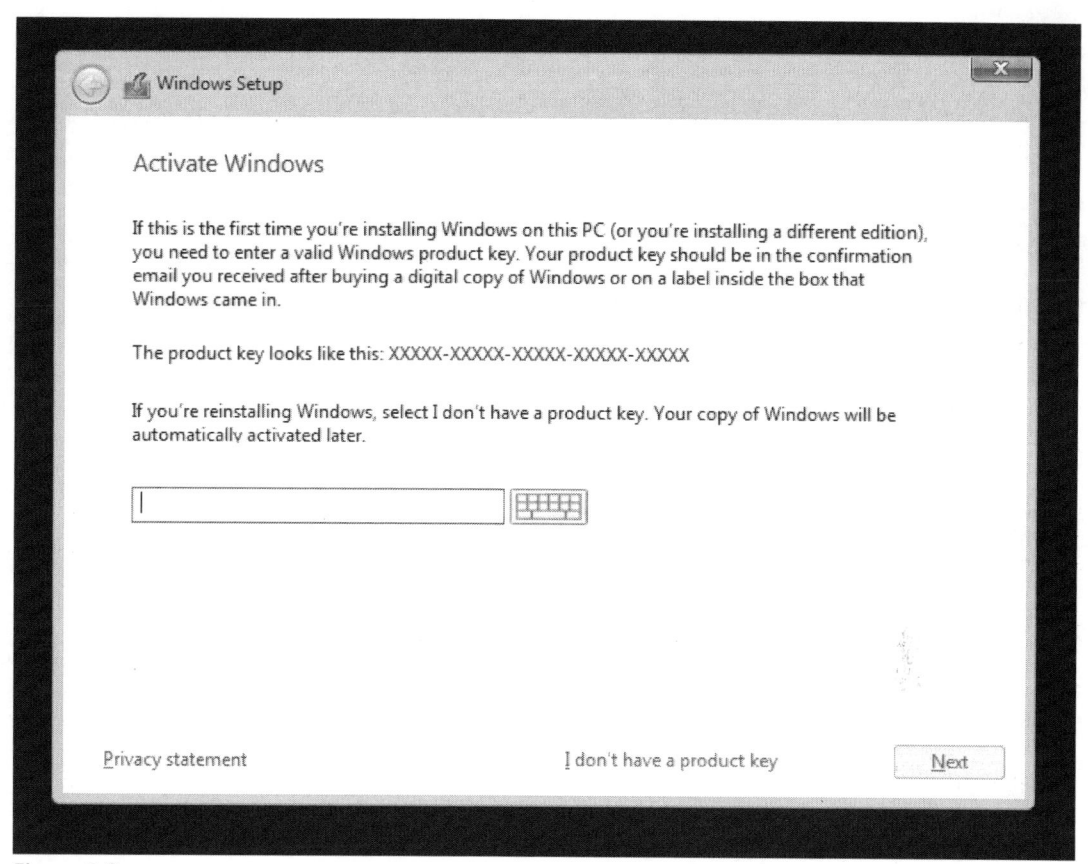

![Figure 1.2 - Windows Setup Activate Windows screen]

Figure 1.2

Next, you will be able to choose which edition of Windows you want to install. The choices you see here will vary depending on your installation media (figure 1.3). Just make sure to choose the one that matches your product key. If you entered the product key, then you might not see this screen because it will choose the edition for you based on that key.

Chapter 1 – Installing Windows

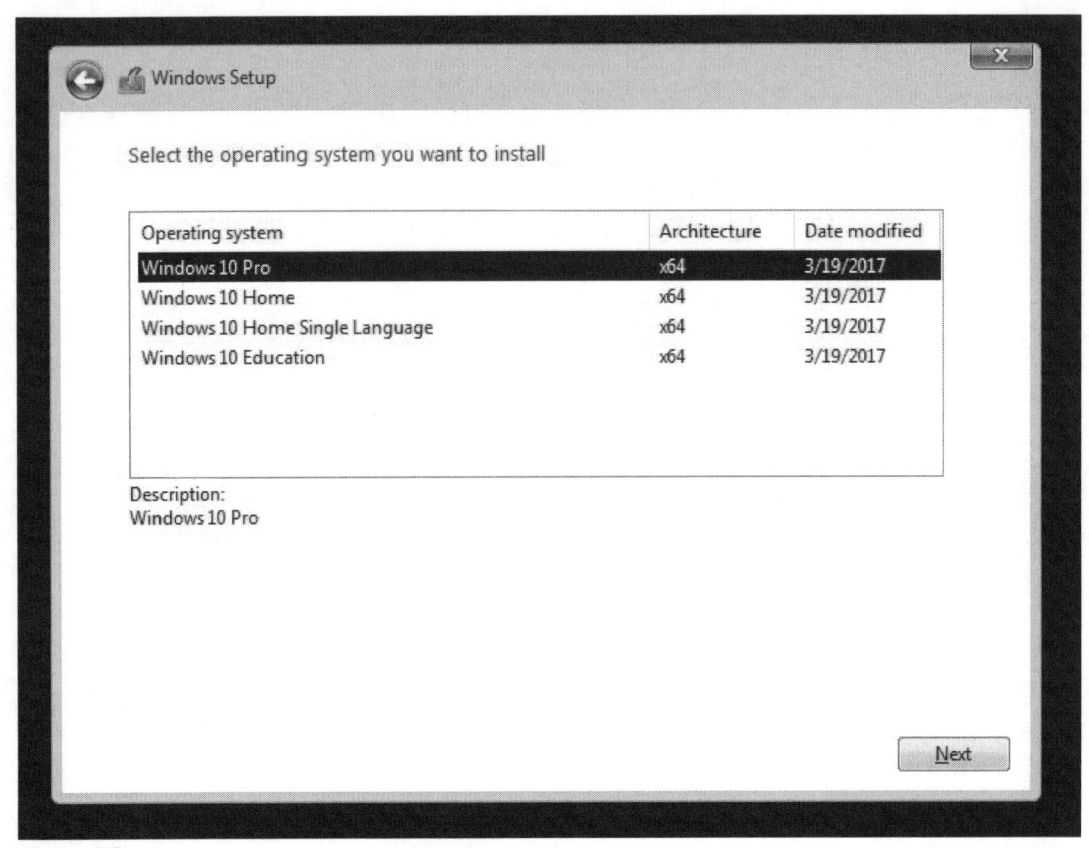

Figure 1.3

Next, you will check the box that says you accept the license terms that are listed. (Most people don't read them, but you can if you are feeling up to it!)

The next window is where you will have to make a choice based on what type of installation you are doing (figure 1.4). Since we are doing a clean installation, we will pick the second option that says *Custom: Install Windows only (advanced)*. You will notice in the description that it says that your files, settings, and applications will not be moved to Windows with this option, so make sure you back up your files!

> **Tip:** When installing a clean version of Windows on your existing computer, another thing to remember is that you will need to reinstall any programs that don't come with Windows, so make sure you have your installation media for your software.

Chapter 1 – Installing Windows

Windows Setup

Which type of installation do you want?

Upgrade: Install Windows and keep files, settings, and applications
The files, settings, and applications are moved to Windows with this option. This option is only available when a supported version of Windows is already running on the computer.

Custom: Install Windows only (advanced)
The files, settings, and applications aren't moved to Windows with this option. If you want to make changes to partitions and drives, start the computer using the installation disc. We recommend backing up your files before you continue.

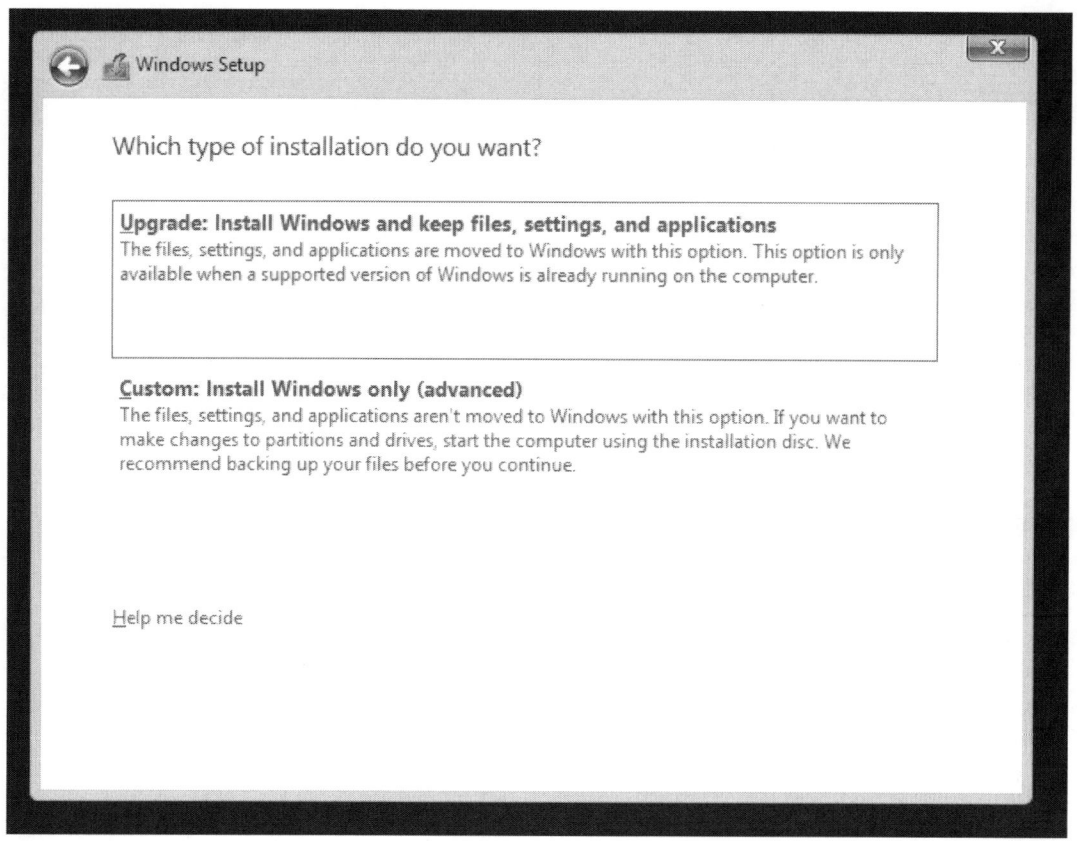

Help me decide

Figure 1.4

The next section is where you will need to choose what hard drive you are going to install Windows 10 on, as well as how much of the hard drive you are going to use (figure 1.5). If you click on Next, it will use the selected hard drive and create a partition using all of the space on the drive. Then it will format the drive to get it ready to install Windows on.

If you click on New, then you can decide how much of the total drive capacity will be used for Windows. Then the rest will be listed as "unused" and you can create additional drives with it after Windows is installed.

Chapter 1 – Installing Windows

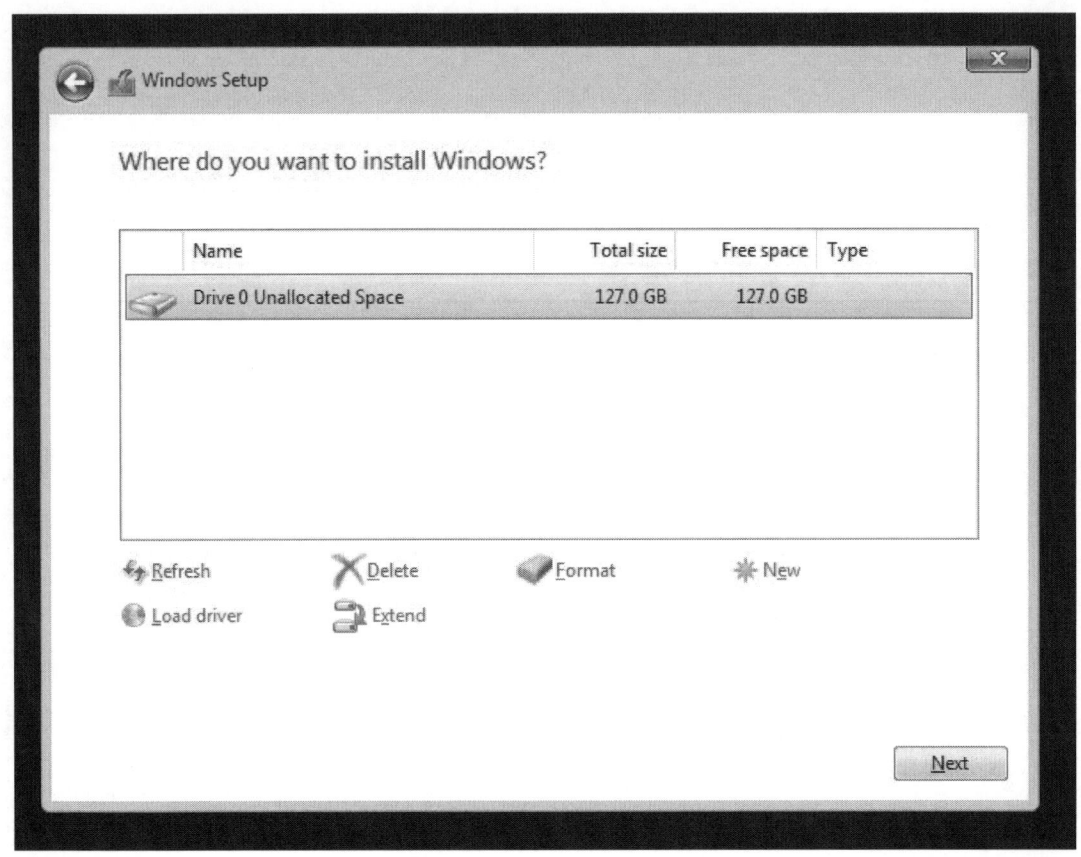

Figure 1.5

Now you can see in figure 1.6 that the installation is running. This process will take a bit of time depending on the performance of the hardware of your computer (such as processor speed, hard drive type, and the amount of RAM installed).

Chapter 1 – Installing Windows

![Windows Setup - Installing Windows screen showing status: Copying Windows files, Getting files ready for installation, Installing features (all checked), Installing updates (in progress), Finishing up]

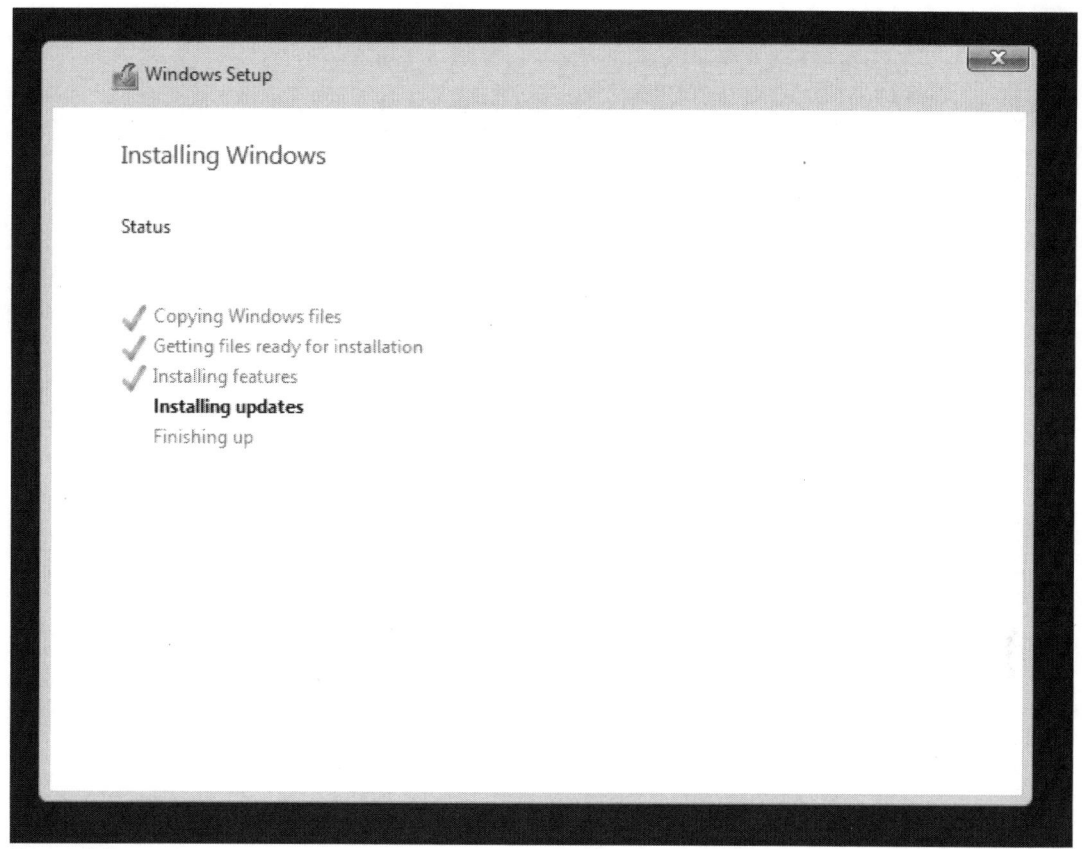

Figure 1.6

After the installation is complete, Windows will restart the computer and prepare your hardware for use with Windows. Then Windows will start up and begin its basic configuration where it will ask you to specify your region, keyboard layout, network (Internet) connection settings, and at the end will ask you to create a username and password for Windows. You will also be prompted to enable Cortana, which is the built in "personal assistant" for Windows 10, and is similar to Siri used on Apple devices.

Next, you will be presented with a bunch of privacy settings that you can disable if you are the type that wants to stay under the radar and doesn't want everything you do shared with Microsoft (figure 1.7). I usually turn all of these settings off because it doesn't really help you to have them enabled. There are even more of these privacy settings that you can change after Windows is installed.

Chapter 1 – Installing Windows

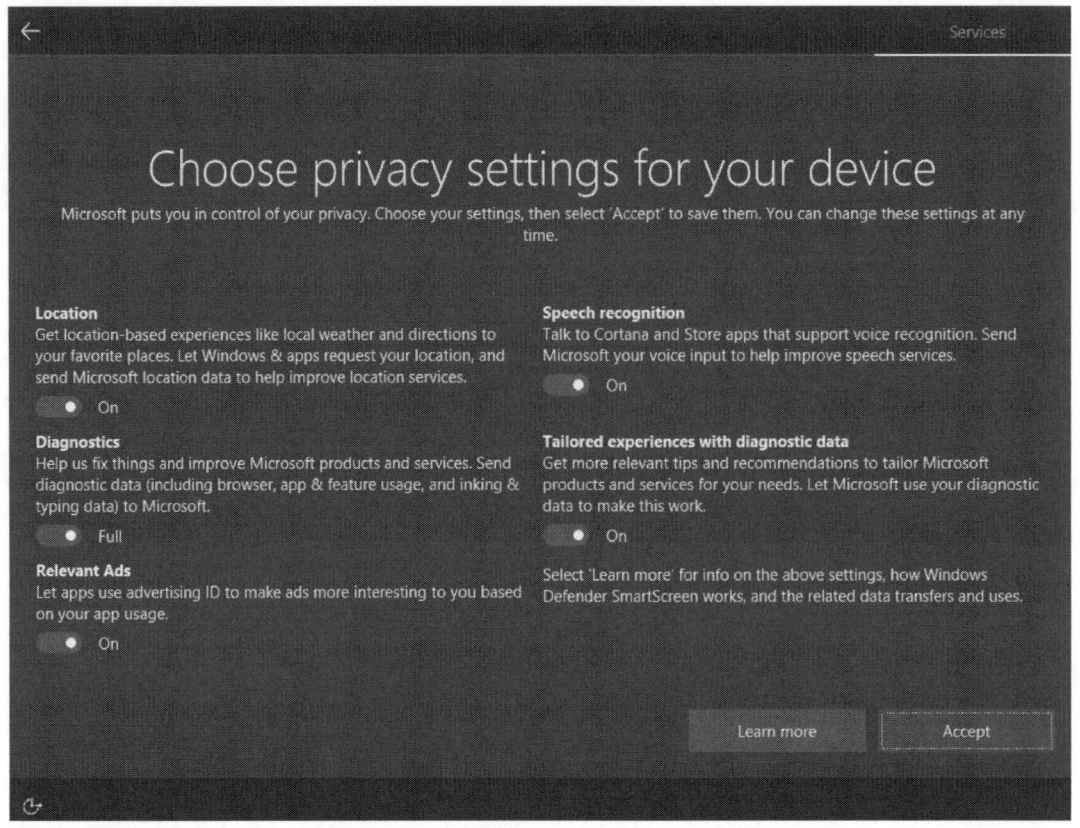

Figure 1.7

After a few more minutes of waiting for Windows to finish configuring itself, you will be presented with a login screen where you will log in with the username and password that you created during the installation, and you are ready to go!

Windows Update
One last thing I want to mention in this chapter is Windows Update and what these updates do to your computer. Windows Updates consist of fixes, patches, and upgrades that are applied to your computer to fix bugs, patch security holes, and add new features to Windows. If your computer is connected to the Internet, then these updates are downloaded and installed automatically.

One downside to the way Windows does its updates is that you can't stop them from being installed like you could with previous versions of Windows. Also, if you are not in front of your computer to stop the reboots that are required after many of these updates, then you might lose any unsaved documents that you have open

Chapter 1 – Installing Windows

during the reboot. (It's always a good idea to save your work before walking away from your computer for any extended period of time.)

You can view the Windows Update settings and update history from the Windows settings, then *Update & Security*, and then *Windows Update*. You can click on *Change active hours* to tell Windows what time period you are active on your computer so it won't automatically restart it during that time period (figure 1.8). You can choose a time span of up to 18 hours.

Active hours

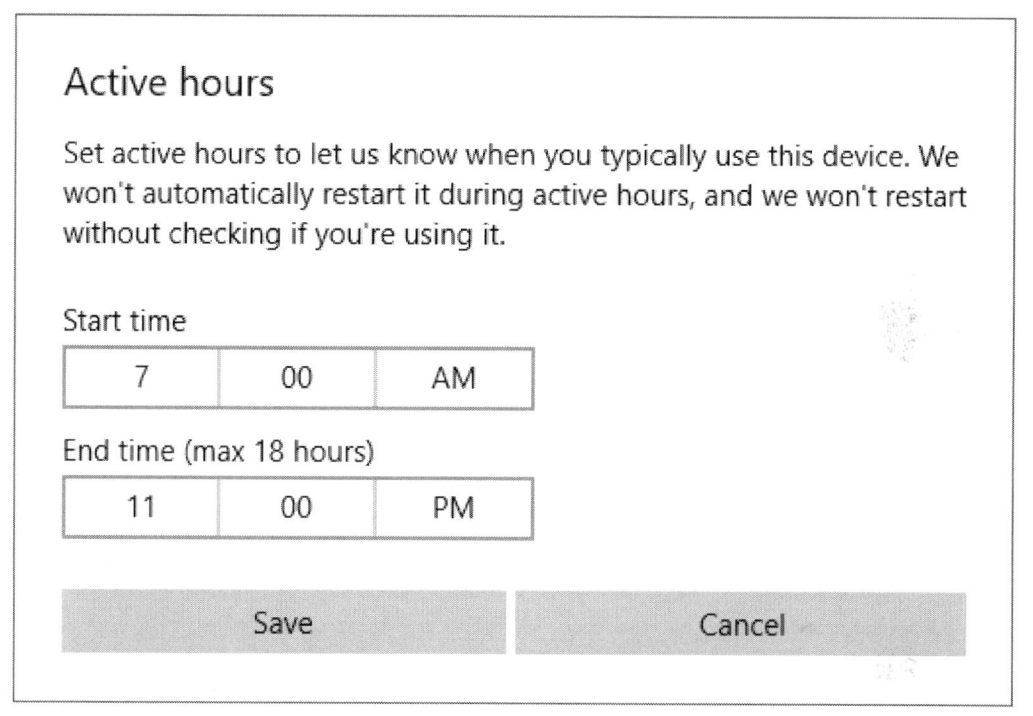

Set active hours to let us know when you typically use this device. We won't automatically restart it during active hours, and we won't restart without checking if you're using it.

Start time

| 7 | 00 | AM |

End time (max 18 hours)

| 11 | 00 | PM |

Save   Cancel

Figure 1.8

Chapter 2 – Networking Basics

Before getting started networking our computers, it's a good idea to get an overview of how networking works and some of the tools you can use to help troubleshoot issues. This book is not meant to be an advanced networking book, but there are still some advanced topics that I would like to go over to get you one step closer to the more advanced topics.

IP Addresses and Configuration
Computers and other devices on a network use IP addresses to communicate with each other. MAC (media access control) addresses are also used for network communication, but that's a story for another day!

An IP address is a number (for the sake of simplicity) that is assigned to a computer that is then used to communicate with other computers and devices that also have an IP address assigned to them. It consists of four sets of numbers (called octets) and looks something like this – 192.168.10.240. There are several types of address classes, and things can get really complicated, so I will just stick with the basics so you have an understanding of how IP addresses are used. For now, we are mostly using IPv4, but soon will be using IPv6 since we are out of public version 4 addresses.

When you want to connect to another computer on the network (or even to a website), you can type in its name, and then a service called DNS (Domain Name System) translates that computer or website name into the IP address of that computer or web server. That way you don't have to memorize IP addresses and only need to know the computer name or website name. On a network, you can't have the same IP address assigned to two devices otherwise there will be a conflict.

There are also what is known as public and private IP addresses. Public IP addresses are used for things such as web servers, and are unique to that server (meaning that IP address can't be used on any other public\Internet device in the world). Private IP addresses, on the other hand, can be used by anyone on their internal network and assigned to devices that only communicate with other internal devices. That doesn't mean these internal devices can't connect to the Internet or other public devices. To do this, the private IP address is translated to a public IP address through the process of NAT (Network Address Translation), which is usually done on your router. This process is beyond the scope of this book, but feel free to look it up if you want to learn more about it.

So, the bottom line is that your computer needs an IP address to communicate on the network, and even to get on the Internet. There are a few ways to find the IP

Chapter 2 – Networking Basics

address of your computer, and I will now go over what I think is the easiest one. If you open a command prompt (which is a way to run text based commands on your computer like they did before Windows), you can type in a certain command to find your IP address information. To open a command prompt, simply type in **cmd** from the search box or from Cortana and you will be shown a window with a black background and flashing cursor (figure 2.1).

Figure 2.1

From this box, all you need to do is type in the command **ipconfig** to be shown the basic IP configuration of your computer (figure 2.2). Keep in mind that the information given here will vary from computer to computer based on how many network connections you have, such as wireless and Ethernet (plugged in), and so on.

Chapter 2 – Networking Basics

```
C:\Windows\System32\cmd.exe

Microsoft Windows [Version 10.0.17134.165]
(c) 2018 Microsoft Corporation. All rights reserved.

C:\Windows\System32>ipconfig

Windows IP Configuration

Ethernet adapter Ethernet:

   Connection-specific DNS Suffix  . :
   IPv6 Address. . . . . . . . . . . : 2605:e000:7ec8:800:353c:bf16:b407:5333
   Temporary IPv6 Address. . . . . . : 2605:e000:7ec8:800:85:8694:7ad5:a86
   Temporary IPv6 Address. . . . . . : 2605:e000:7ec8:800:741f:bf72:8974:11cf
   Link-local IPv6 Address . . . . . : fe80::353c:bf16:b407:5333%8
   IPv4 Address. . . . . . . . . . . : 192.168.0.2
   Subnet Mask . . . . . . . . . . . : 255.255.255.0
   Default Gateway . . . . . . . . . : fe80::2ac:e0ff:fe89:5227%8
                                       192.168.0.1

Ethernet adapter VirtualBox Host-Only Network:

   Connection-specific DNS Suffix  . :
   Link-local IPv6 Address . . . . . : fe80::8889:8166:8ac0:5383%24
   IPv4 Address. . . . . . . . . . . : 192.168.56.1
   Subnet Mask . . . . . . . . . . . : 255.255.255.0
   Default Gateway . . . . . . . . . :

Wireless LAN adapter Local Area Connection* 3:

   Media State . . . . . . . . . . . : Media disconnected
```

Figure 2.2

As you can see in my example, the IP address is **192.168.0.2**. For now, you only need to be concerned with the IPv4 address, but as I mentioned, soon we will all be using IPv6 addresses since we are out of publicly available IPv4 addresses to assign to new public devices. You might also notice that I have a network connection for a VirtualBox host and Wireless LAN adapter. You need to know which network interface you are dealing with when running this command to get the information you need.

> There is a more advanced version of the ipconfig command you can run to get a lot more detailed information about all of your network connections. To run this command just type in **ipconfig /all**.

Another thing to note from figure 2.2 is the Subnet Mask and Default Gateway settings. For a basic home or small business network, these will be the same for all computers. The subnet mask is used to differentiate between different subnets or networks if you have more than one. You will need something with routing capabilities to communicate between these different networks.

The gateway address is the IP address of the device that will take you out of your network to a different network. So, for larger networks, this would be the address of your router, and for your home or small office network it will be the address of the modem or router used to connect to your ISP so your computers can send and receive traffic back and forth from the Internet.

Dynamic and Static IP Addresses
Another thing I want to mention about IP addresses is the difference between a static IP address and a dynamic IP address. Each one has its place in networking, so it's important to know the basic difference between the two.

A static IP address is an address that does not change over time unless changed manually. It is used when you need the IP address or network location to remain the same consistently. A good example of this is for a web server. If you go to www.google.com, you are really going to the IP address of 66.102.7.99 (actually, they have many IP addresses for their web servers). If this were to suddenly change, you would not be able to get to Google unless you knew the new IP address, or until Google updated their DNS records. Most of the time your servers at work will use static IP addresses so you will always be able to access them with the same address, and so that your network administrators will know how to get to them if DNS is not working.

Dynamic IP addresses are what you will most likely be dealing with at home for your computer and other devices on your network. A dynamic IP address is an address that can change from time to time. It is mostly used when having a consistent IP address is not necessary. An example of this would be the IP address your modem or router uses for the internet and assigns to your computer when it boots up. When you reboot your computer, there is a chance that your computer will be assigned a different IP address based on how long the lease for that address was configured. This process is done using DHCP. Your workstation at work most likely has a dynamic IP address since there is usually no need for it to have the same IP address all the time. Dynamic IP addresses are leased from the DHCP server for a period of time, and then your computer will request a renewal or a new IP address when the lease expires. At home, your router typically acts as the DHCP server.

Chapter 2 – Networking Basics

Manually Configuring an IP Address

IP addresses can be assigned statically (manually by you) or dynamically (automatically) by a DHCP server, but if you are the type that likes to do things yourself, then it's easy to assign an IP address to your computer manually. Before doing so, you just need to make sure you have all the appropriate information handy, otherwise you could be looking at communication problems.

There is more than one way to configure a manual IP address, but I will go over one of the easier methods. What you need to do is go into the Windows Control Panel and find *Network and Sharing Center*. Then click on the link on the left that says *Change adapter settings*. Find the network adapter that you are currently using in the list. (You might only have one, and if that's the case, it makes things easier.)

Next, you should right click on the appropriate adapter and choose *Properties*, and from the Networking tab click on *Internet Protocol Version 4* and click *Properties* again.

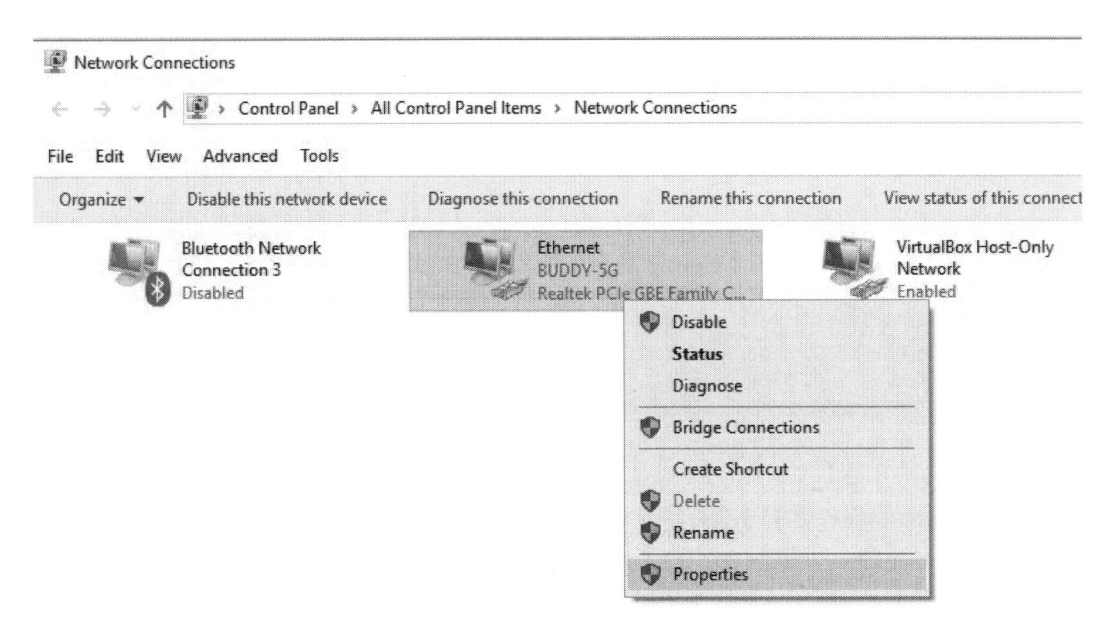

Figure 2.3

If your computer is set to get its IP address automatically from a DHCP server, then your properties box will look similar to figure 2.4.

20

Chapter 2 – Networking Basics

Figure 2.4

To manually assign an IP address to your computer, click on the radio button that says *Use the following IP address* and enter in the appropriate information for the IP address, subnet mask, and default gateway (figure 2.5). Just make sure the IP address you use is not in use on your network by any other device. For the DNS settings, you will need to find out what DNS servers are being used on your network, which will most likely be the public DNS servers used by your ISP.

> **Tip**
> You can see your DNS settings by running the **ipconfig /all** command before manually changing your IP address. Or you can just leave the radio button for *Obtain DNS server address automatically* checked.

21

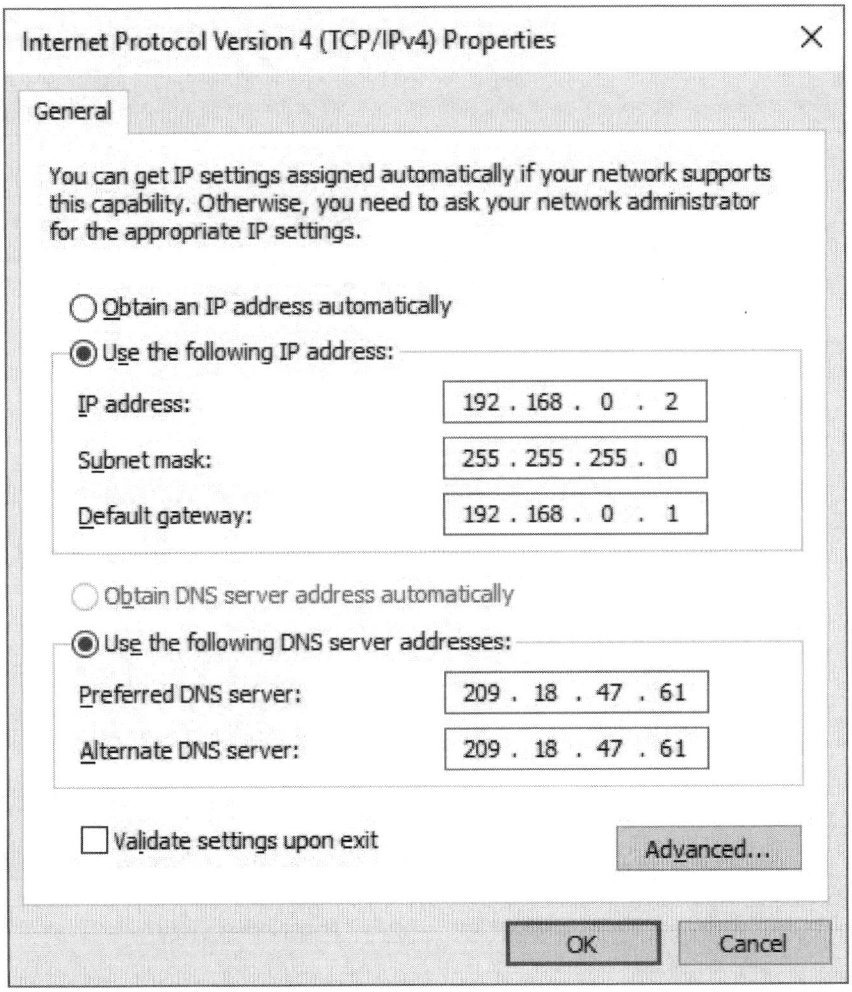

Chapter 2 – Networking Basics

Figure 2.5

If your network is using a DHCP server for IP address distribution, then you can leave the DNS settings set to automatic while having the IP settings set to manual, and you will get the DNS settings configured automatically for you.

Another way to get to the IP address settings in Windows 10 is to go to your Windows 10 Settings, click on *Network & Internet,* and then on *Change adapter options* in the *Status* section (figure 2.6).

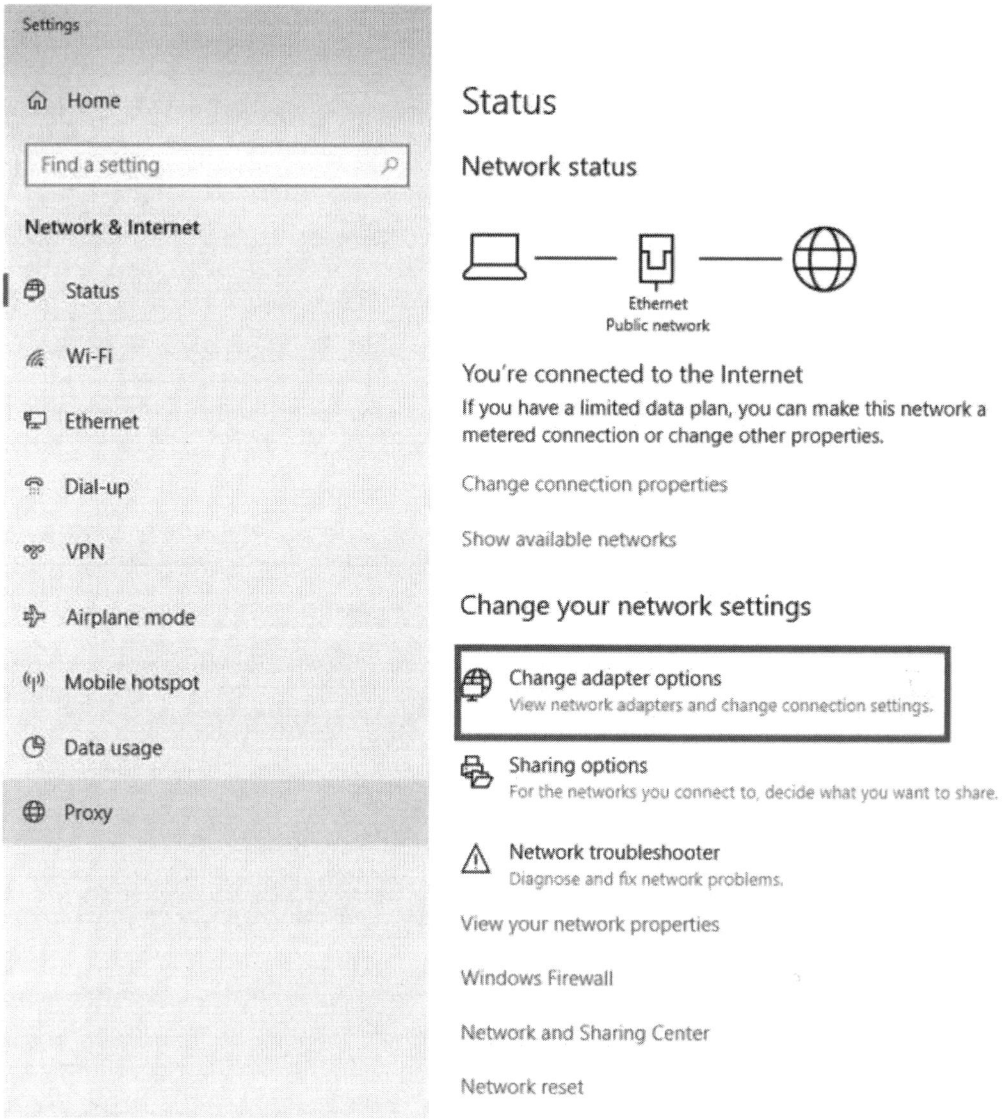

Chapter 2 – Networking Basics

Figure 2.6

DHCP
I want to mention DHCP really quickly since I was just talking about it in the last paragraph. DHCP (Dynamic Host Configuration Protocol) simplifies the management of IP address configuration by automating address configuration for network clients. In order for DHCP to work, you need to have a device acting as a DCHP server. This device can be a computer, router, or other type of network device. The DHCP server is configured with a range or ranges of IP addresses that can be used to give to clients that request one. It can also be configured with other network parameters. For a client to be able to obtain information from a DHCP server, it must be DHCP enabled. When it is configured this way, then it will look for a DHCP server when it starts up.

DNS

DNS (Domain Naming System) translates hostnames to their IP addresses so we don't need to remember IP addresses when connecting to other network devices. Like I mentioned earlier with my Google IP address example, we use DNS so we don't have to remember IP addresses when accessing websites. DNS also works for hostnames (computer names) on the network so you don't need to know their IP addresses to connect to them either. So, if you have a computer called Workstation1 with an IP address of 192.168.0.25, you just need to remember the name Workstaion1 when connecting to it.

DNS requires a DNS server that stores these hostnames to IP address relationships, otherwise you won't be able to connect to a computer or other device by its name. If you don't have a DNS server, you can use the local host file (discussed in Chapter 3), which is a text file on your computer, to store this information, but for the most part, it is a manual process to set this up and keep it updated.

Wireless Setup

Nowadays people seem to use wireless (Wi-Fi) for their Internet connection rather than plugging into a modem with a cable. This makes sense because everything is wireless enabled, and that way you don't have to be tied down by cables. With Windows 10, it's pretty easy to get your computer connected to your wireless connection and online. The first thing you need to check for is to make sure you actually *have* a wireless adapter in your computer, and that it's enabled. To do so, go to the Windows 10 Settings, then to Network & Internet, and finally to the Wi-Fi section (figure 2.7). Once there, you will see the status of your Wi-Fi adapter (as in is it on or off), as well as some links to show you other wireless information. You can also get to these settings from the Control Panel.

Chapter 2 – Networking Basics

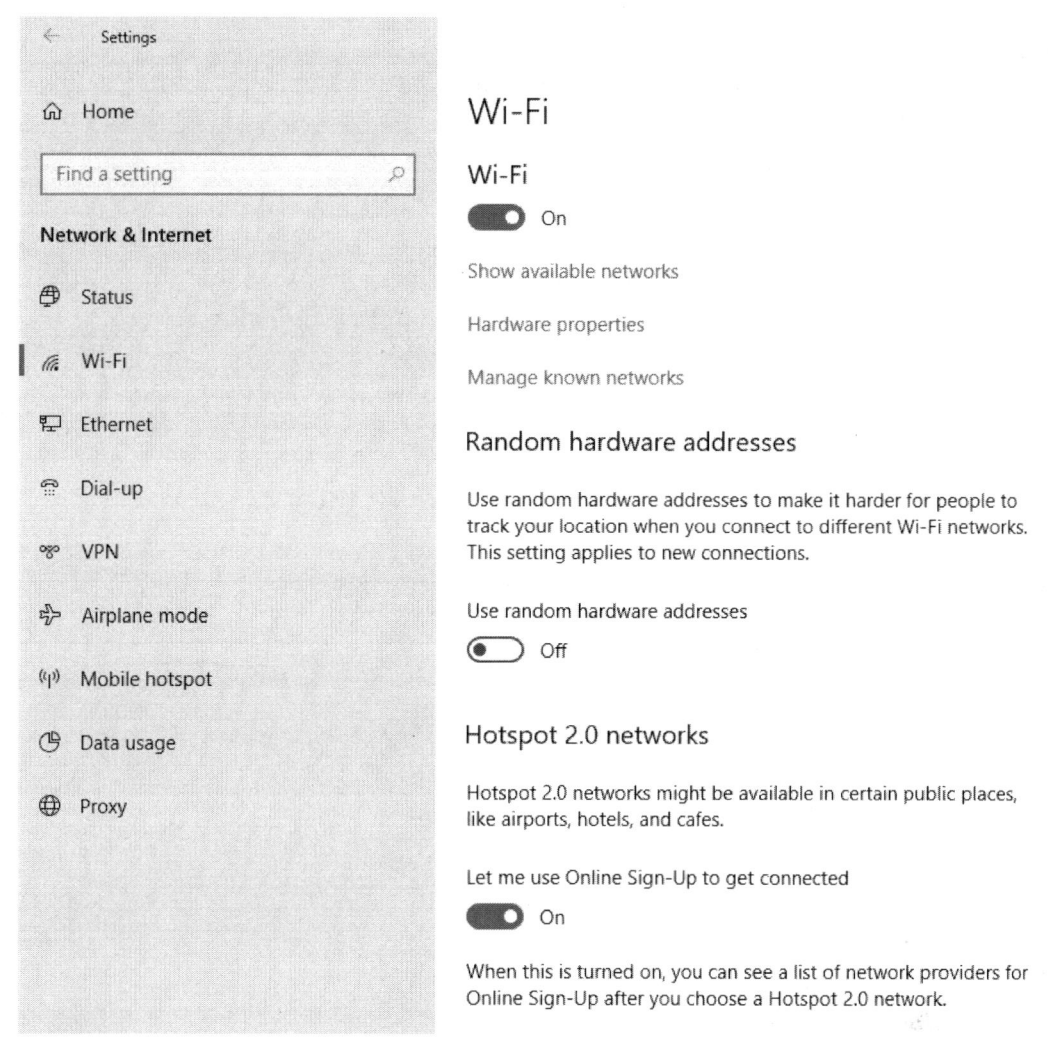

Figure 2.7

Clicking on the *Show available networks* link will show you what Wi-Fi networks are in range of your computer and their signal strength (figure 2.8). Then you will be able to connect to one of the networks in range assuming you have permission to do so, because most of the time they are password protected and if they aren't, then it's probably not a good idea to connect (it might be trap from someone looking to hack into your computer). If it's somewhere like a Starbucks that offers free Wi-Fi with no password, then you are usually okay to connect to it.

Chapter 2 – Networking Basics

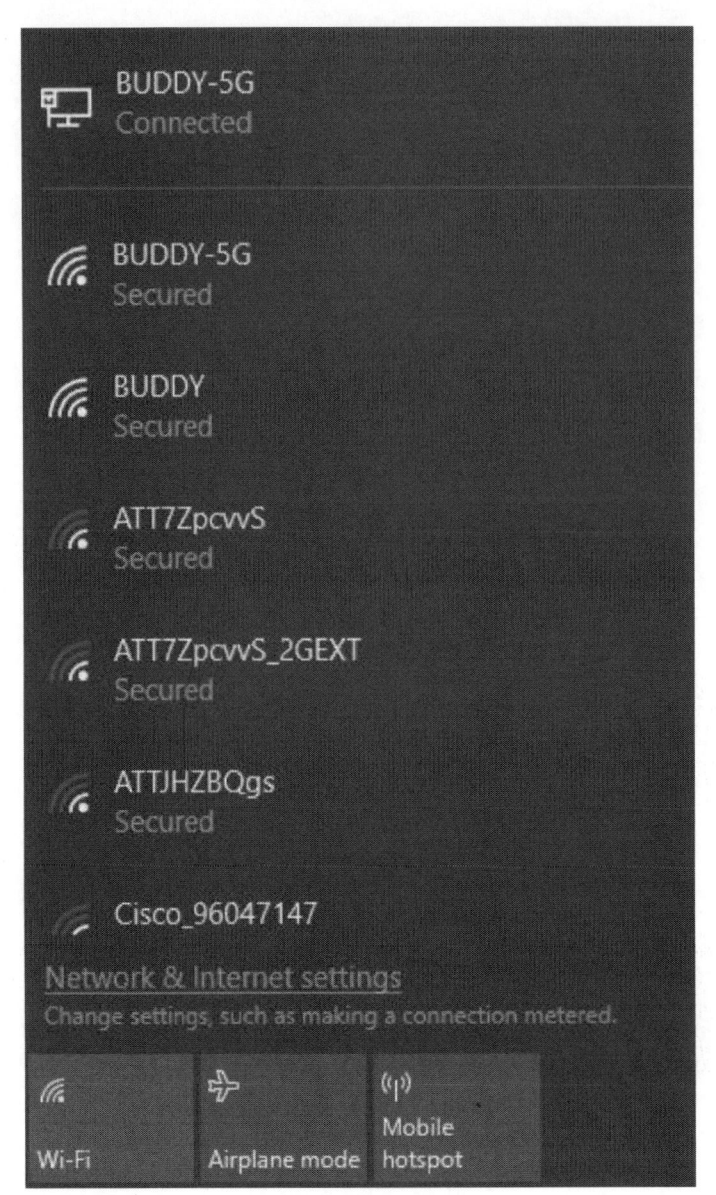

Figure 2.8

If you've ever heard the term SSID used when talking or reading about wireless connections, it is referring to the name of the connection itself. SSID stands for Service Set Identifier, and this name can be customized within your modem or router to make it easy to identify your network when adding a device to connect to it.

You can also see in figure 2.8 that the Wi-Fi button the bottom left of the box is a lighter grey, meaning it's enabled. So, if you don't see any network connections, make sure that your Wireless adapter is enabled.

Chapter 2 – Networking Basics

Another thing I want to mention from figure 2.7 is the *Manage known networks* link. If you click on this, it will bring you to an area where it will show all of the remembered networks that you have connected to either currently or in the past. If you have some connections in there that shouldn't be there or that you don't want to have remembered anymore, you can click on it and then click on the *Forget* button (figure 2.9).

← Settings

⌂ Wi-Fi

Manage known networks

+ Add a new network

[Search this list]

Sort by: Preference ∨   Filter by: All ∨

⏶ BUDDY-5G

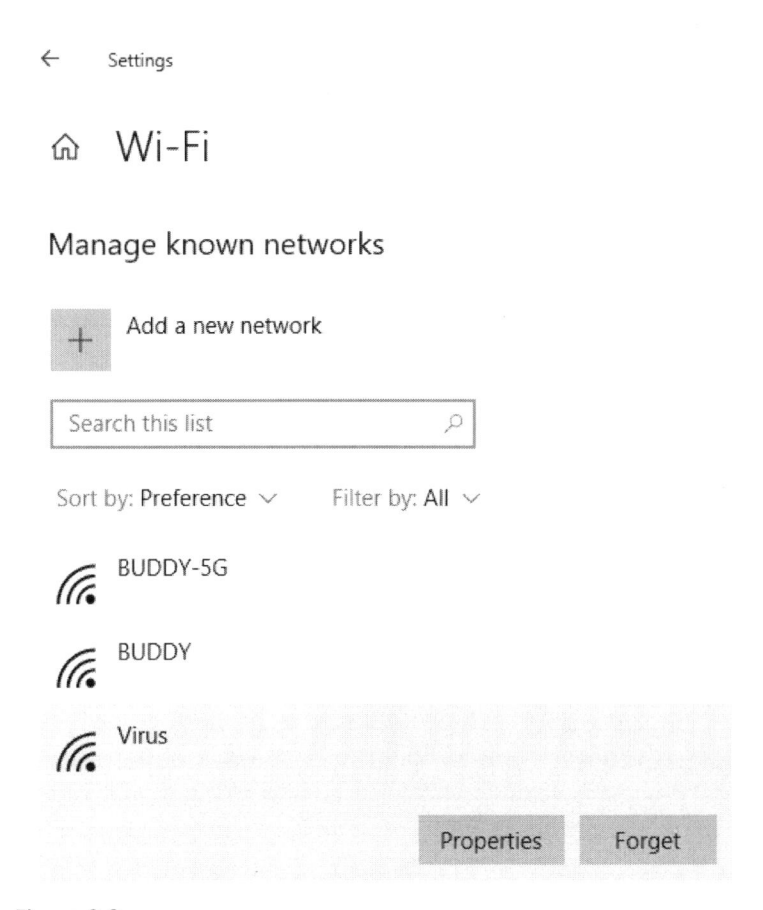

⏶ BUDDY

⏶ Virus

[Properties] [Forget]

Figure 2.9

Don't expect wireless Internet access to be completely trouble free because there will be time when you can't connect to your wireless connection or to the Internet.

> **Tip:** Even though today's modern wireless adapters boast speeds that are higher than what most people have for their broadband connection, don't expect to have as fast of a connection compared to using a cable.

Chapter 2 – Networking Basics

LAN vs. WAN
If you've done any type of networking or IT work, then you will most likely have heard the term Local Area Network (or LAN), and maybe even Wide Area Network (or WAN). But what is the difference between the two? Well, I'm glad you asked!

A LAN is a network that spans one location such as your home, office, or even an entire building. Some people also consider networks that span a location like a school campus a LAN. The network devices can be connected via cabling, or by using a wireless connection. The network may consist of one network segment or multiple network segments with different IP address ranges assigned to them. To use different IP address ranges on a network requires the use of a layer 3 device (like a router) or layer 3 switch to allow the segments to communicate with each other.

A WAN, on the other hand, is a network that extends over a large geographical distance such as between cities, states, or even countries. Since it's not possible to use standard networking media such as Ethernet cables or Wi-Fi connections, WANs rely more on leased lines from entities like phone companies and cable providers to cover the larger distances. These connections usually consist of long fiber optic cable runs designed for long distance communications.

Network Adapter
Network adapters are used as the interface between the network and the computer, server, printer, or whatever device that the adapter is installed in. A computer (etc.) can have several network adapters, and network adapters can come with several network ports on one adapter. Common ports for these adapters include RJ45, which is used for Ethernet cables. The cable connects to the port on the back of the card, and then the card itself plugs into a slot on the motherboard in the computer.

Chapter 2 – Networking Basics

Figure 2.10

Many desktop computers have built-in network adapters that are integrated with the motherboard similar to the way laptops are designed. However, this doesn't mean that you can't upgrade your network adapter with a faster model or one with more ports.

Hub
Next, I want to briefly mention a network device that is pretty much obsolete, but you might run into one of them at some point in your networking career. Hubs (figure 2.11) are devices with four or more ports (usually not more than sixteen ports) that simply transfer the packets from the network cable out all the ports. Hubs are layer 1 devices and also act as repeaters, meaning they regenerate the signal, allowing it to travel further down the cable than it would if it was just a straight cable run.

Chapter 2 – Networking Basics

Figure 2.11

The problem with hubs is that they are "dumb", meaning they don't know anything about any of the devices on the network, and that's why they just forward all the traffic out all the ports (which is also known as broadcasting). This is why they are not practical on larger networks and usually only seen on small home networks.

> **Tip:** If you ever encounter a situation where someone is using a hub on their home or small office network, feel free to replace it with even a cheap switch to improve performance.

Switch

Network switches (figure 2.12) are what we use instead of hubs when we want to build a network the right way. Switches have built-in intelligence, and some more so than others.

Figure 2.12

The way a switch functions is by keeping track of the MAC addresses of devices that pass traffic through it. MAC addresses are the burned-in hardware address that every network device has. This MAC address information is stored in MAC filter tables (also known as Content Addressable Memory tables).

By referencing these tables, they avoid broadcasting all network traffic out all ports whenever some device on the network decides it wants to start communicating. Once a MAC address is stored on the switch with its associated\connected port number, the switch will only pass traffic through that port when traffic comes into the switch for a device with a known MAC address. One downside is when the switch is powered off, the information on the MAC filter table is lost, and it has to be rebuilt as connections are made after the switch is turned back on.

Chapter 2 – Networking Basics

You can get a basic 8 switch for around $40, and don't need to go with the high end brands like Cisco or Brocade for a simple home or small office network. You can stick with brands like NetGear, Linksys, and D-Link.

Router
Even though you will most likely not be using a router on your network, I want to briefly discuss their purpose. Routers are used to perform a variety of functions to keep data flowing on the network. The purpose of a router (figure 2.13) is to "route" traffic from one network to the other. If you want to communicate with a computer or other device on a network that is different from your own, then the traffic will need to be routed between them.

When some data (network packet) comes in on one of the ports on the router, the router reads the network address information in the packet to determine its destination. Then, using information in its routing table or policy, it sends the packet to the next network to ultimately get to its final destination. It might have to go through several routers (with each step called a hop) to get to its destination.

Routing tables are databases stored in RAM that contain information about directly connected networks. These tables can be updated and maintained dynamically (automatically) by routing protocols, or statically (manually). Routing tables will keep track of information such as the network address assigned to interfaces, subnet masks, route sources, destination network, and the outgoing interface etc.

Figure 2.13

So, the bottom line is that if you have different networks (such as 192.168.1.0 and 192.168.2.0) and want to send data between the two, then you will need a router to do so, or at least a layer 3 switch that can perform routing functions.

Chapter 2 – Networking Basics

> **Tip:** Your home wireless router is actually doing the same thing as your network router in the office (to a degree) by routing traffic from your home network to the Internet, which, of course, is a network itself.

Making Physical Network Connections
Connecting all of your devices to your network is an important step to get right so everything works correctly and there are no communication problems. If you have a lot of devices you plan on connecting, you might want to make some sort of network diagram to make sure you don't miss anything.

You will most likely be using wired (cables) and wireless connections for your devices, which is perfectly fine as long as they are configured correctly. Figure 2.14 shows a typical home or small office setup using a switch as the center of connectivity. For the laptop and printer, I have put a solid line, indicating a wired connection, *and* a dotted line, indicating a wireless connection. I did this to show you that you can use either one with these types of devices (assuming it's supported), but that doesn't mean you should use both at the same time. Choose one type or the other to avoid communication problems.

Chapter 2 – Networking Basics

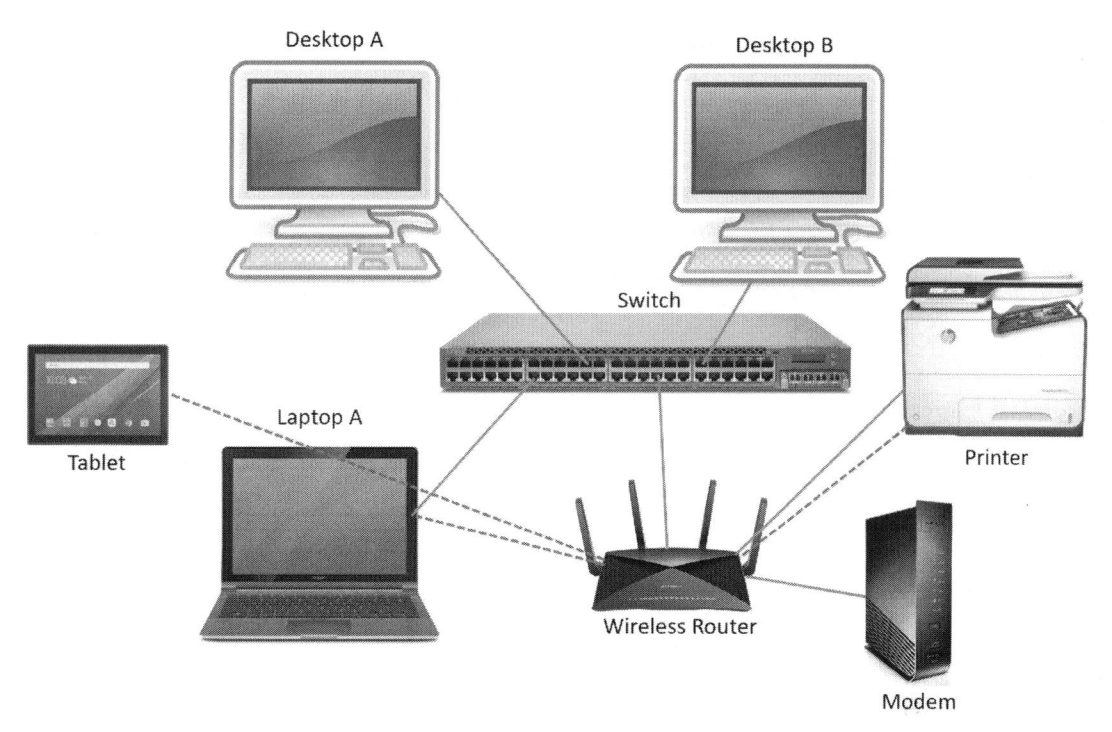

Figure 2.14

If your wireless\broadband modem\router has network ports on the back of it, then you can use those to connect devices rather than a separate switch to save some money and reduce some complexity. Figure 2.15 shows the back of a typical wireless router with four network ports. Some wireless routers will come with eight ports, giving you more connection options. The standalone port on the right is used to connect to your modem.

Figure 2.15

Chapter 2 – Networking Basics

> **Tip:** Many broadband modems have wireless capabilities built in so you don't need to have a separate modem and router for your Internet connection, which cuts down on the number of devices and connections on your network.

Here is a more simplified diagram using a modem\wireless router device instead of a separate device for both (figure 2.16). Then I took out the switch and used the switch ports on the back of the modem for network connectivity. I still included the wired and wireless connections for the laptop and printer. This method should work fine, but if you want better performance, I would stick with a separate switch so all the network traffic doesn't have to pass through the modem.

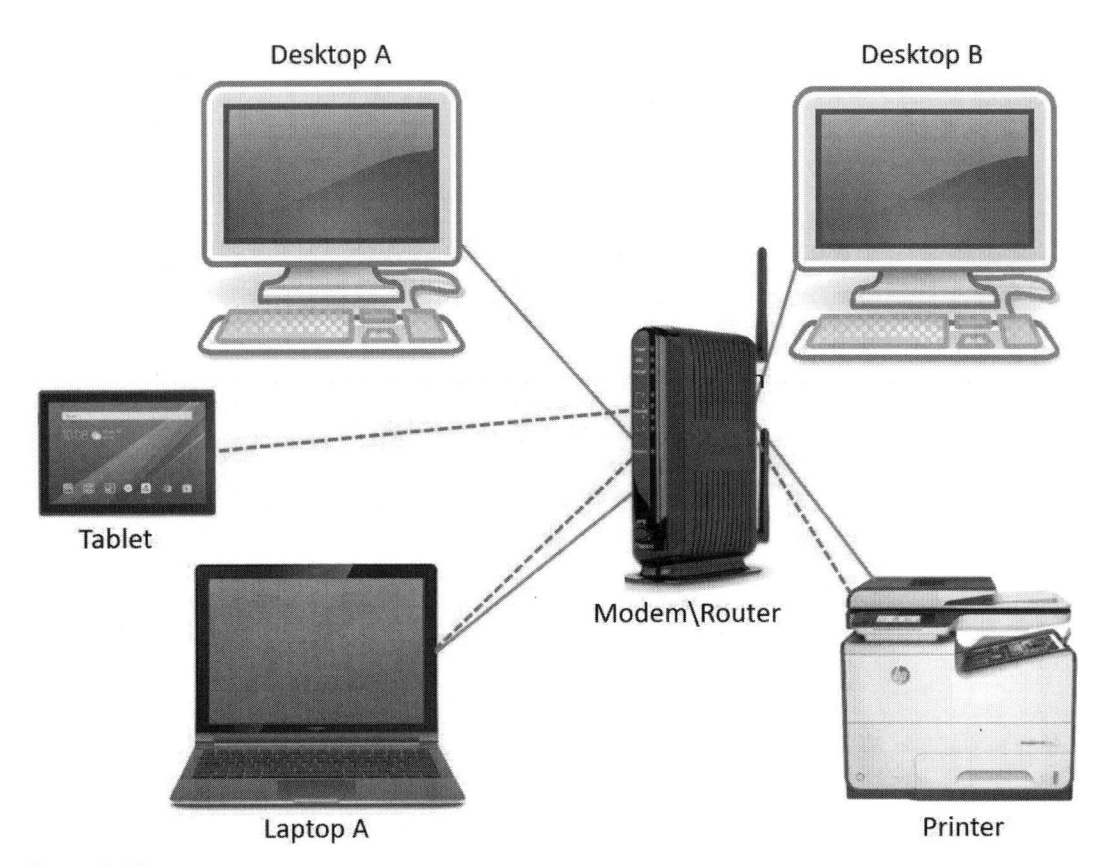

Figure 2.16

Chapter 2 – Networking Basics

For the network (Ethernet) cables, try to use at least Category 5e (Cat 5e) or better cables so you will get the proper speed going over your network. Cat 5e supports 1GB (gigabit) speeds, which is what any newer device will run with at the minimum. High end equipment can run at much higher speeds such as 10GB, 40GB, and even 100GB. (1GB should be just fine for home and small office needs.) If you get a Cat 6 or even Cat 7 cable, then you will be assured you are getting the speed you paid for.

(Keep in mind that Ethernet cables have a range limit of about 300 feet before the signal starts to degenerate and has to be repeated using a device such as a hub\router\repeater, so don't run your cables too long or you will run into problems.)

Chapter 3 – Setting up Workgroups

Networking with Windows is not all that difficult if you are just setting up a basic home network or small office network. When you start dealing with domains (discussed next) and multiple sites and networks connected together, then things get a little more interesting. But if you just want to network a few computers together, then it's fairly easy to do.

Peer to Peer vs. Client-Server Networks
Before I get started on the network configuration, I want to discuss the two main types of networks. Each one serves a similar purpose, but they are configured and managed differently.

Peer to peer networks (also called workgroups) were the first type of network to be used. In this type of network, there is no centralized management or security, and each computer is in charge of its own local users and file and folder permissions. Since there is no centralized user management, any user who wants access to resources on another computer will need to have an account on that specific computer. So, if a user wants access to files on ten different computers, then that user will need ten separate user accounts. Computers on a peer to peer network are usually connected together through a simple hub or network switch (figure 3.1).

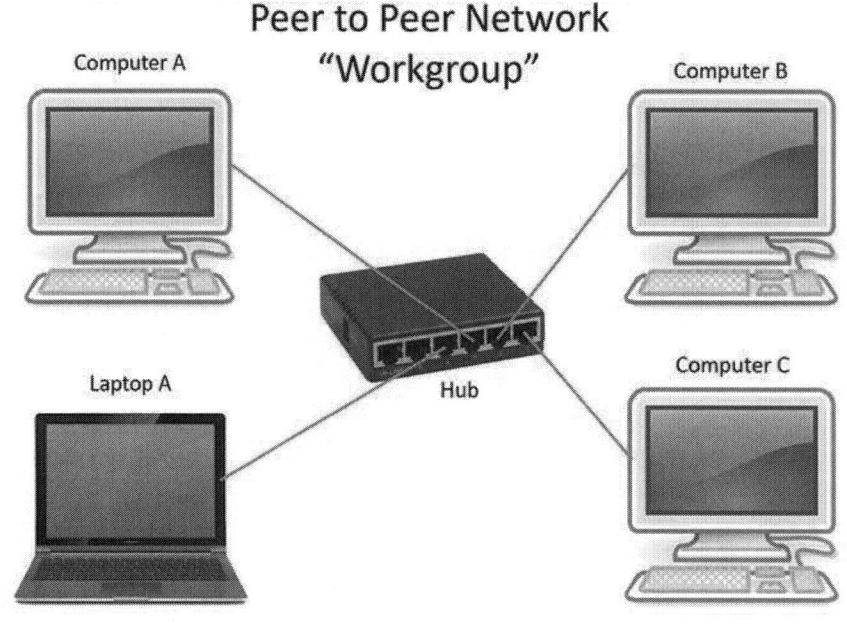

Figure 3.1

Chapter 3 – Setting up Workgroups

So, if Sally is a user on Computer A and she wants to access files on Laptop A and Computer C, then an admin on Laptop A and Computer C will need to make a user account for her, and then assign the permissions she needs to be able to access those resources. (You can imagine how complicated this would get as the number of computers on the network grows.)

When the number of computers in a peer to peer network starts to go past ten, then you can run into problems such as slowdowns from network broadcasts and other traffic because all the traffic goes to each computer, even though only the computer that it was meant to go to will accept the information. Plus, many workgroup configured operating systems can only accept ten concurrent connections at a time. So, if you have a computer acting as a file server for twenty users, then only ten of them can connect to that file server at a time.

Peer to peer networks work fine for home networks or small office networks where there are not a lot of users and computers to manage. But once you get to a certain limit, that is where you need to implement something more, such as a client-server network.

A *client-server network* has clients (workstations) as well as a server (or many servers). As you can see in figure 3.2, the clients are labeled Computer A, Computer B, Laptop A, and so on. There is also a file server and a directory server, which is used to manage user accounts and access controls.

Client-Server Network

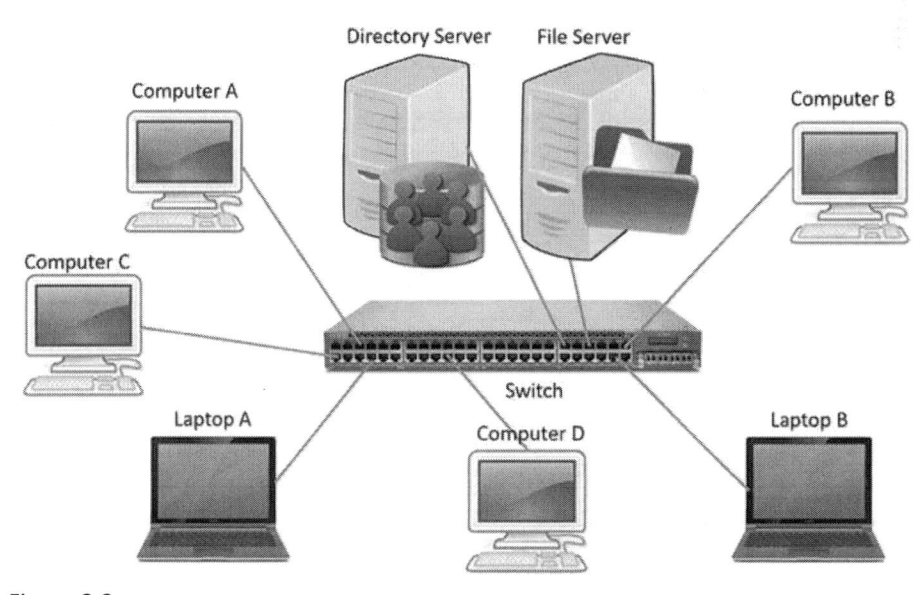

Figure 3.2

Chapter 3 – Setting up Workgroups

All the computers and servers connect to each other via a network switch rather than a hub like we saw in the peer to peer network, even though you can use a switch for a peer to peer network as well. The main advantage here is that every user account is created on the directory server, and then each computer, laptop, and other servers are joined to a domain where authentication is centralized for logins and resource permissions. A domain is a centralized way to manage computers, users, and resources, and each computer joins the domain, and each user is created as a domain user. So, if a user named Joe on computer C wants to access files on Laptop B, they can do so assuming their user account is allowed to. There is no need to make a user account for Joe on Laptop B or any other computer on the network besides the initial user created on the directory server.

Using a switch rather than a hub reduces broadcast traffic because the switch knows what port each computer is connected to, and doesn't have to go to each computer or server to find the one it is trying to get to. Switches can be thought of as "smart" hubs, or hubs can be thought of as "dumb" switches.

The client-server model is also very scalable, and the amount of concurrent connections to a server is only limited to the licensing model in place, and eventually the hardware limits in regards to network bandwidth and server capacity. Directory servers can handle managing thousands of users with little hardware resources needed.

The downsides of the client-server model include:

- Increased costs, because servers are more expensive than computers and network switches are more expensive than hubs.

- More difficult to implement and maintain because of its complexity.

- Single point of failure if a directory server goes down and none of your users can log in. This is often bypassed by having multiple directory servers (or domain controllers).

Overall, if your environment has many resources and you want to centralize the management of your users and computers, then you should go with the client-server model. If you only have a few computers and users, then a peer to peer configuration should work just fine. Plus, you can reconfigure it to a client-server model in the future if needed.

Chapter 3 – Setting up Workgroups

Workgroups

In order for your computers to be able to communicate with each other on a network, they need to be in the same, let's say "club" if you will. For Windows, this club that your computers are a part of is called a Workgroup. These workgroup computers are all equal when it comes to who is in charge, and no computer has any authority over another computer. The default workgroup name for Windows is actually called Workgroup, but you can change it to whatever you like as long as all the computers you want in the workgroup have the same workgroup name as well. All the computers have their own local user accounts, and if you want to access another computer from yours, then you need to have an account on that computer as well.

> **Tip:** If you are wondering what happened to the Windows Homegroup network sharing feature, it was removed in one of the Windows 10 major updates, so we are now back to just Workgroups.

Domains

If you work at a company with a reasonable amount of computers that run Windows, then you are most likely part of a Windows domain. In a domain, all access and security is controlled by centralized servers called domain controllers. You log into your computer with your domain username and password and that determines what level of access you have to all network resources like file servers and printers. Using domains makes it easy for network administrators to control user accounts and permissions since it can all be done from one place and apply to the entire network.

To check your workgroup name or to see if you are a part of a domain, you can type in *system* in the search box or in Cortana and open the *System properties* box as shown in figure 3.3. Next to the word Workgroup will be the workgroup name. (In my example it's called WORKGROUP.) If your computer was joined to a domain, it would say *domain* rather than *Workgroup* in this section.

Chapter 3 – Setting up Workgroups

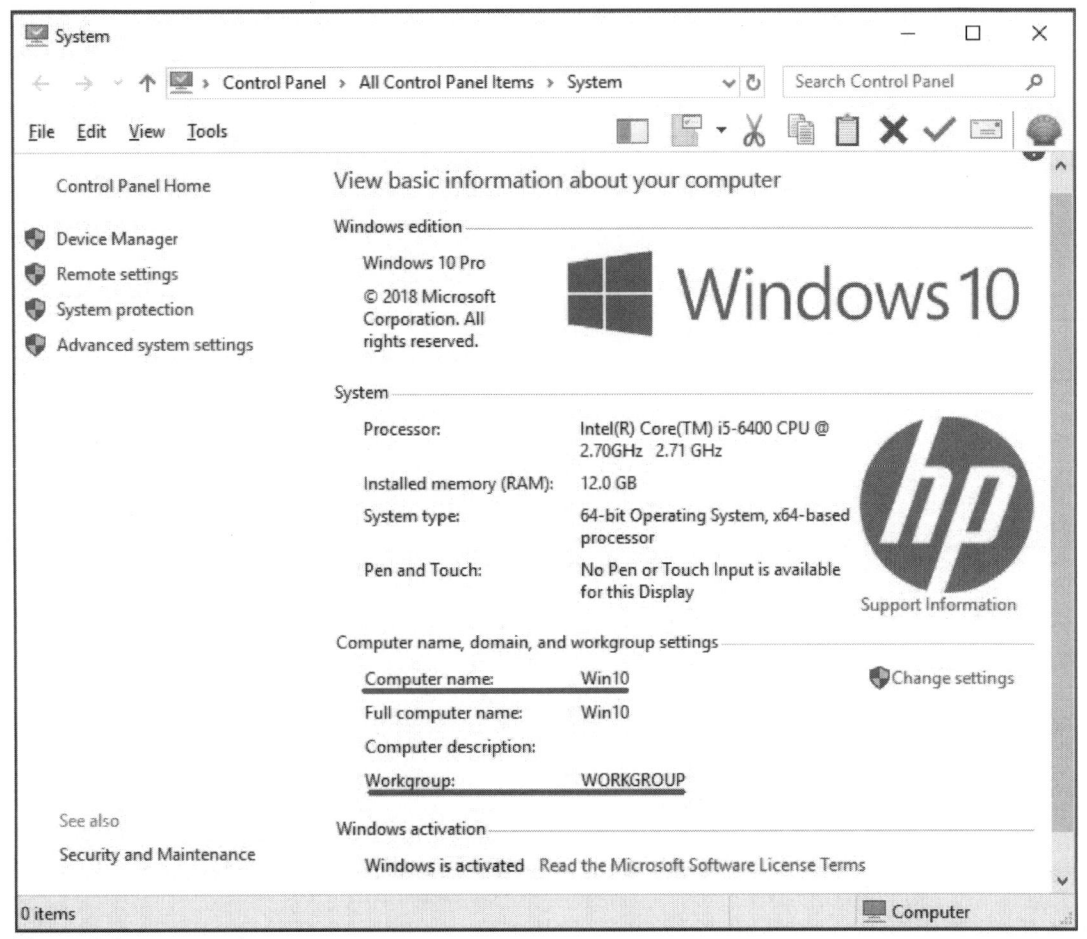

Figure 3.3

You can also find your computer's name (discussed next) from the System properties, which is something you will want to know for networking purposes because you will most likely access other computers by their name rather than something like their IP address.

Computer Names
Naming your computers is an important step to make your networking life easier on yourself. Computers will have a name and an IP address, and you can use either one for connection purposes. But, as I mentioned before, it's much easier to remember a name rather than an IP address.

If you are planning a new network from scratch or have a lot of computers, you might want to come up with a naming scheme before naming your computers so things make sense after everything is ready to go. For example, you can use the names of the people who are assigned to that computer as the computer name. You can also

Chapter 3 – Setting up Workgroups

name your computers based on their tasks or location such as *front desk* or *sales computer*.

> **Tip:** Computer names are commonly referred to as hostnames, and the terms can be used interchangeably. In larger networks, hostname is the more common term. Hostname can also apply to other devices on the network besides computers.

There are a few ways to see the hostname of your computer, and I will now go over a couple of ways to find this.

One easy way is to open a command prompt (cmd), type in the word hostname, and press enter. As you can see in figure 3.4, the hostname or computer name is *Win10*.

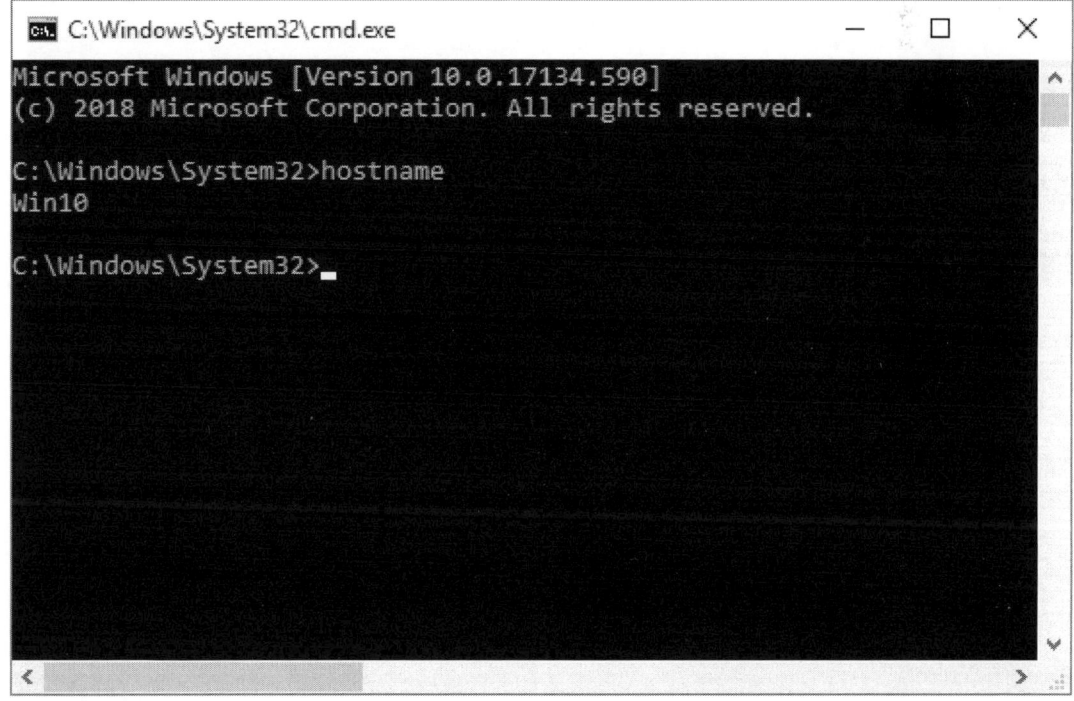

```
C:\Windows\System32\cmd.exe

Microsoft Windows [Version 10.0.17134.590]
(c) 2018 Microsoft Corporation. All rights reserved.

C:\Windows\System32>hostname
Win10

C:\Windows\System32>
```
Figure 3.4

Another method is to go look at your System Properties in Control Panel and get the name from there. As you can see in figure 3.5 (which is basically the same thing you saw in figure 3.3), it shows the same Win10 computer name here. If you were on a domain rather than a workgroup, then the full computer name might say something like *win10.yourcompany.com*.

Chapter 3 – Setting up Workgroups

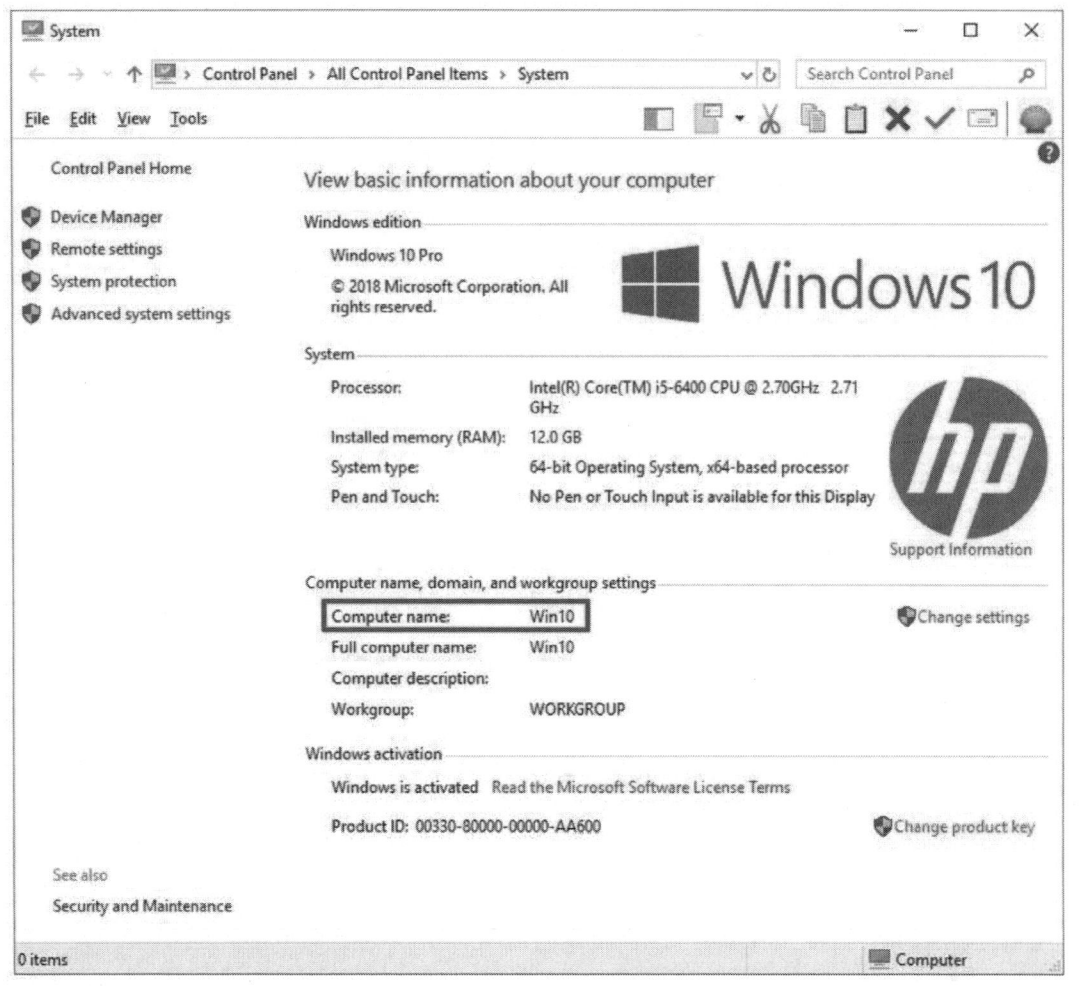

![System control panel window showing computer information including Windows 10 Pro, Intel i5-6400 CPU, 12.0 GB RAM, computer name Win10, and Workgroup WORKGROUP]

Figure 3.5

Changing Your Computer's Name
You will most likely need to change the names of your computers to make things easier, especially since the names given to computers by their manufacturers don't make too much sense and usually look something like HBMRR-34358-RW, which doesn't help anyone!

Just like with most things in Windows, there is more than one way to change your computer's name. If you look back at figure 3.5, to the right of the computer name you will see a link that says *Change settings*. When you click on that, you will get a box similar to figure 3.6.

42

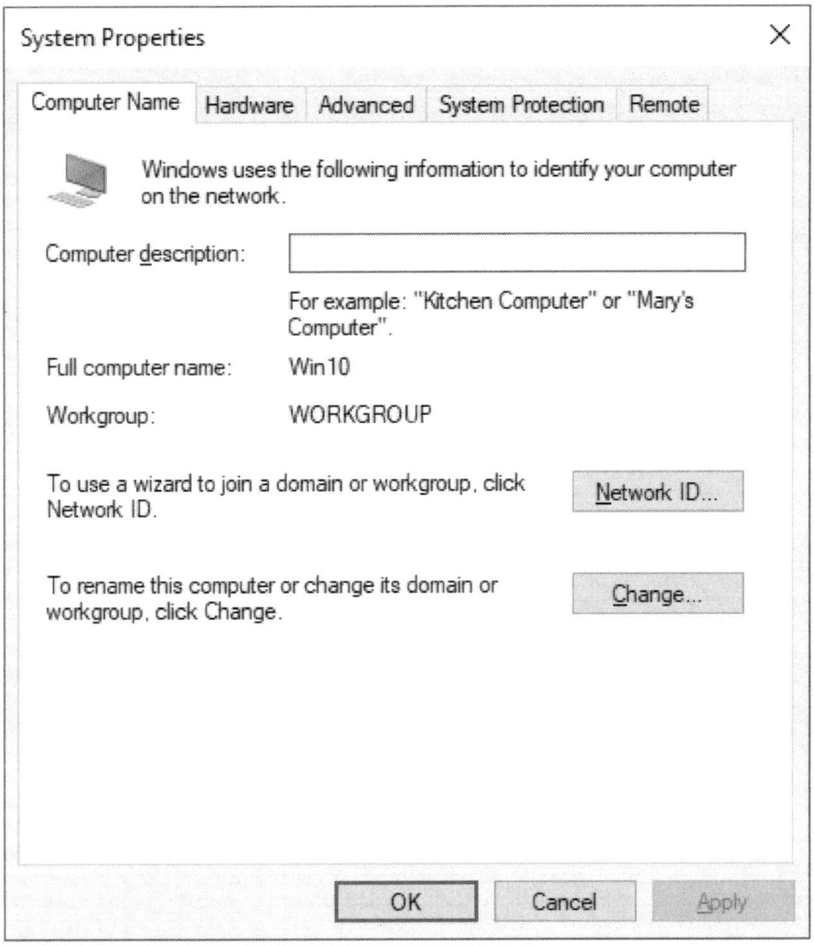

Chapter 3 – Setting up Workgroups

Figure 3.6

From here you want to click on the *Change* button. It's easy to just type the new name in the box above, but that will only add a description to the computer and not change its name. (Believe me, I have done this many times!)

After clicking on the *Change* button, you will then be able to change the computer name to whatever you wish (figure 3.7).

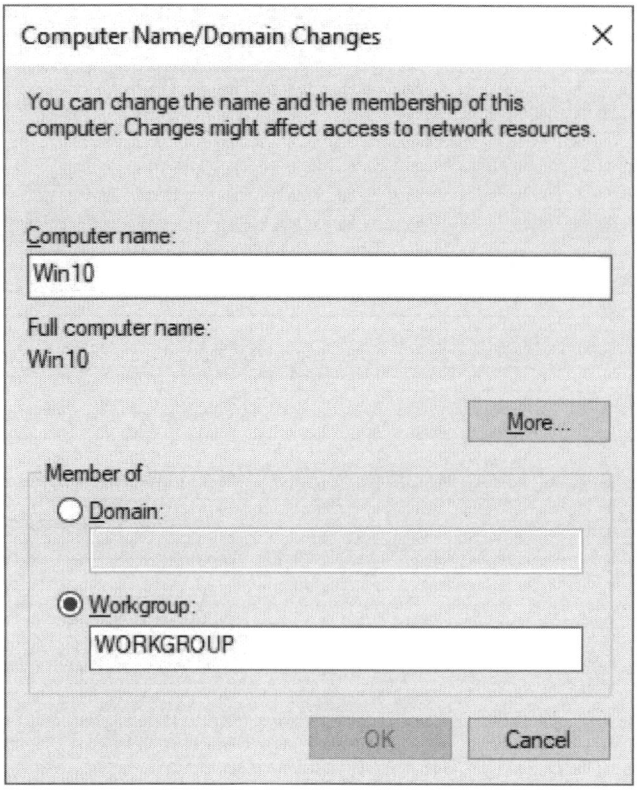

Chapter 3 – Setting up Workgroups

Figure 3.7

There are limitations to what you can name your computer. You shouldn't use more than fifteen characters for networked computers, and you should avoid spaces and special characters such as $ # %. Also make sure not to give the same name to more than one computer or you will be asking for trouble. When you are done with the name, change simply click on *OK* and you will be prompted for a reboot. After you restart your computer, the new name will be applied.

You can also do this from the Windows 10 settings by going to *System* and then clicking on *About*. From there, click on the *Rename this PC* button, enter in a new name, and click on *Next* (figure 3.8).

Chapter 3 – Setting up Workgroups

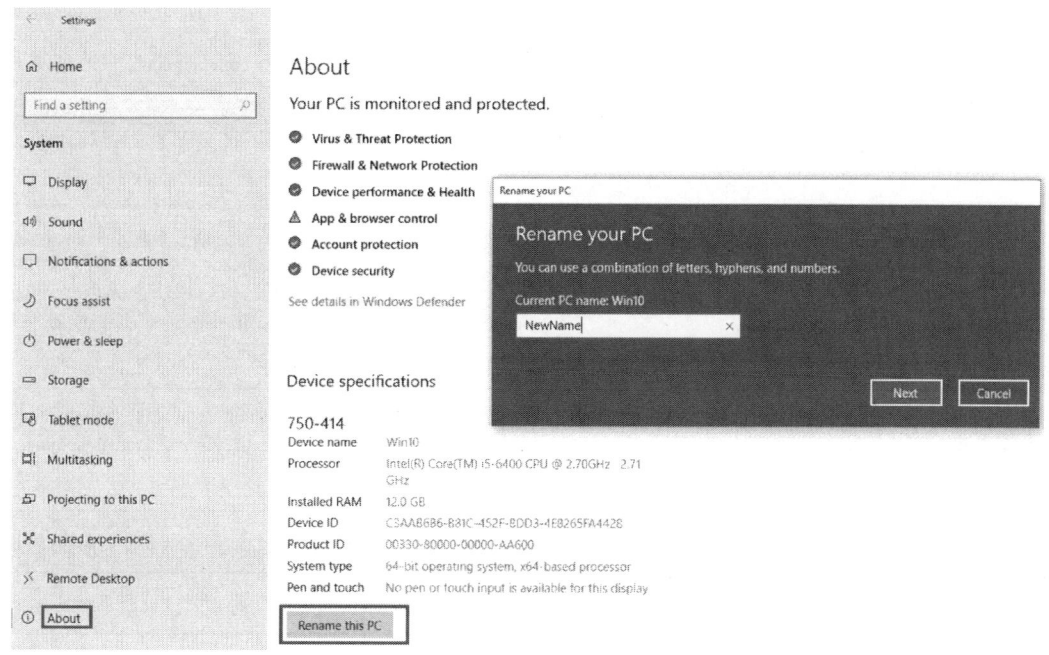

Figure 3.8

Then you will be prompted to restart your computer to have the name change take effect.

Another way to change your computer's name is from a command prompt. But to do this you will have to use an elevated command prompt, which means running the command as an administrator. To get to an administrative command prompt, you simply need to right click on the cmd icon and choose *Run as administrator*.

Once you have the command prompt open, use the following command:

WMIC computersystem where caption='current_pc_name' rename new_pc_name

Before running it, change **current_pc_name** to the current name of your computer, and **new_pc_name** to the name you want to change it to.

So, in my example, I would be using:

WMIC computersystem where caption='*Win10*' rename *Sales*

Chapter 3 – Setting up Workgroups

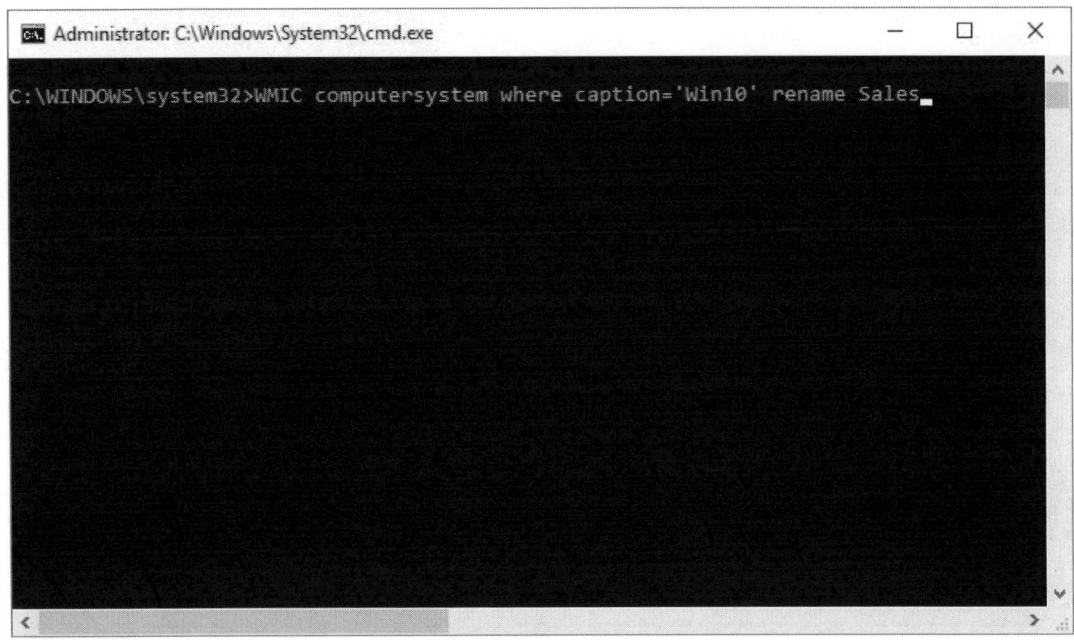

Figure 3.9

If you get a *ReturnValue* of 0, then you know the command ran successfully.

Figure 3.10

Then you will need to reboot your computer for the name change to take effect. To test the changes, you can open up a command prompt again (it doesn't have to be as an administrator), and run the *hostname* command (figure 3.11).

46

Chapter 3 – Setting up Workgroups

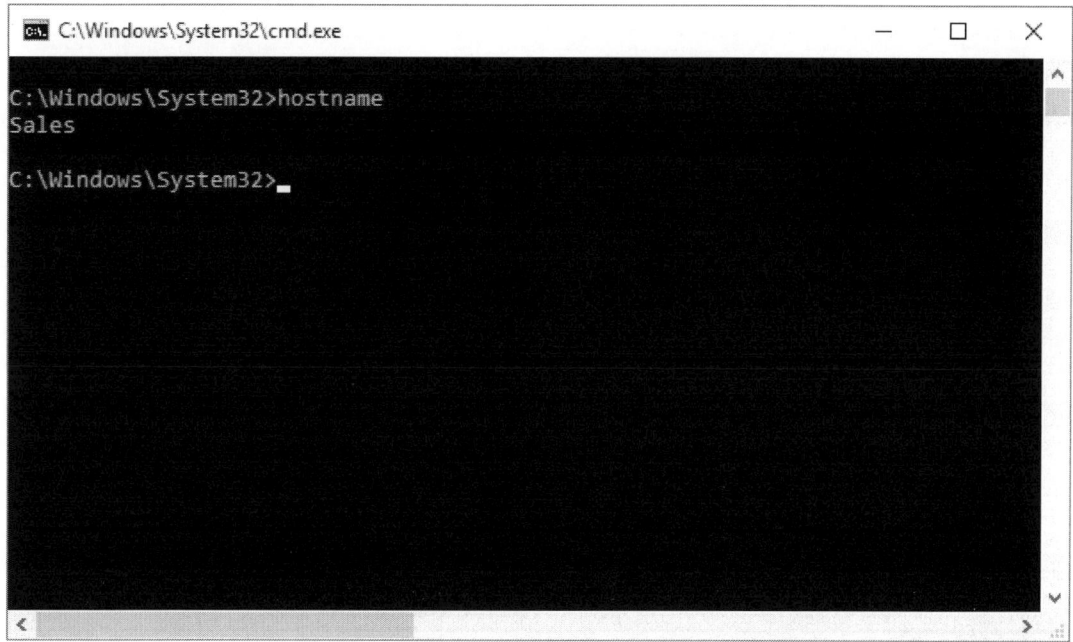

Figure 3.11

> **Tip:** If you find that a command is not working properly or gives you a permission error, make sure that you are logged in using an account that has admin privileges. If it *still* won't work, then try the right click on the cmd icon **Run as administrator** method.

Setting Up Your Workgroup

Now that you know how to rename your computers so things will make more sense, it's time to choose a Workgroup name that makes sense as well. Many people like to leave the default name of Workgroup as their Workgroup name, which is completely fine. In fact, it might even be a good idea because if you need to add a new computer, you won't need to worry about changing it to match your other computers.

To save a step, you can actually change the Workgroup name at the same time you are changing the computer name and get them both done with only one reboot. Otherwise, when you change the Workgroup name, you will have to reboot in order for those changes to take effect. (I have heard cases where this can cause problems, so you might want to do them separately if you have the time.)

Chapter 3 – Setting up Workgroups

To make this change, you go to the same place that you saw earlier where you changed the computer name in your System Properties in Control Panel.

Figure 3.12

> **Tip:** If you want a quick way to get to your System Properties, then you can simply type in **SystemProperties** (no spaces) in the Run box and it will take you right there.

Once you are at the computer name change screen, simply type in the new name for your Workgroup where it says Workgroup (as seen in figure 3.12). Then click on OK and reboot and you will be ready to go.

Chapter 3 – Setting up Workgroups

Hosts File

Windows has a file called the hosts file that is used to manually configure computer names to IP address mappings if needed. This method is not really used anymore, but the file is still in Windows in case you need to make some kind of manual entry, or if your current name resolution method is not working properly.

For typical name resolution, Windows uses what they call NetBIOS (a Microsoft name resolution protocol), which is a broadcast protocol that allows computers to find each other without any central server. In a domain situation, you will need to use DNS servers for your name resolution, and these DNS servers are typically the same servers that are used as your domain controllers.

The hosts file is located on your Windows drive under:

C:\Windows\System32\drivers\etc

Notice in figure 3.13 that the file is just called *hosts* with no file extension. There is no Windows program associated with the hosts file, so when you try to open it, you will be asked what program you want to use to view the file. For the most part, people use Notepad to view and edit this file.

Chapter 3 – Setting up Workgroups

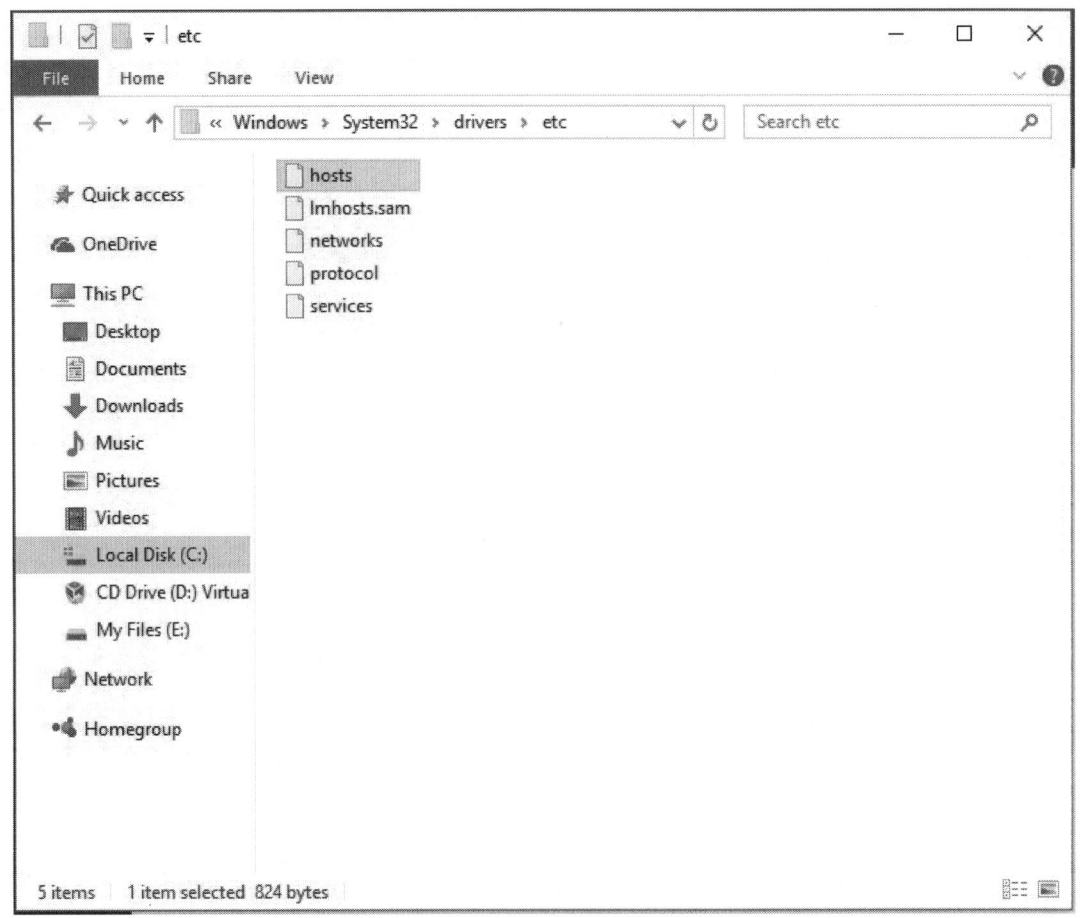

Figure 3.13

Once the file is open (figure 3.14), you will see a description of what the file is used for along with some examples. Any text with # in front of it is ignored and just treated as plain text and will not affect what the host file does. If you look at the example text, you will see that the IP address of 102.54.94.97 is mapped to the hostname called rhino.acme.com, which is saying that when you contact rhino.acme.com, the host file will resolve that name to the IP address of 102.54.94.97.

Chapter 3 – Setting up Workgroups

```
hosts - Notepad                                                    —    □    ×
File  Edit  Format  View  Help
# Copyright (c) 1993-2009 Microsoft Corp.
#
# This is a sample HOSTS file used by Microsoft TCP/IP for Windows.
#
# This file contains the mappings of IP addresses to host names. Each
# entry should be kept on an individual line. The IP address should
# be placed in the first column followed by the corresponding host name.
# The IP address and the host name should be separated by at least one
# space.
#
# Additionally, comments (such as these) may be inserted on individual
# lines or following the machine name denoted by a '#' symbol.
#
# For example:
#
#      102.54.94.97     rhino.acme.com          # source server
#       38.25.63.10     x.acme.com              # x client host

# localhost name resolution is handled within DNS itself.
#       127.0.0.1       localhost
#       ::1             localhost
```

Figure 3.14

You can put any information in here you like, but you need to make sure it's accurate, otherwise it won't do you any good. If you look at figure 3.15, you can see that I entered a new line that maps the IP address of 1.2.3.4 to a hostname\computer name of BobsComputer.

Chapter 3 – Setting up Workgroups

```
# Copyright (c) 1993-2009 Microsoft Corp.
#
# This is a sample HOSTS file used by Microsoft TCP/IP for Windows.
#
# This file contains the mappings of IP addresses to host names. Each
# entry should be kept on an individual line. The IP address should
# be placed in the first column followed by the corresponding host name.
# The IP address and the host name should be separated by at least one
# space.
#
# Additionally, comments (such as these) may be inserted on individual
# lines or following the machine name denoted by a '#' symbol.
#
# For example:
#
#      102.54.94.97     rhino.acme.com          # source server
#      38.25.63.10      x.acme.com              # x client host

# localhost name resolution is handled within DNS itself.
#      127.0.0.1        localhost
#      ::1              localhost
       1.2.3.4          BobsComputer
```

Figure 3.15

Now when I go to a command prompt and ping BobsComputer, it will attempt to use 1.2.3.4 as its IP address. As you can see in figure 3.16, it attempts to ping, but since this is just a made up entry, the ping fails. However, it does use 1.2.3.4 for the IP address.

> **Tip:** Editing the hosts file requires administrative permission, so you may run into trouble saving the file. One workaround is to save it as a hosts.txt in Notepad. Then rename the original hosts file, and then rename your hosts.txt file to just hosts.

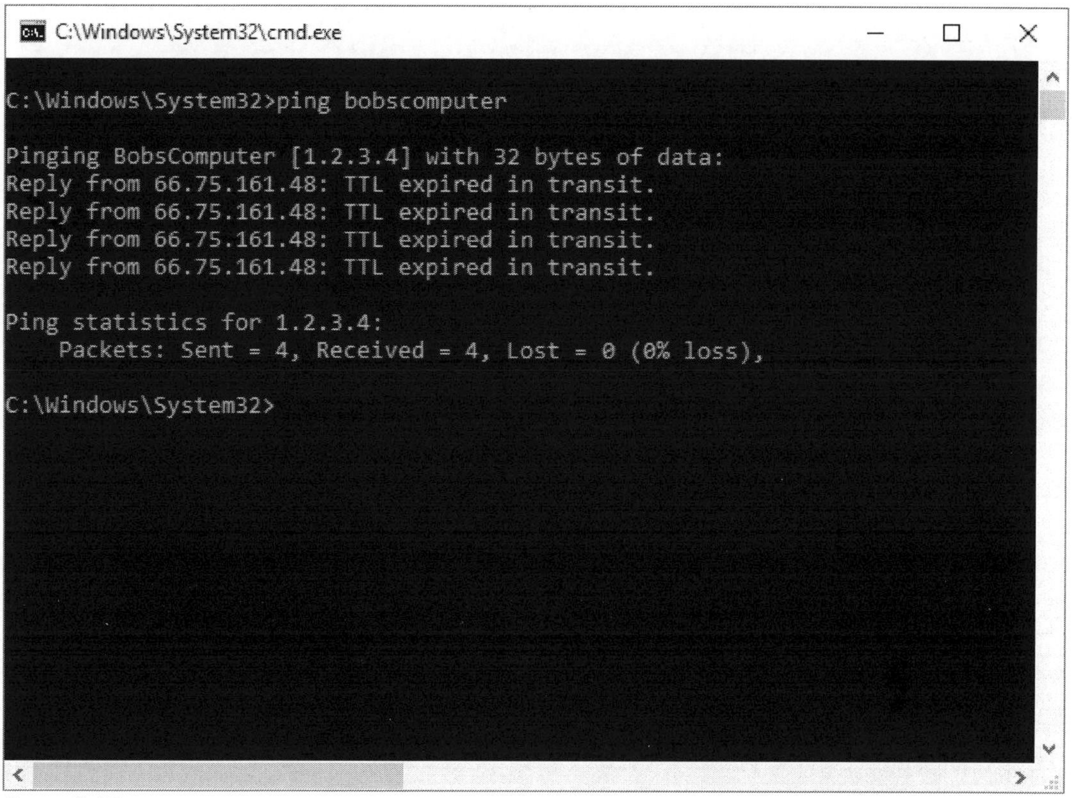

Chapter 3 – Setting up Workgroups

```
C:\Windows\System32>ping bobscomputer

Pinging BobsComputer [1.2.3.4] with 32 bytes of data:
Reply from 66.75.161.48: TTL expired in transit.
Reply from 66.75.161.48: TTL expired in transit.
Reply from 66.75.161.48: TTL expired in transit.
Reply from 66.75.161.48: TTL expired in transit.

Ping statistics for 1.2.3.4:
    Packets: Sent = 4, Received = 4, Lost = 0 (0% loss),

C:\Windows\System32>
```

Figure 3.16

Chapter 4 – User Accounts

One thing you definitely need to have to use a Windows computer is a user account (but I'm sure you know this since you use one to log into your computer every time you power it on). User accounts are required to make sure people are allowed to access the computer only if the owner wants them to. In order to use a Windows computer, you will need a user account that has been configured for you by an administrator, or when you first set up your new computer. There are many reasons why Windows has user accounts, including the following:

- Having a way to protect their personal files from being accessed from others (unless they want them to be accessed);

- Providing a way to assign permissions to shared files and folders on the local computer or network;

- Determining what type of functions that person is allowed to perform on the computer itself;

- Tracking things such as login times, failed login attempts, and file access using event logging;

- Setting allowed times for users to be able to log onto a computer or network;

- Saving the personal settings of your computer, such as your desktop background and installed printers etc.;

- Assigning levels of access for software usage.

Keep in mind as a Workgroup user you won't have to worry about most of these because your user account will mainly be used to save personalization settings that you customized for your user account, and to keep your documents from being accessed by other users. As usual, Microsoft has given us a couple of ways to work with user accounts, and each way works a little differently (but I will get to that later on in this chapter).

User Account Types
There is more than one type of account for a Windows user, and this makes sense because different people need different levels of access and permissions. The two

Chapter 4 – User Accounts

main types of user accounts that you will be dealing with are the standard user and the administrator user accounts.

Standard user accounts are for people who need to do everyday tasks on the computer such as run programs, go online, print, and so on. Standard users can also install and uninstall certain software as well. It's usually a good idea to make everyone on your computer a standard user, and then if they need something done that requires higher privileges, they can have an administrator do it. (And by administrator, I mean you!)

Administrator user accounts have full control over the computer, and can do things such as install or uninstall any software, add or remove user accounts, add or remove hardware, and make changes that affect Windows itself. If you are logged in as a standard user and need to do something that requires administrator access, many times you will get prompted to enter the username and password of an administrator so you don't need to actually log out and then back in as an administrator to get the job done.

> **Tip**
> Windows has a built-in account that is actually called Administrator, but it is disabled by default. However, it is pretty easy to enable. Here is how you do it.
>
> https://www.onlinecomputertips.com/support-categories/windows/360-windows-enable-admin-account

Local Accounts vs. Microsoft Accounts
Starting with Windows 8, Microsoft has been trying to get people to use an actual Microsoft account to log into their computer rather than the usual local account many of us were used to using. By using a Microsoft account, you can transfer personalization settings and certain files (like pictures) between devices that you use this account to log into. A Microsoft account uses an email address to login rather than a standard username.

You can see your Microsoft account sync settings by going to the Windows 10 settings, choosing *Accounts,* and then clicking on the *Sync your settings* section (figure 4.1).

55

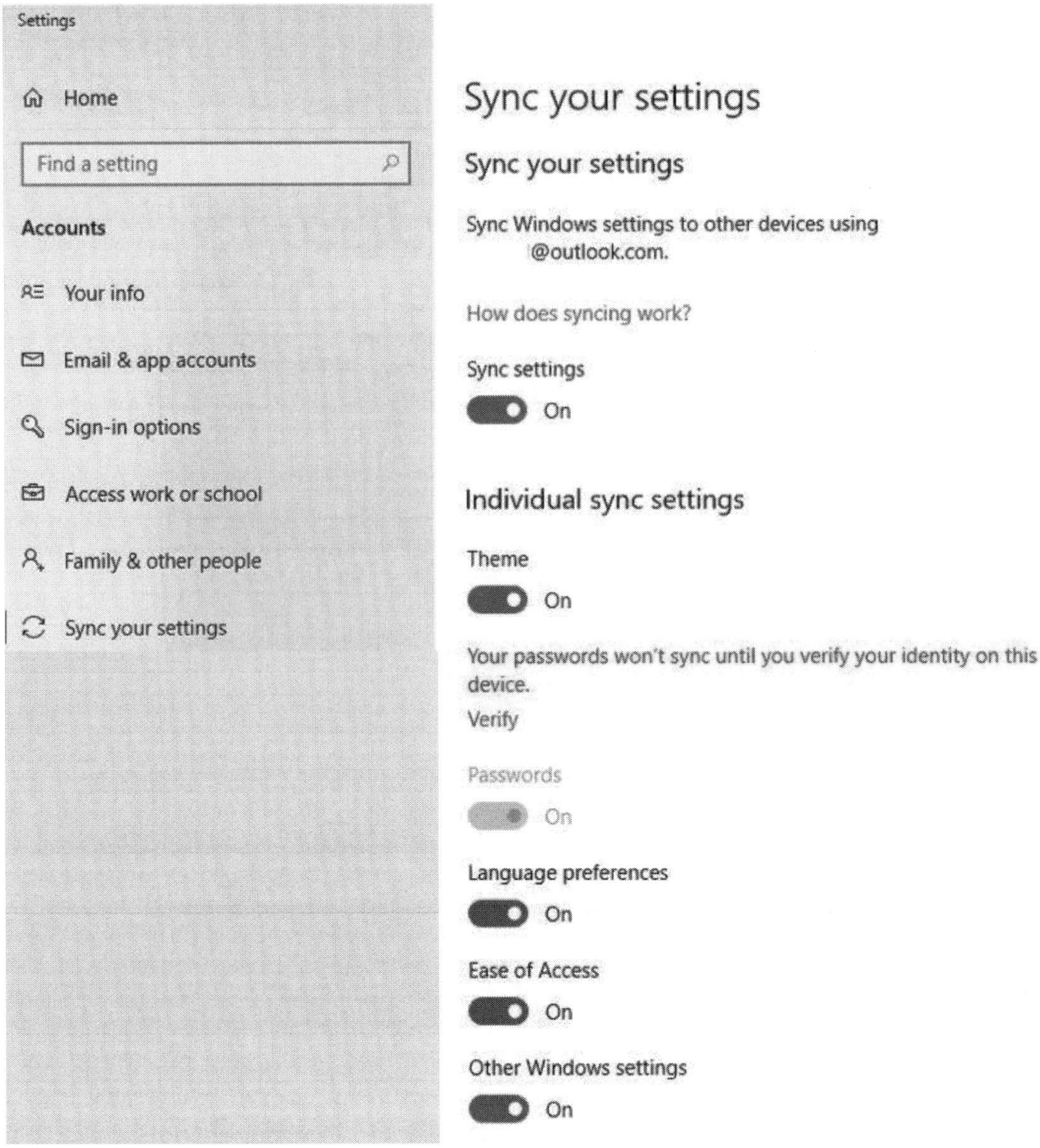

Chapter 4 – User Accounts

![Figure 4.1 Settings - Sync your settings]

Figure 4.1

If you are the type that likes to keep things old school (and simple), then you can still use a standard user type to log in with. Standard users can only log into the computer they have an account on (unless you are using domain), and can perform functions like use and install software, printers, and other devices based on whether they are a standard user or a local administrator.

Even if your computer was initially configured with a Microsoft account, you can convert it to a standard account pretty easily. I find that local accounts are much easier to troubleshoot when it comes to login problems, plus you don't need to

Chapter 4 – User Accounts

worry about your users syncing their personal files that they might use on their other devices with computers that are meant to only be used for work.

Creating User Accounts

To view the user accounts on your computer, go to the *Windows 10 Settings*, click on *Accounts,* and then on *Family & other people*. From this screen you will see your account and any other accounts configured on the computer (figure 4.2). If you click on the *Your info* section, you can see information about the account you are logged in with.

To create a new user account, you will click on either *Add a family member* or *Add someone else to this PC*. The family member option is used to add members of your family (like kids) where you want to restrict access to things like certain websites or games. The *someone else* option is where you would go to add a new standard or administrator user.

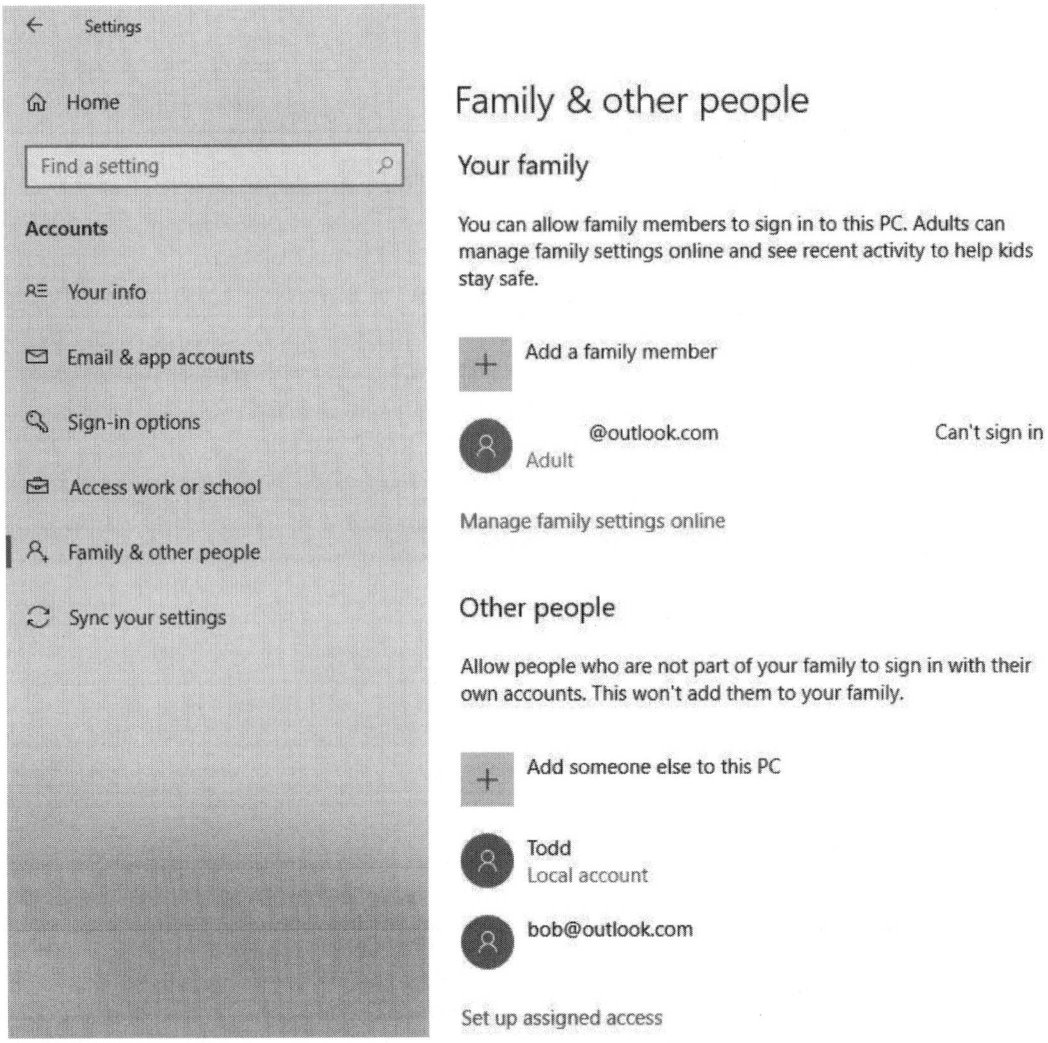
Settings
Home
Find a setting
Accounts
Your info
Email & app accounts
Sign-in options
Access work or school
Family & other people
Sync your settings
Family & other people
Your family
You can allow family members to sign in to this PC. Adults can manage family settings online and see recent activity to help kids stay safe.
Add a family member
@outlook.com
Adult
Can't sign in
Manage family settings online
Other people
Allow people who are not part of your family to sign in with their own accounts. This won't add them to your family.
Add someone else to this PC
Todd
Local account
bob@outlook.com
Set up assigned access

Figure 4.2

Let's add a new standard user to Windows by clicking on *Add someone else to this PC*. Here I will create a local user account rather than a Microsoft account. To do so, click on **I don't have this person's sign-in information** on the bottom of the window (figure 4.3).

Chapter 4 – User Accounts

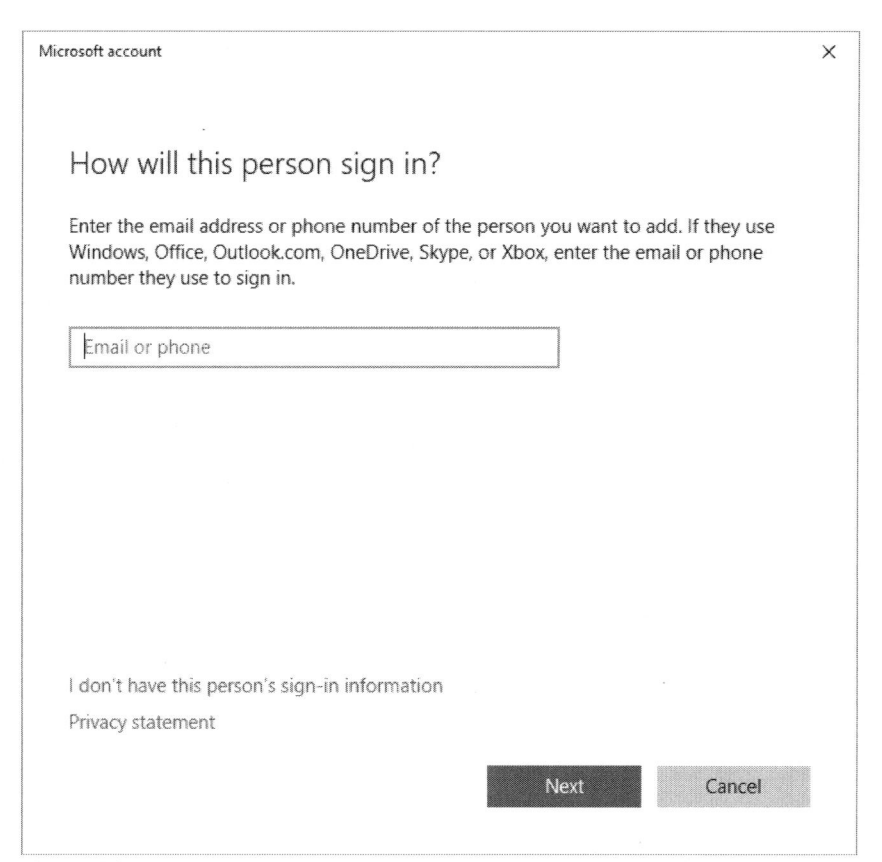

Figure 4.3

Then, on the next window where it asks for an email address again, click on the link that says **Add a user without a Microsoft account** (figure 4.4).

59

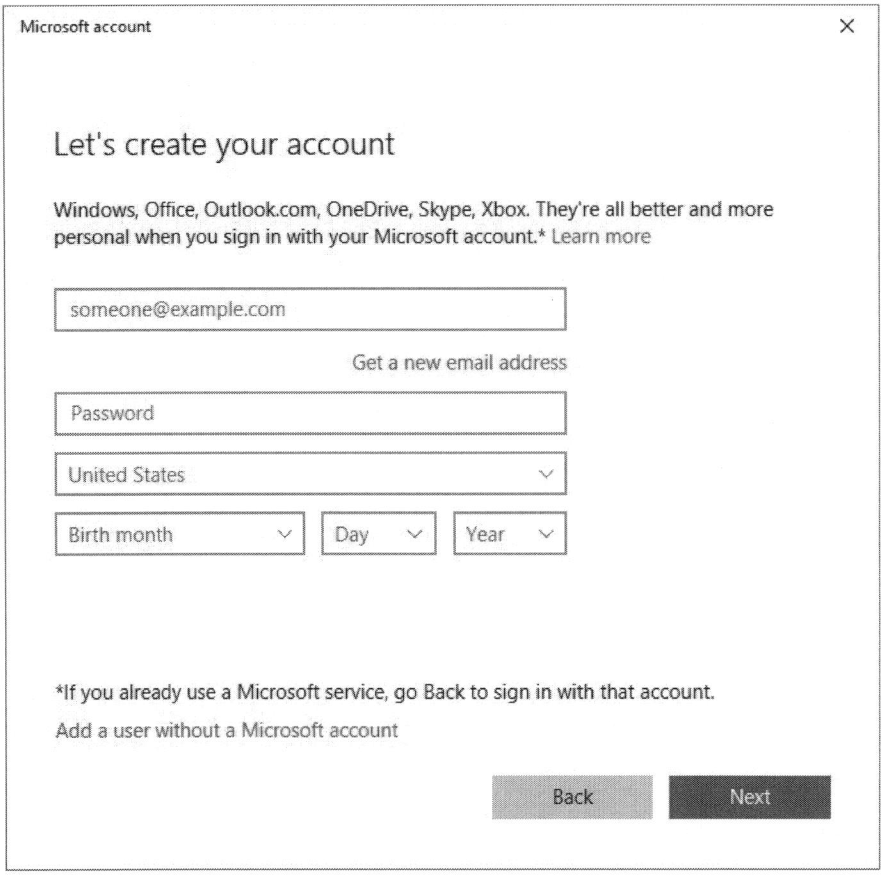

Figure 4.4

Next, you will be able to type in the username and password for your new local user. For the password hint section, choose something that will remind you of what the password is in case you forget it, but at the same time doesn't give the password itself away. Windows will also want you to answer some security questions in case you forget your password and want to try and recover it (figure 4.5).

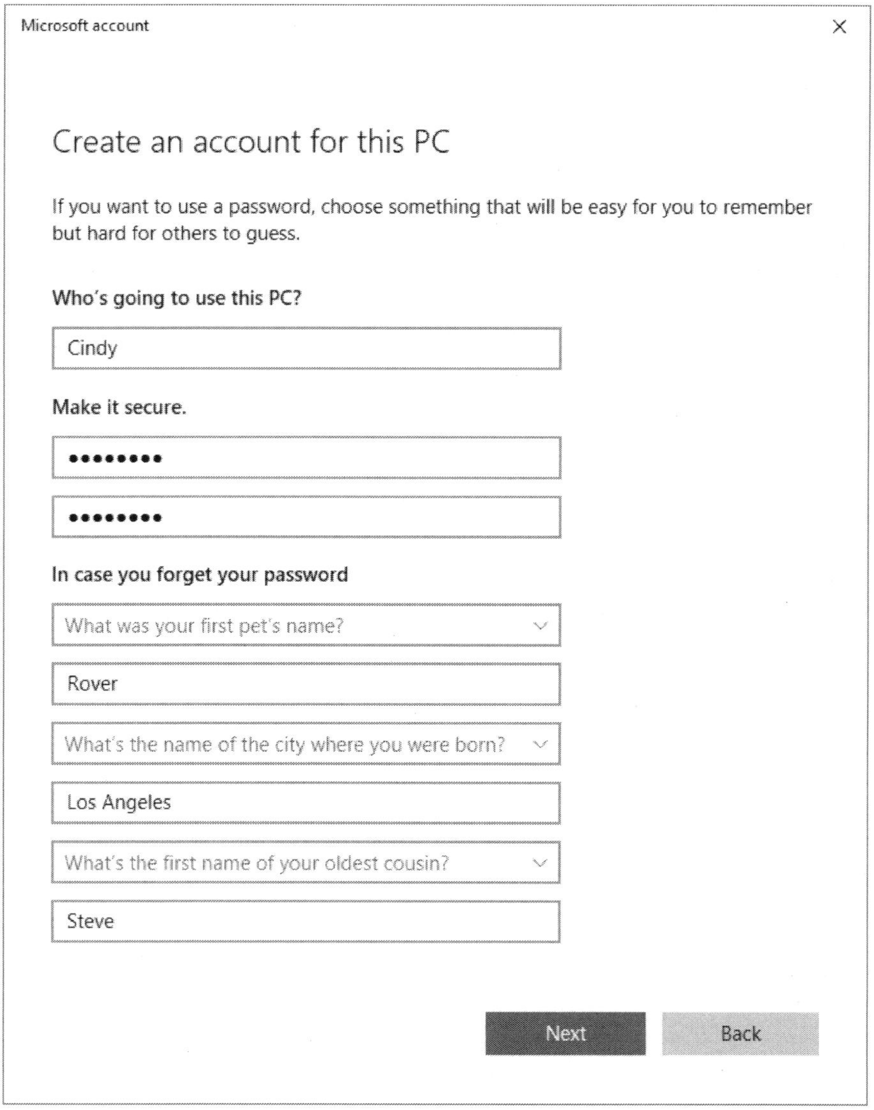

Chapter 4 – User Accounts

Figure 4.5

Once you have the account created, you can go back to the *Other people* section where your user accounts are listed, click on the user account, and then click the *Change account type* button to make the user an administrator if needed (figure 4.6).

61

Chapter 4 – User Accounts

Other people

Allow people who are not part of your family to sign in with their own accounts. This won't add them to your family.

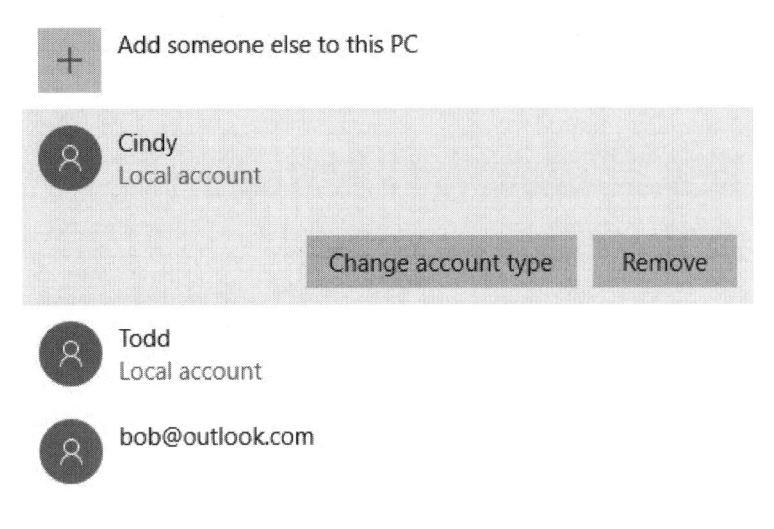

+ Add someone else to this PC

Cindy
Local account

Change account type   Remove

Todd
Local account

bob@outlook.com

Set up assigned access

Figure 4.6

You can also remove user accounts from this section. One thing to keep in mind when removing a user account is that it will also delete their data (such as documents, downloads, photos, and so on), so it's a good idea to back up their files first.

Now I will add a Microsoft account to a computer to show you how that process is done in case you want to go that route. Before you can add your Microsoft account to your computer, you will need to create one online so you will have the correct information handy when adding your account to the computer.

Back in the Family & other people section of the Windows 10 settings, you should see a link that says *Sign in with a Microsoft account*. If you are already signed in with your Microsoft account, you might not see this link.

Chapter 4 – User Accounts

Family & other people

Your family

Sign in with a Microsoft account to see your family here or add any new members to your family. Family members get their own sign-in and desktop. You can help kids stay safe with appropriate websites, time limits, apps, and games.

Sign in with a Microsoft account

Figure 4.7

The first thing you will need to do is enter the email address associated with your Microsoft account. In my case I created a new Outlook.com email address to use for this account and have entered it (as seen in figure 4.8).

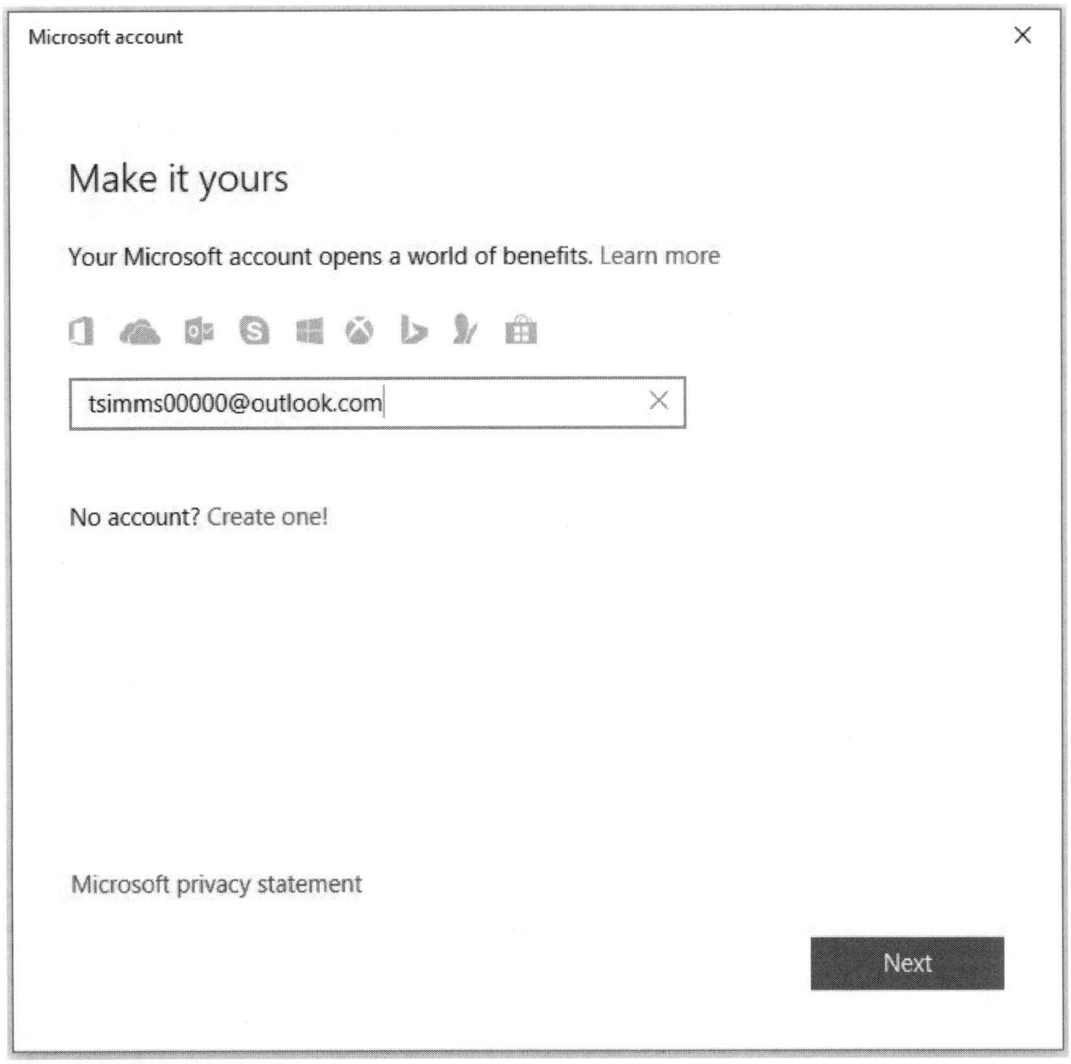
Microsoft account
Make it yours
Your Microsoft account opens a world of benefits. Learn more
tsimms00000@outlook.com
No account? Create one!
Microsoft privacy statement
Next
Figure 4.8

Next, I will enter the password associated with that Microsoft account (figure 4.9). At this step you are not making a new password, but entering the one used when you setup your account, so if you don't know it, then you will have to go online and have it reset.

Chapter 4 – User Accounts

![Microsoft account password entry dialog]

Microsoft account

Enter password

Enter the password for tsimms00000@outlook.com

••••••••

Forgot my password

Microsoft privacy statement

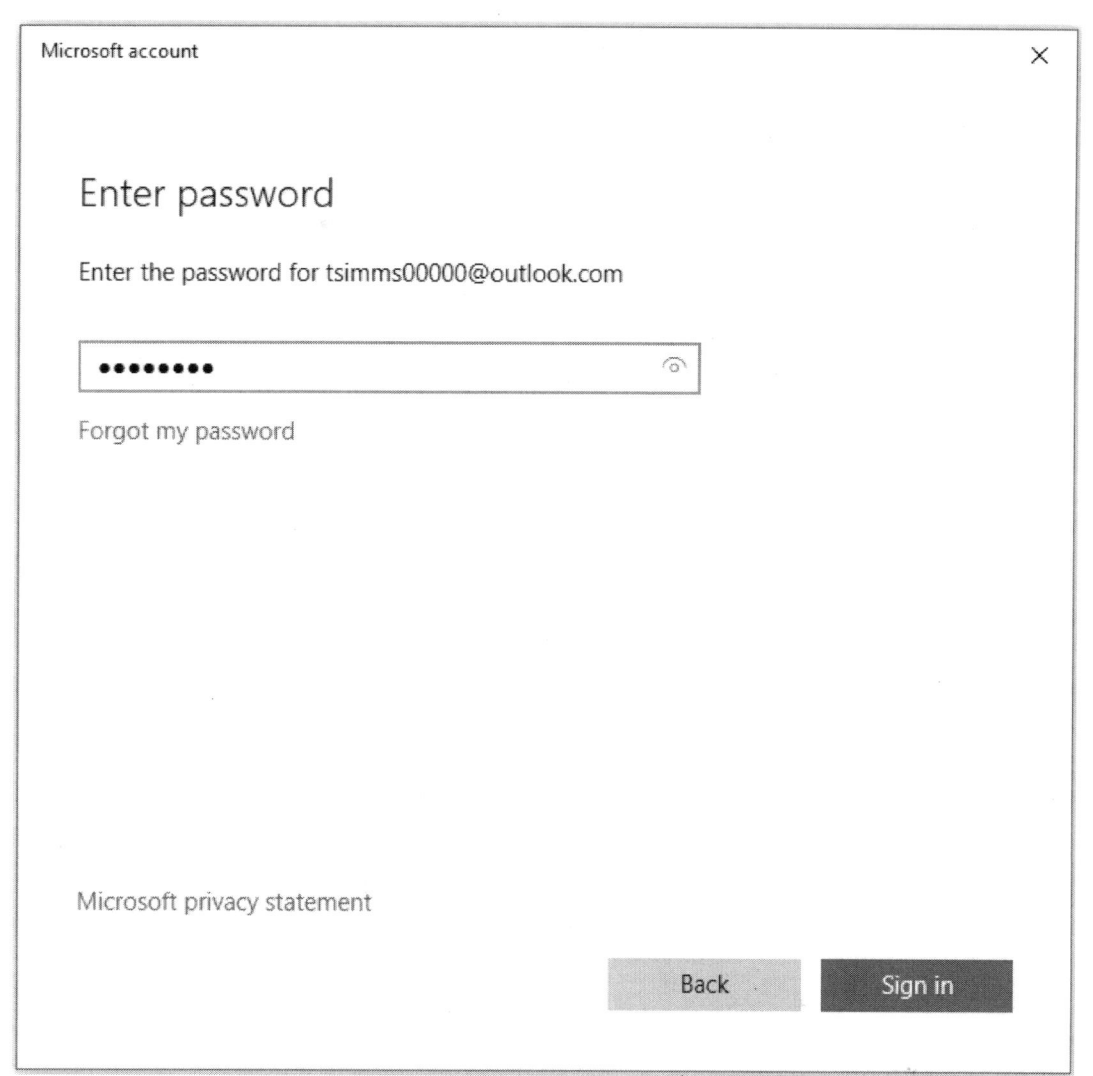

Back   Sign in

Figure 4.9

Next, you should get prompted to enter your current Windows password so the computer knows that it's actually *you* who is trying to add this Microsoft account to the computer (figure 4.10)

Chapter 4 – User Accounts

![Microsoft account sign-in dialog]

Microsoft account

Sign into this computer using your Microsoft account

From here on out, you'll unlock this device using either the password for your Microsoft account or, if you've set one up, your PIN. That way, you can get help from Cortana, you can find your device if you lose it, and your settings will automatically sync.

To make sure it's really you, we'll need your current Windows password one last time. Next time you sign into Windows you'll use your Microsoft account password.

If you don't have a Windows password, just leave the box blank and select Next.

Current Windows password

••••••••

Next

Figure 4.10

Finally, you may be asked to create a PIN to go along with your account (figure 4.11). This PIN is the same type that you would use with your ATM card, so that way you can type that in to get into Windows rather than your password if you want to make things a little easier on yourself.

Chapter 4 – User Accounts

![Create a PIN dialog]

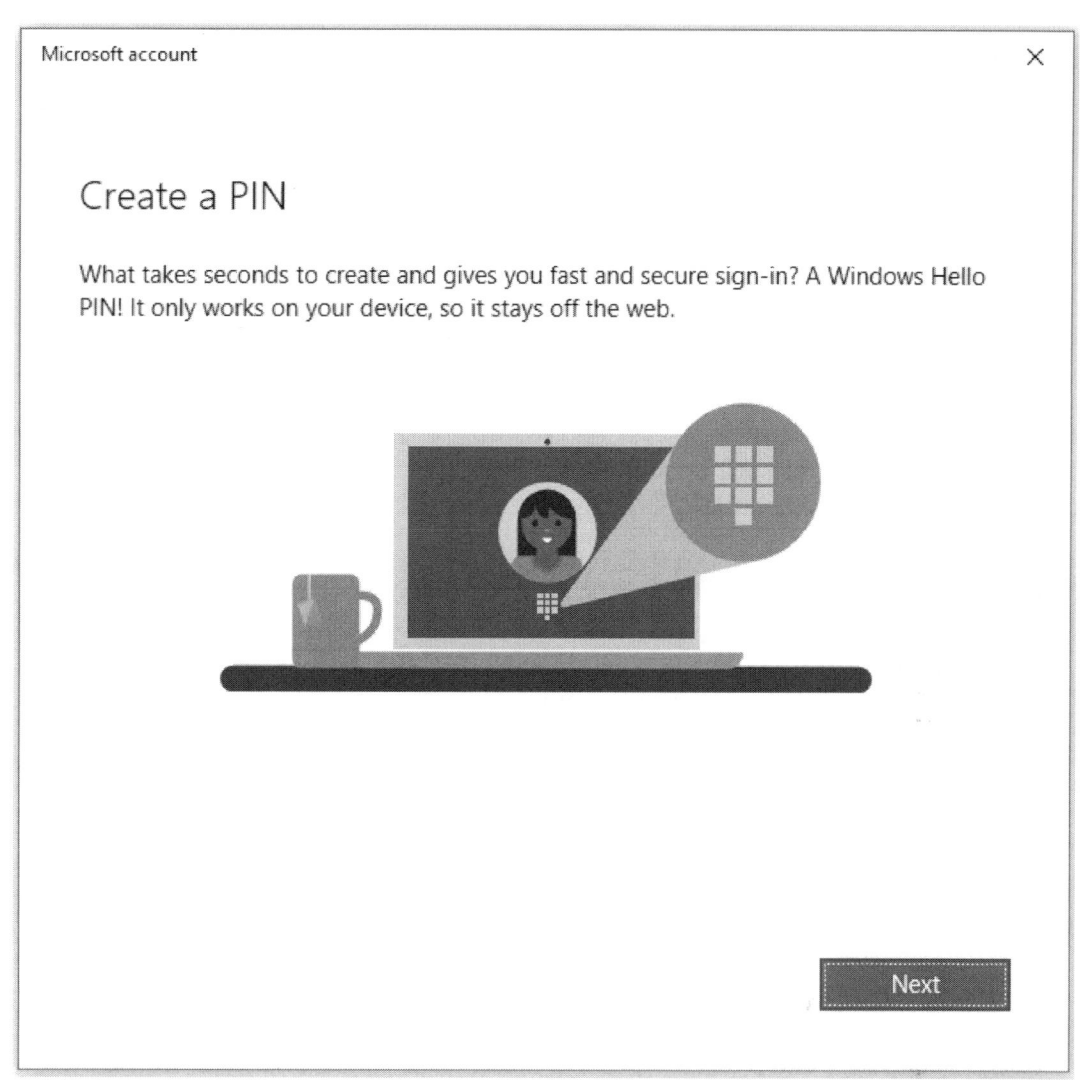

Figure 4.11

After taking all of these steps, you can go back to the *Your info* section in the user account settings and see that you are not using your Microsoft account on this computer (figure 4.12)

Chapter 4 – User Accounts

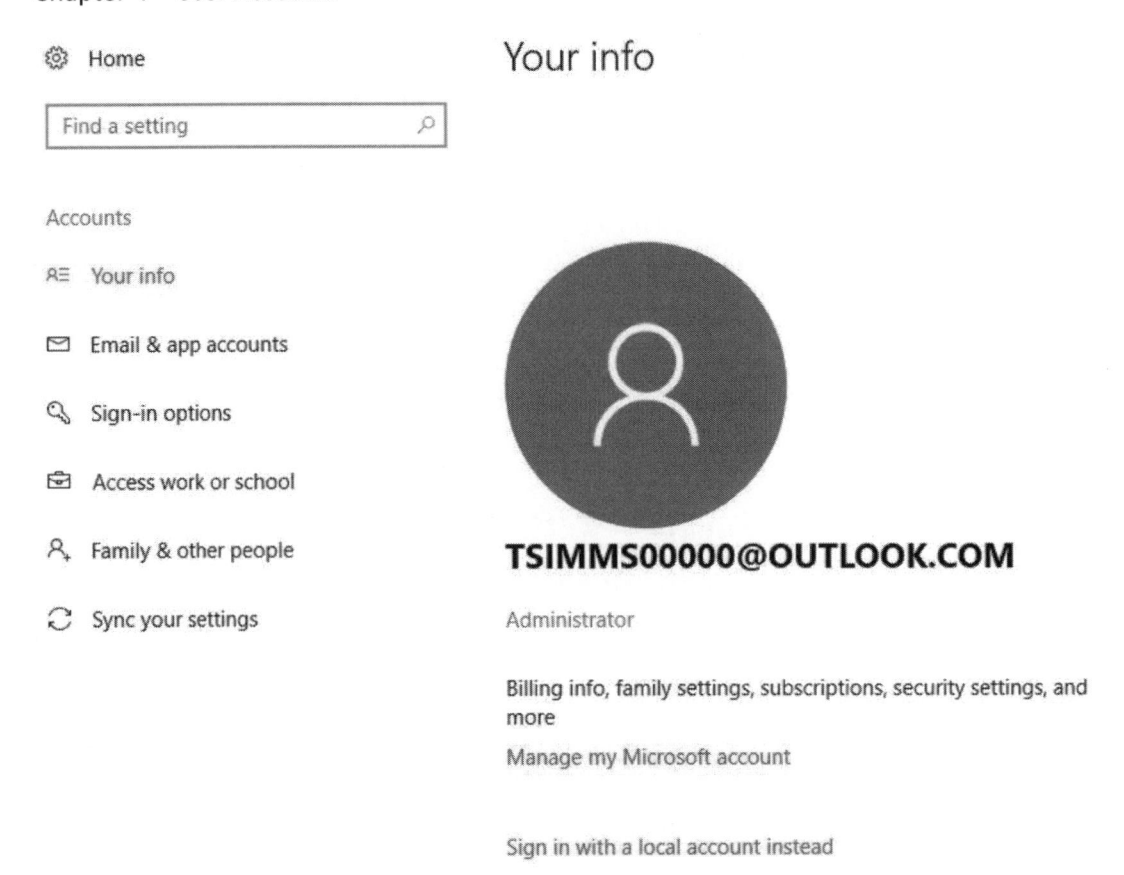

⚙ Home	**Your info**
Find a setting 🔍	
Accounts	
ᛎ≡ Your info	
✉ Email & app accounts	
🔑 Sign-in options	
🗂 Access work or school	
👪 Family & other people	**TSIMMS00000@OUTLOOK.COM**
🔄 Sync your settings	Administrator
	Billing info, family settings, subscriptions, security settings, and more
	Manage my Microsoft account
	Sign in with a local account instead

Figure 4.12

One thing I want to stress with Workgroup networking is that each user needs to be configured on each computer that they need to access, so if Bob needs to use three out of ten computers, he will need to be manually added to each one of those three computers (preferably with the same password so they don't have to remember three of them).

Groups
I wanted to quickly go over Windows groups since you can use them with Workgroup networking, although they are not really used that much compared to domain networking, where they really come in handy.

Windows has its own default users and groups that you can view if you know how to get to them. These are not shown in the usual places such as the User Accounts setting in Control Panel, or the Accounts setting in the Windows 10 Settings. The easiest way to get to this section is to type in **lusrmgr.msc** from the Run box, and you will see a Microsoft Management Console (MMC) similar to figure 4.13 where you can view the local users, and figure 4.14 where you can see the local groups.

Chapter 4 – User Accounts

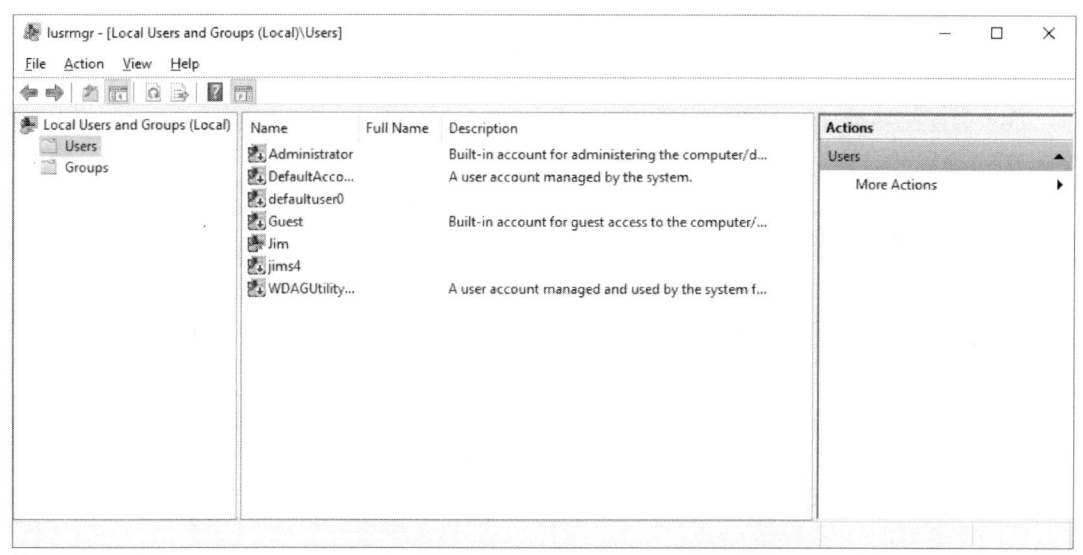

Figure 4.13

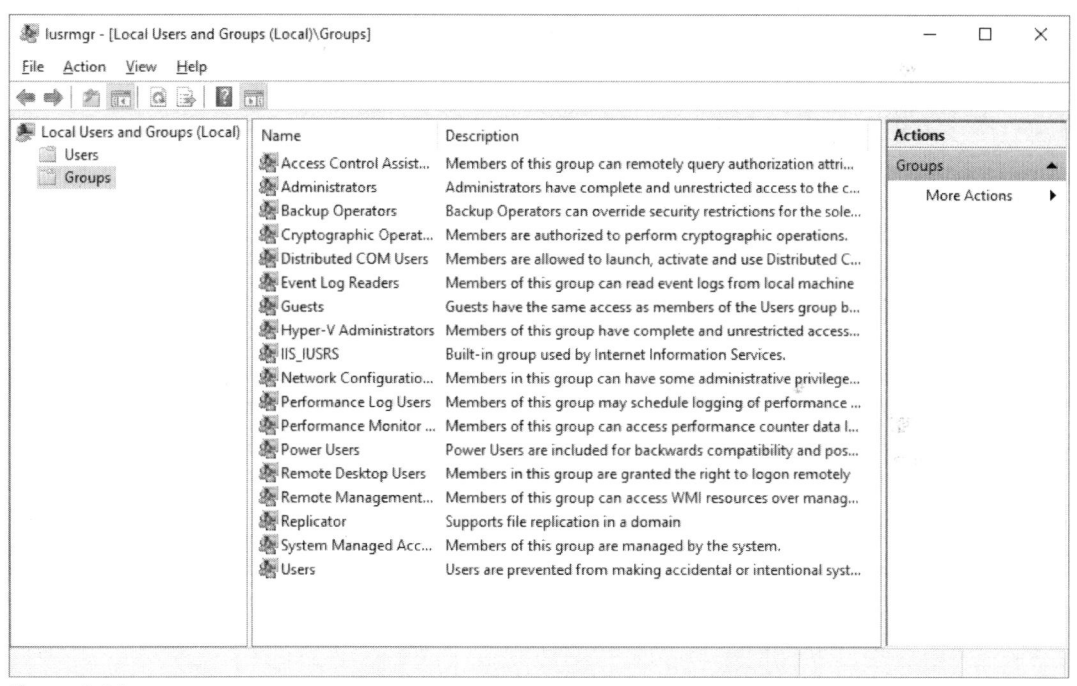

Figure 4.14

This console can only be accessed by Windows 10 Pro and above and unfortunately can't be used with Windows 10 Home Edition. For the most part, you won't be messing with any of these groups except for maybe Administrators and Remoted Desktop Users, which I will be discussing in the next chapter.

69

Chapter 4 – User Accounts

> **Tip:** Microsoft has been trying to update the way administrative tasks are done in Windows while trying to keep the functionality that admins have been used to for years, so you will find that there are several ways to do things in Windows, and sometimes the old ways are still the best. I assume they will consolidate things

If I open up the Administrator group, for example, it will show me what users are contained within that group (figure 4.15).

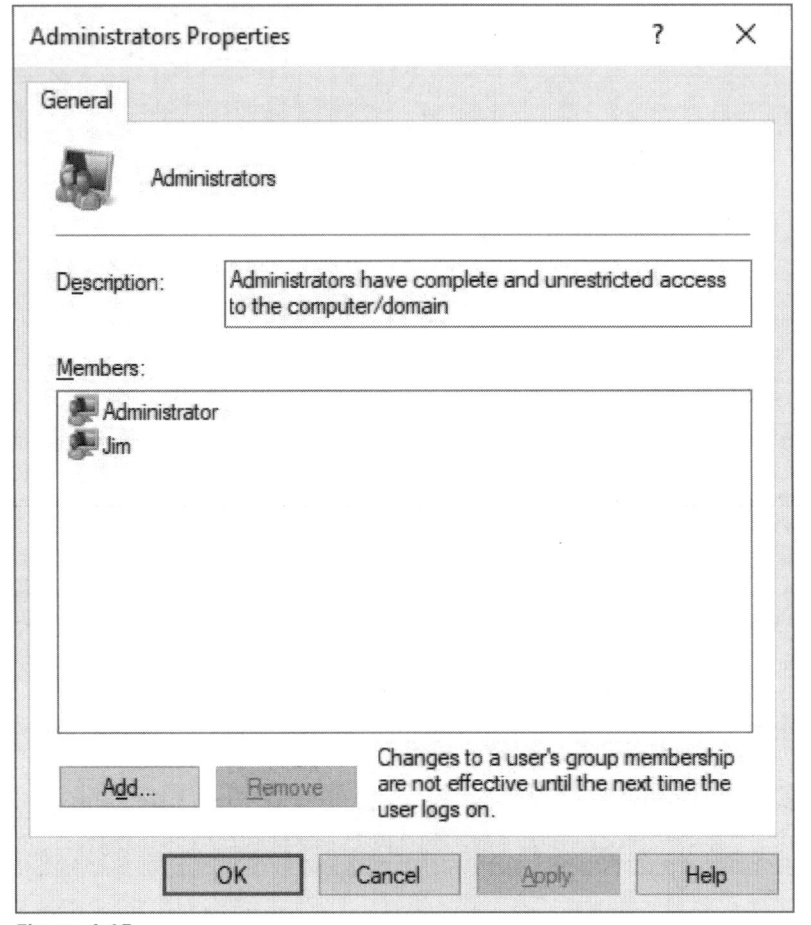

Figure 4.15

Now let's say I wanted to add another user from this computer to this group so they can have local administrative rights to the computer. All I need to do is click on the *Add* button, type in the user name or do a search, and that's it. Then, the next time that user logs in to this computer, they will officially be a local administrator. They

Chapter 4 – User Accounts

won't notice anything looking different with this new power, but will be able to perform tasks that they couldn't before.

You can create your own groups and then add local users to those groups in order to consolidate tasks. For example, let's say you had a sales printer that you only wanted sales people to be able to use. You can make a group called *Sales*, add all of your sales users to that group, and then only allow the Sales group access to the sales printer. This way you don't have to add each user individually to the printer, but rather just add the group. Then, if you have new sales people later, you can add their accounts to that sales group and they will automatically be able to access the sales printer.

Like I mentioned before, using groups in Workgroups is not nearly as effective as in a domain environment, and it's a lot more work setting them up since users are configured on a computer-by-computer basis rather than network-wide like they are on a domain.

Chapter 5 – Sharing Resources

Now that you have your users setup on all of your computers, it's finally time to discuss the reason you set up your network to begin with: sharing resources. For the most part, you will be sharing files and folders, but you can also share things like printers, external drives, software databases, and so on.

Resource Sharing and Permissions
No matter what type of network configuration you are configuring, you should come up with a plan on what users will have what type of access to your shared resources. Permissions need to be set properly, otherwise you will have users who are able to access things they shouldn't, and users who will be blocked from using resources they should be able to use.

I will first begin by discussing file and folder shares and the different types of permissions that go along with them. Then I will dive into some sharing examples between networked computers.

For files and folder sharing and permissions, the easiest way to begin is by right clicking on the item you want to share, and then choosing *Properties*. From there, you will need to assign share level permissions and then Security (or NTFS) permissions.

Share permissions are what you use to have the resource be shared on the network for other users to access. Security permissions are the levels of access you can give to those users who are allowed to use the shared resources. Just keep in mind that when share and NTFS permissions are used simultaneously, the most restrictive permission will always apply. Also know that NTFS permissions apply to users who are logged on to the computer locally (and over the network), while share permissions don't apply because you are not accessing a shared resource while logged on locally to the computer that hosts that share. Here is a summary of the share and NTFS permissions available on a Windows network. These apply to workgroups and domains.

Below is a summary of the share and NTFS permissions you can assign to your resources. Figure 5.1 shows the permissions screens for each one.

Chapter 5 – Sharing Resources

Share Permissions

- **Read** - Users can view file and folder names, open files, and run programs. The *Everyone* group is assigned *Read* permissions by default.

- **Change** - Users can do everything allowed by the *Read* permission, as well as add files and subfolders, edit files, and delete subfolders and files.

- **Full Control** - Users can do everything allowed by the *Read* and *Change* permissions, as well as change permissions for NTFS files and folders only. The *Administrators* group is granted *Full Control* permission by default.

NTFS Permissions

- **Full Control** - Users can add, modify, move, and delete files and directories, as well as their associated properties. Users can also change permissions for all files and subdirectories.

- **Modify** - Users can view and modify files and their properties, including adding files to or deleting files from a directory, or file properties to or from a file.

- **Read & Execute** - Users can run executable files, including scripts, as well as open files.

- **List folder contents** - Permits viewing and listing of files and subfolders as well as executing files.

- **Read** - Users can open files and view file properties and directories.

- **Write** - Users can write to a file as well as create files and folders.

Chapter 5 – Sharing Resources

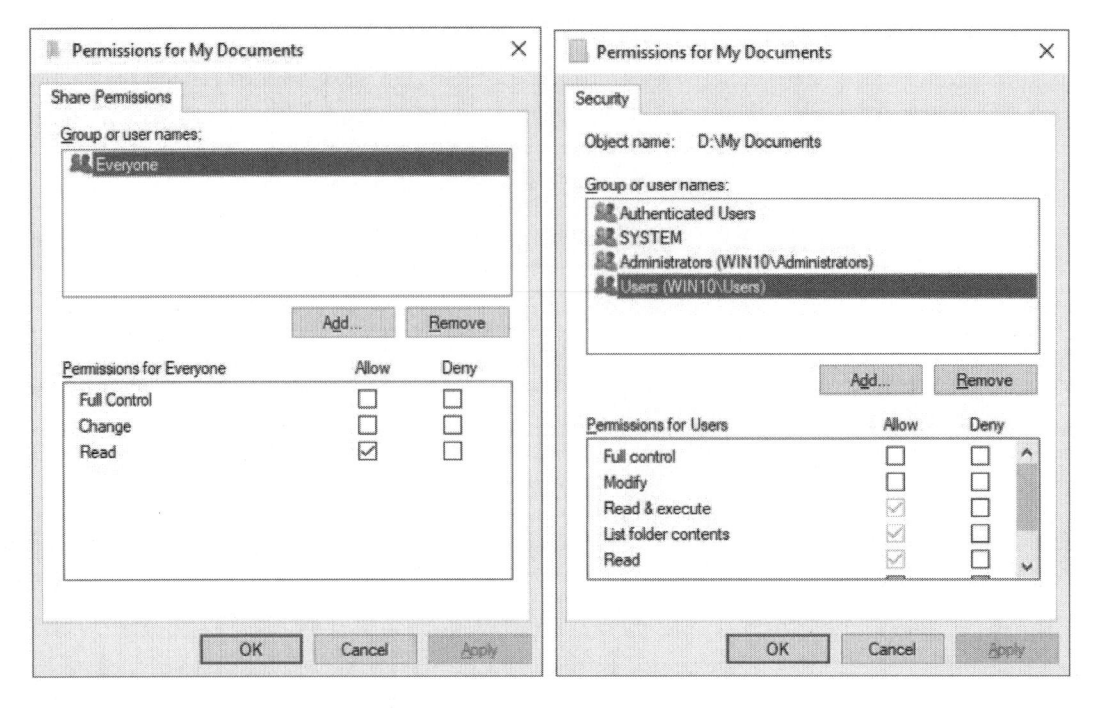

Figure 5.1

If you plan on sharing many folders with many users, you might want to come up with a game plan first and write it all down so you are not trying to remember what you wanted to do during the process itself.

UNC Paths
If you plan on accessing shared resources on other computers on a regular basis, then you will need to know about UNC (Universal Naming Convention) paths. These paths are used to navigate directly to a shared resource without having to browse to find it. They are similar to website addresses (URLs) that take you to a particular page.

For example, here is a URL (Uniform Resource Locator) for a website:

https://www.onlinecomputertips.com/support-categories/networking/298-mapping-a-network-drive

And here is a UNC path example for a shared folder:

\\computer-name\share-name\folder

Chapter 5 – Sharing Resources

A more specific example would look like this:

\\Server1\SalesFiles\Reports

Notice how the URL and UNC path both use a similar format, except the URL uses forward slashes (/) and the UNC path uses backslashes (\). Also take note how they start with the main server or website and work their way down to a more specific destination.

So, for the website URL, it starts with the *www.onlinecomputertips.com* website, then goes to the *support-categories* level, then the *networking* level, and then finally the page on mapping a network drive.

For the UNC path, it starts at *Server1,* which is the name of the computer the share is located on, and then goes down to the next level, which is the *SalesFiles* share itself, and finally reaches the *Reports* folder, which is inside the SalesFiles share.

To use UNC paths, you can either type them into your Windows Explorer address bar, or even in the Run dialog box. If you take a look at figure 5.2, you can see that I entered the UNC path in the address bar, and then Windows recognized it as one and brought up the *Computer* tab, where I have options to do things like map a network drive or add a network location.

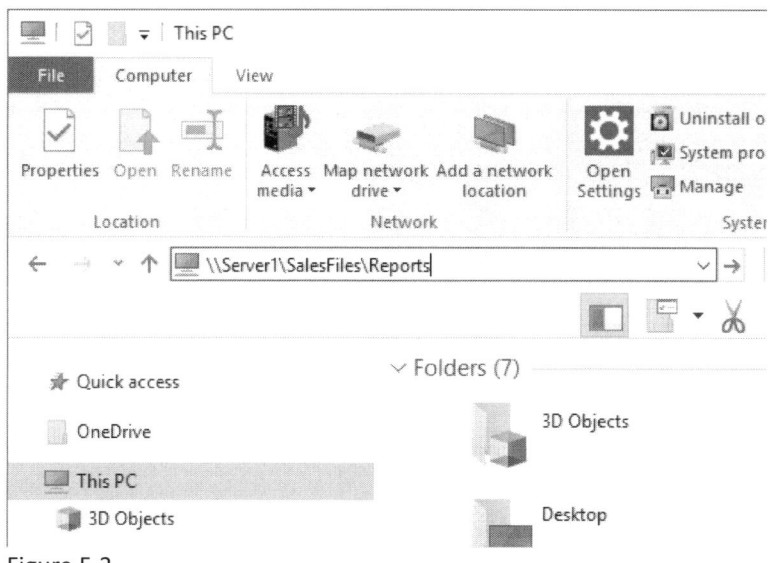

Figure 5.2

Speaking of mapping a network drive, this can be used to add a permanent (until you remove it) placeholder on your computer for that particular UNC path so you don't have to type it in each time or even remember it! (I will demonstrate this as well coming up next.)

Windows Firewall

Before you can start sharing resources, you will need to make sure that your computers will allow other computers to connect to them, and many times the Windows Firewall will prevent that, so I want to spend a moment talking about the Windows Firewall and what you need to do to allow the access you need to be allowed through the firewall.

When working with Windows networking, you will still need to account for security measures and realize that Windows computers will not just let any traffic pass from computer to computer without being checked. If it did allow everything through unfiltered, then Microsoft wouldn't have much of a reputation for being a secure operating system.

Windows comes with a built-in software firewall that is designed to filter incoming and outgoing traffic on your computer to help the overall security of your computer. For the most part, it's something you won't really need to mess with, and you can usually just let it do its job in the background. But if you need to allow or deny a certain application or service, then you can do it from the firewall. For example, you may come across a situation where a Windows computer on your network is not pingable, and it can be a case of the firewall blocking ICMP traffic. In this case, you can go into the firewall and allow it so you are able to ping the computer.

Chapter 5 – Sharing Resources

To open the Windows Firewall, you can do so from Control Panel, or simply type *firewall* in the Start menu search box to open the firewall application. As you can see in figure 5.3, the Windows Firewall is divided up into different panes that show you certain types of information and also allows you to make configuration changes.

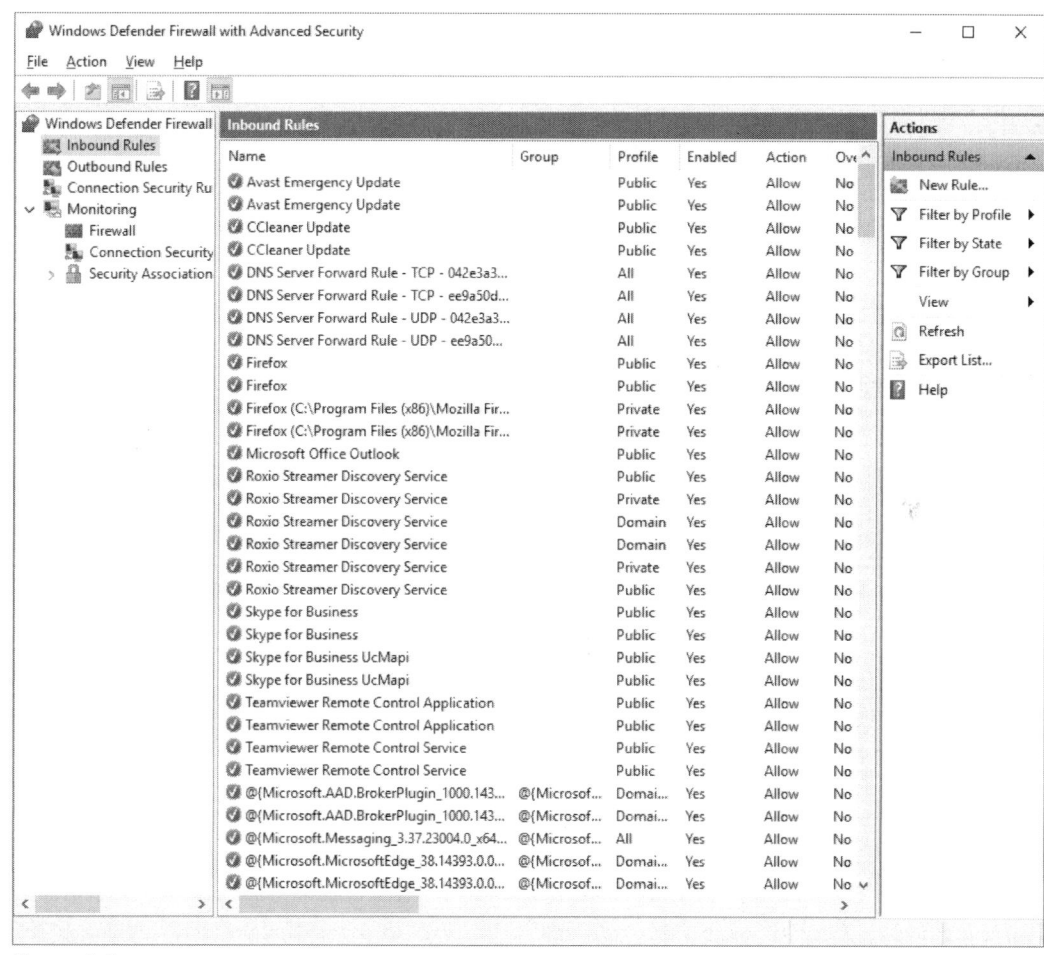

Figure 5.3

On the left side, you have your inbound and outbound rules, which are used to control what comes into your computer over the network or Internet and what your computer is sending out over the network. The Connection Security Rules section is where you can create a custom rule that determines how computers are authenticated using IPsec. IPsec (Internet Protocol Security) is a framework of standards for ensuring private, secure communications over IP networks. The Monitoring section is where you can see stats on how the firewall is working as well as set up things like notifications and configure logging options.

Chapter 5 – Sharing Resources

The middle pane shows things like your inbound and outbound rules depending on what you click on from the pane on the left. So, if you were to click on Inbound Rules on the left, it would show you all of the rules for incoming traffic in the middle pane like figure 5.3 shows. You can then do things from the right pane such as disable the rule, or copy it to create a new rule from the existing rule settings. If you click on *Properties* (figure 5.4), it will show you a bunch of information relating to that rule, such as what program it applies to, the protocols and ports it uses, what IP addresses it applies to, and so on.

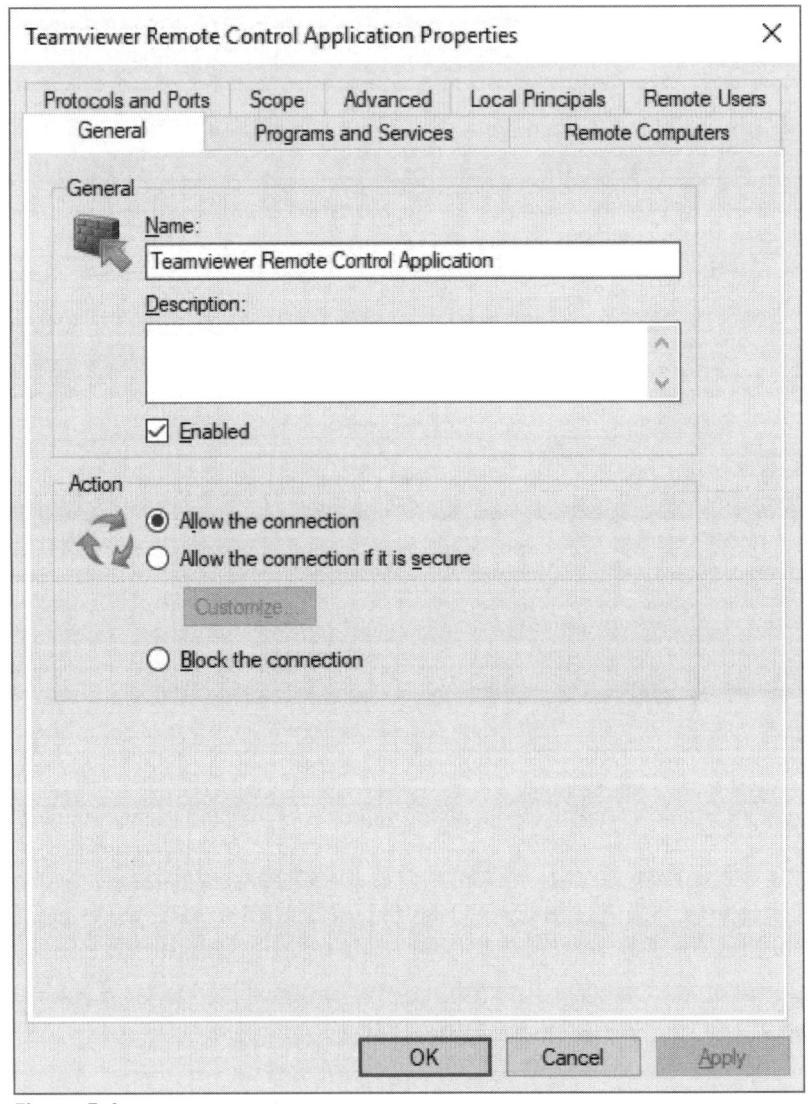

Figure 5.4

To make a new rule, you would first click on *Inbound Rules* or *Outbound Rules* (depending on which direction you want the rule to apply to) and then click on *New Rule* in the right pane. Then you will have to choose if the rule applies to a program,

Chapter 5 – Sharing Resources

port, predefined Windows experience, or a custom rule (figure 5.5). The rule type that you choose will determine what configuration steps you will need to perform next will be.

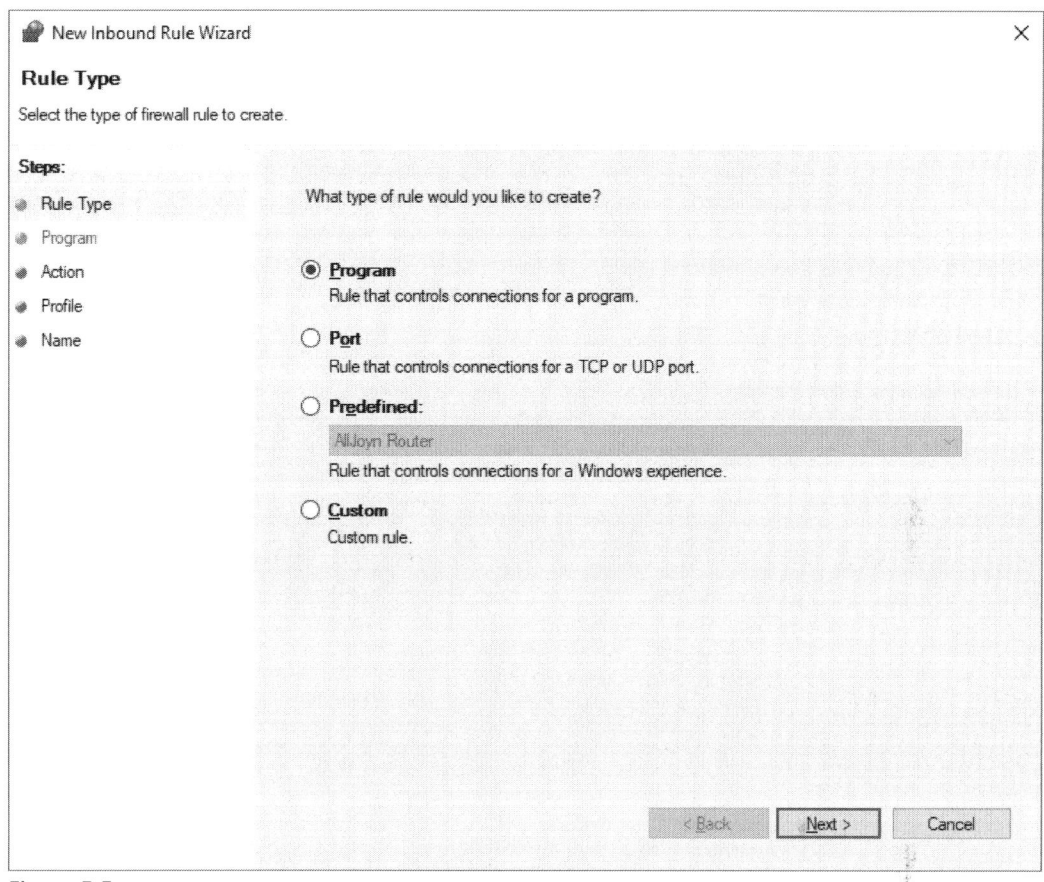

Figure 5.5

If you ever need to see if the Windows Firewall is responsible for blocking a network application or traffic, you can disable it to do some testing. You can do so by clicking on the *Action* menu and then clicking on *Properties*.

One easy way around all of these firewall rules is to disable it completely, but of course that is a security risk. If you have a quality physical firewall between your network and the Internet, then you may be able to get away with it, assuming you trust all of the computers and users within your network. To turn the Windows Firewall off, simply click on the link that says *Turn Windows Firewall on or off*.

Chapter 5 – Sharing Resources

Windows Firewall

← → ˅ ↑ 🛡 › Control Panel

Control Panel Home

Allow an app or feature through Windows Firewall

Change notification settings

Turn Windows Firewall on or off

Restore defaults

Advanced settings

Troubleshoot my network

Figure 5.6

Then select the option to Turn off Windows Firewall for the network type you are using. Then repeat this step on each of the computers in your network.

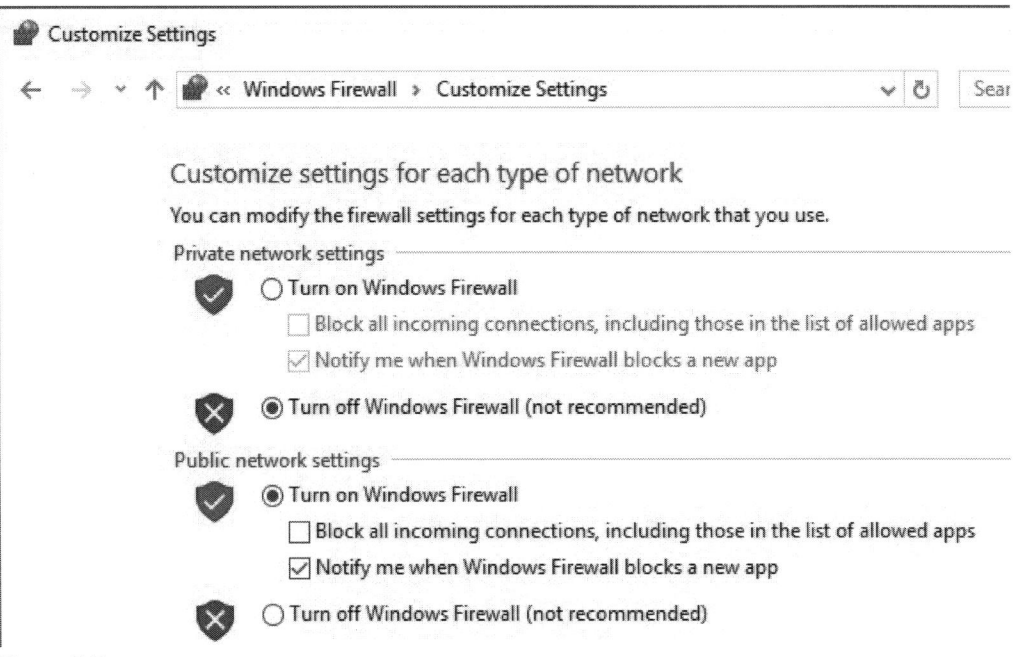

Customize Settings

← → ˅ ↑ 🛡 « Windows Firewall › Customize Settings   ˅ ↻   Sear

Customize settings for each type of network

You can modify the firewall settings for each type of network that you use.

Private network settings
- ○ Turn on Windows Firewall
  - ☐ Block all incoming connections, including those in the list of allowed apps
  - ☑ Notify me when Windows Firewall blocks a new app
- ● Turn off Windows Firewall (not recommended)

Public network settings
- ● Turn on Windows Firewall
  - ☐ Block all incoming connections, including those in the list of allowed apps
  - ☑ Notify me when Windows Firewall blocks a new app
- ○ Turn off Windows Firewall (not recommended)

Figure 5.7

Chapter 5 – Sharing Resources

For those of you who still want to use the Windows Firewall, there are some changes you can make to allow your traffic through so you can still share your files, folders, and printers. In the firewall, click on the link for *Advanced settings* (as seen in figure 5.6). Then click on Inbound Rules and find the rules named *File and Printer Sharing (NB-Session-In)* and *File and Printer Sharing (SMB-In)* and enable them like shown in figure 5.8. Just be sure you are enabling them for the network that you are using. So, in my case, it's for the Private network and not the Public or Domain networks.

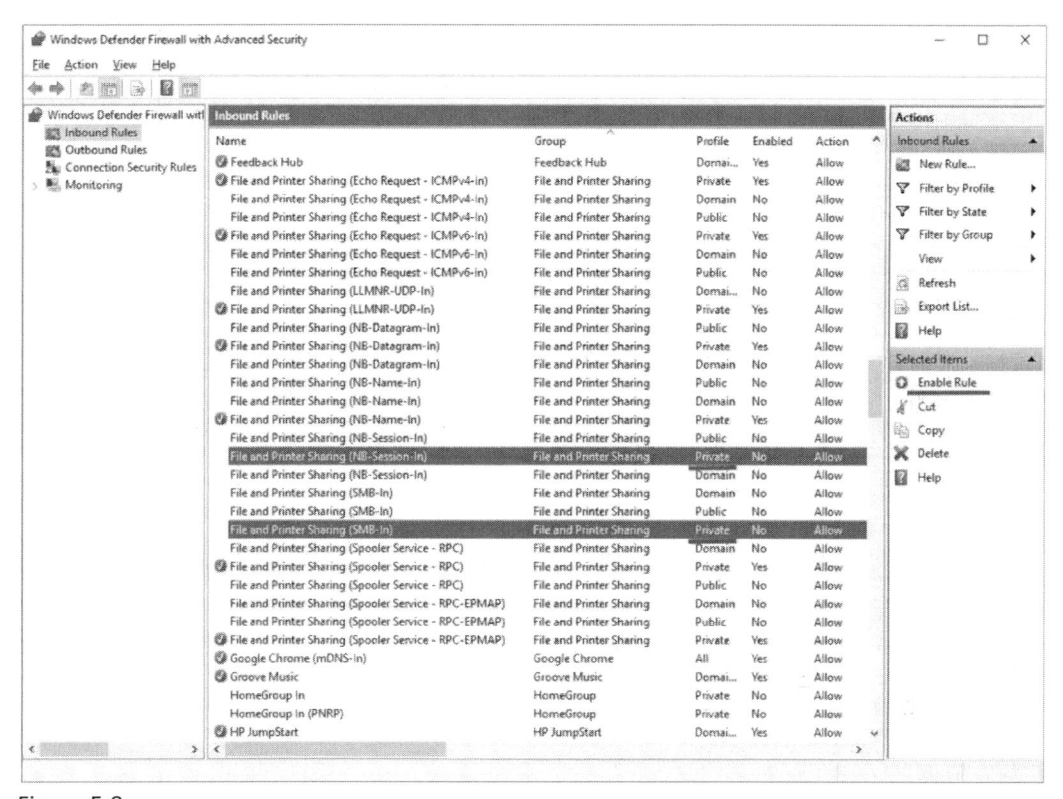

Figure 5.8

Another way to make this change and also to confirm that it is configured is to click on the link that says Allow an app or feature through Windows Firewall (figure 5.6), and make sure that File and Printer Sharing is checked for the network that you are using (figure 5.9).

Chapter 5 – Sharing Resources

Allow apps to communicate through Windows Defender Firewall

To add, change, or remove allowed apps and ports, click Change settings.

What are the risks of allowing an app to communicate?

Allowed apps and features:		
Name	Private	Public
☑ DNS Server Forward Rule - UDP - ee9a50d7-c90b-4e83-9827-2077028adee7 - 0	☑	☑
☑ dpdecoder	☐	☑
☑ Email and accounts	☑	☑
☑ Facebook	☑	☑
☑ Feedback Hub	☑	☑
☑ File and Printer Sharing	☑	☐
☑ Firefox	☐	☑
☑ Firefox (C:\Program Files (x86)\Mozilla Firefox)	☑	☐
☑ FusionScript services for Fusion	☐	☑
☑ Get Help	☑	☑
☑ Google Chrome	☑	☑
☑ Groove Music	☑	☑

Figure 5.9

> **Tip:** If you are not using Windows 10, then you might find the wording of these links and items to be a little different, and that's because Microsoft likes to change things for the sake of changing things. But, for the most part, you should be able to figure out what I'm referring to.

Another thing you should enable in the Windows Firewall is ICMP (Internet Control Message Protocol), which is used by PING (Packet Internet Groper) to test the connectivity between network devices. You will be using PING for troubleshooting tasks when computers don't want to communicate with each other. This procedure is performed the same way as the steps for enabling File and Printer Sharing except you will enable the rule called *File and Printer Sharing (Echo Request - ICMPv4-In)* for the appropriate network. (I will be going over PING in more detail in Chapter 6.)

Sharing Files and Folders
Now it's time to set up a few networked computers and get them communicating with each other so we can share some files, folders, and printers. For this

Chapter 5 – Sharing Resources

demonstration, I will have a computer named **Computer1**, **Computer2,** and then my workstation that I have been using so far called **Win10**. They will all be running Windows 10 and using the default Workgroup name of WORKGROUP.

I will create two additional users besides myself on each computer named Cindy and Joe to begin with since we will need people to share our files with! To begin, we will log on to Computer1 as the administrator and create these two users, as well as add myself as a user. This process does not have to be done with the administrator account, and can be done by any user with local administrator privileges on that computer.

There are many ways to add users, and the options you will have will be based on what version of Windows you are running. If you remember back in Chapter 4, I already went over the method used for Windows 10 using the PC Settings interface. I will now go over two other ways you can use to add users to your computer.

The first method I will use is done by going to the *Control Panel* and choosing *User Accounts*. Once you are in the User Accounts section, you will see the user that you are currently logged in as (figure 5.3). In my case, I am logged in with a local user named Admin.

To add a new user, simply click on the link that says *Manage another user account,* and it will take you to another screen where you will have an option that says *Add a new user in PC settings*. You will see this if you are running Windows 10, and that is because you need to make your new users in the PC settings rather than from the User Account settings in Control Panel.

Chapter 5 – Sharing Resources

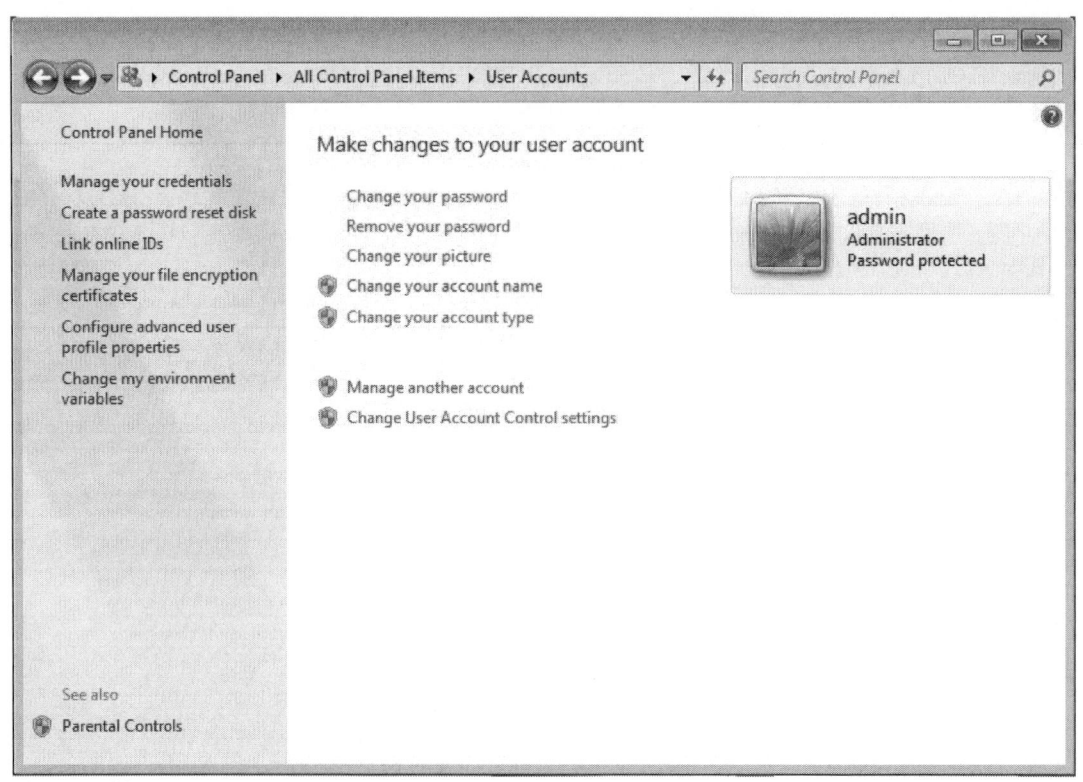

Figure 5.10

If you are running Windows 7, then you will see a link that says *Create a new account* (figure 5.11) after you clicked on the Manage another user account link.

Chapter 5 – Sharing Resources

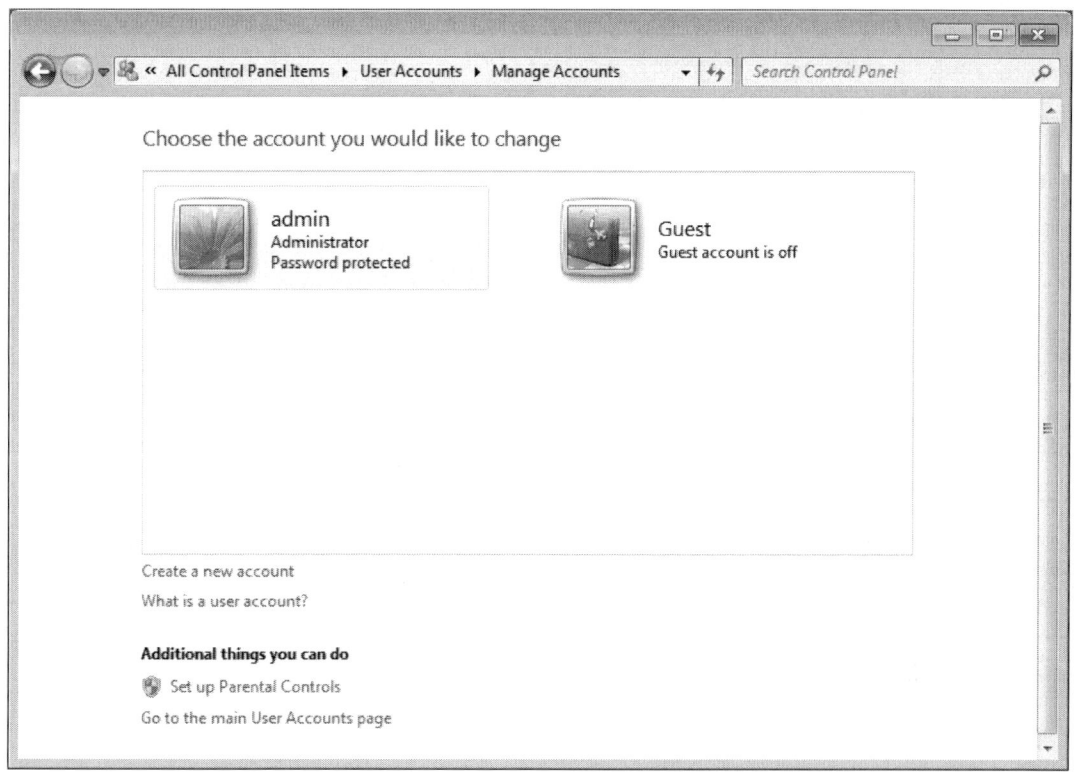

Figure 5.11

Next, you will need to type in the username and then decide if it will be a standard or administrator account, and then click on the *Create account* button (figure 5.12).

Chapter 5 – Sharing Resources

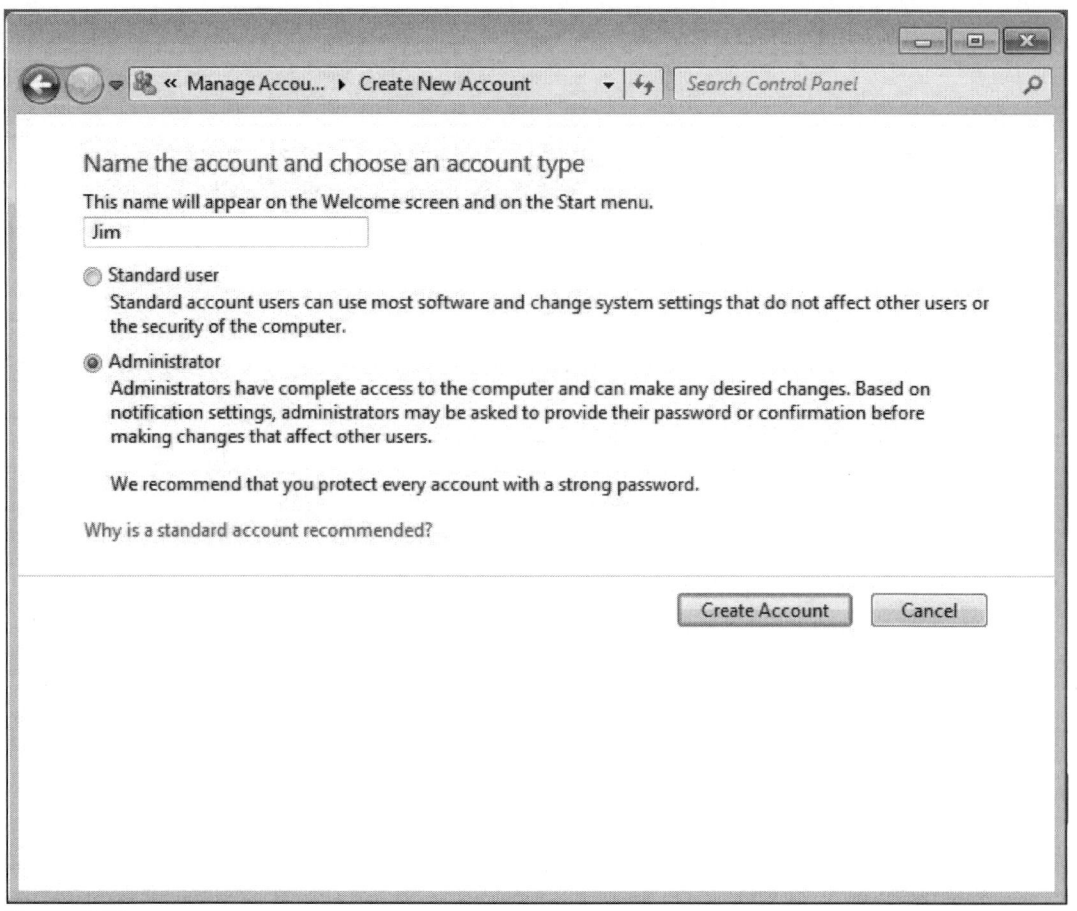

Figure 5.12

Then it will take you back to your accounts list, where you will see the new account that has been added (figure 5.13). You might be wondering why you didn't create a password for this user when you made the account. I often wonder that myself, but to create the password you need to click on the new user, where you will be taken to a screen where you can create a password for that user (figure 5.14).

Chapter 5 – Sharing Resources

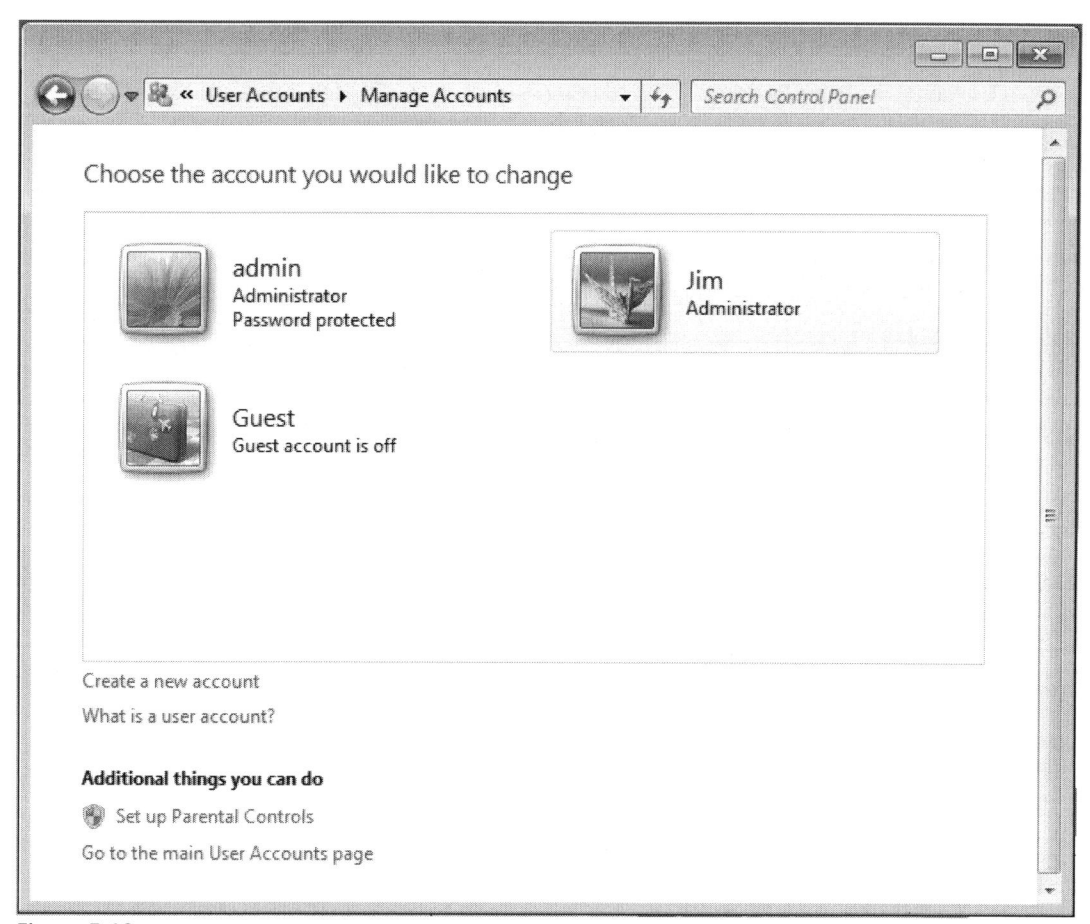

Figure 5.13

Chapter 5 – Sharing Resources

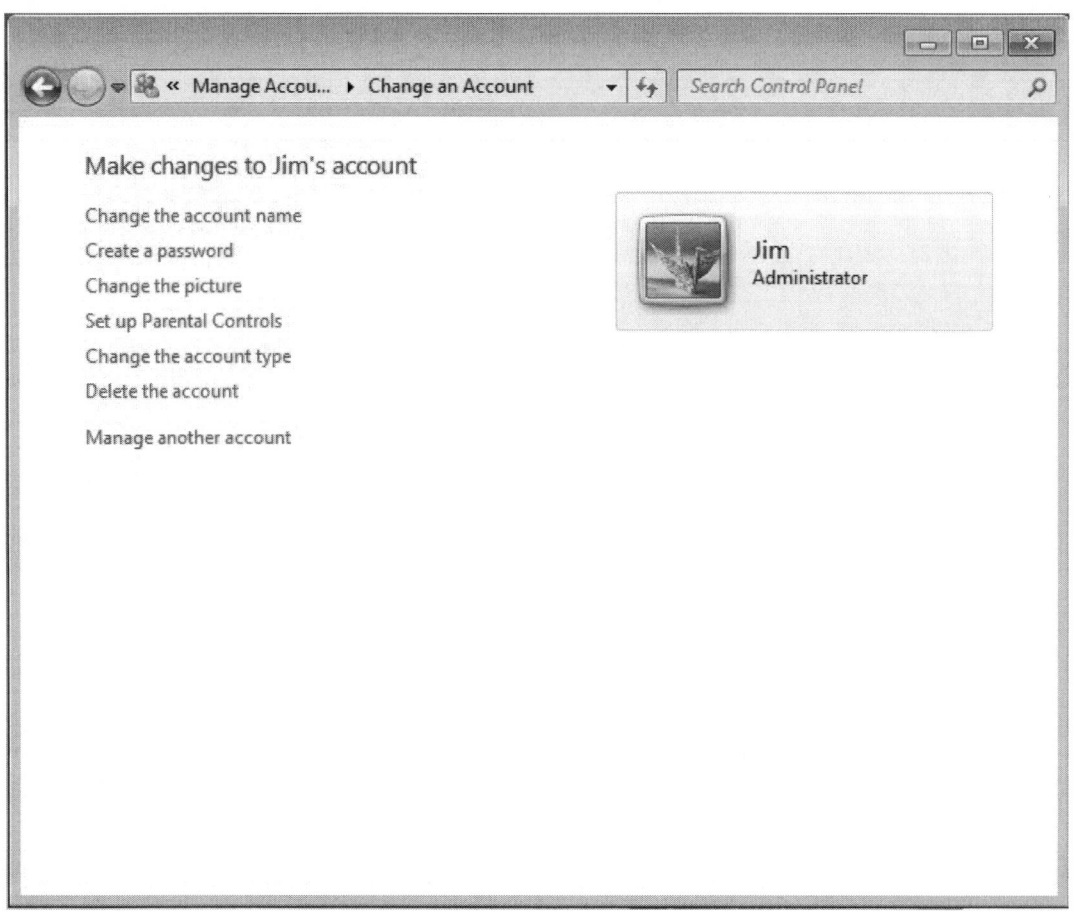

Figure 5.14

Once you click on *Create a password,* you will be prompted to enter the new password, confirm it, and then create a password hint (figure 5.15). Just be sure to make this password the same on all of the computers you want this user to access to avoid issues with accessing resources. When finished, click on the *Create password* button, and you will be ready to go. You will just need to do the same process for all the other users you want to have permission to access this computer.

Chapter 5 – Sharing Resources

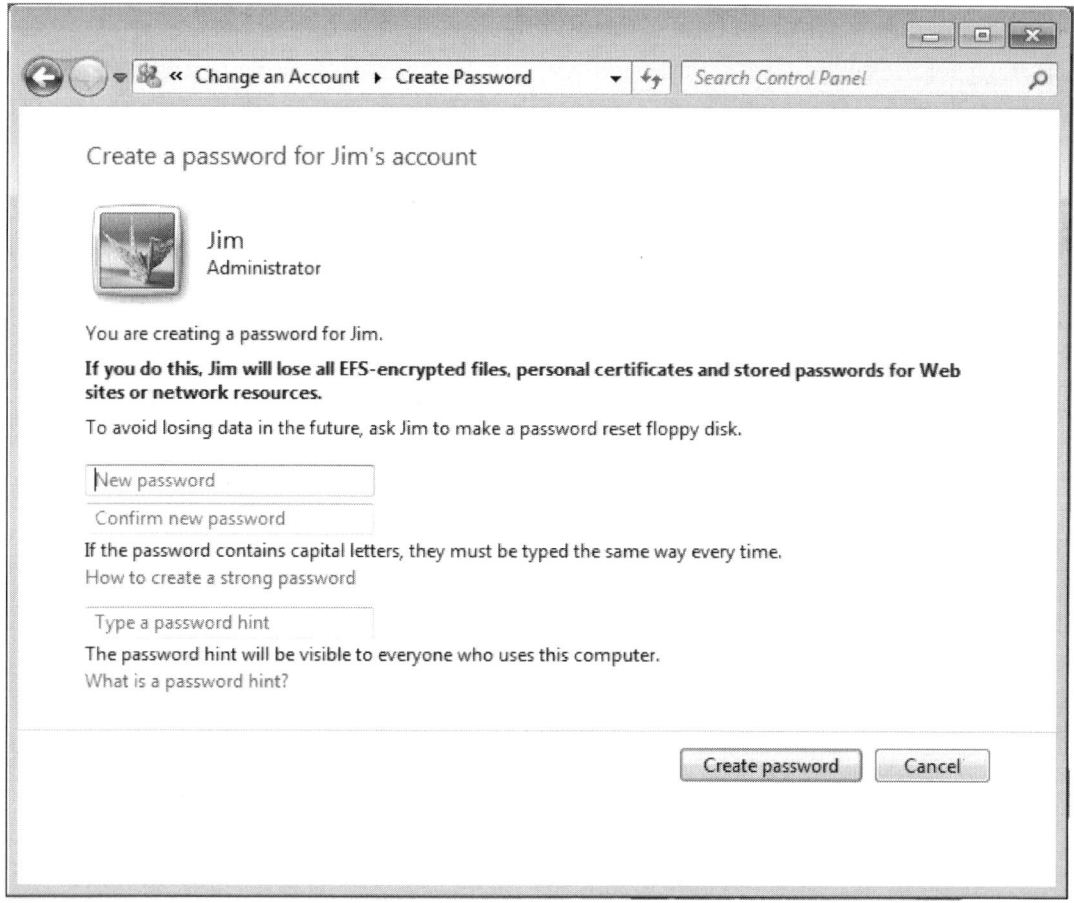

Figure 5.15

The next user account creation method I would like to go over is one that not everyone knows about, but it is an easy way to create user accounts and also give you some additional management features that you don't get from the Control Panel method. This method requires you to type in **netplwiz** from the run menu to bring up this alternate Windows user accounts management tool (figure 5.16). You can use this method to manage users on Windows 10, but if you try and create a new user using this method while running Windows 10, it will just bring up the new user interface I went over in Chapter 4.

The Users tab shows you the users that have been created on this computer. As you can see in figure 5.16, the Jim user account I just made shows up here.

Chapter 5 – Sharing Resources

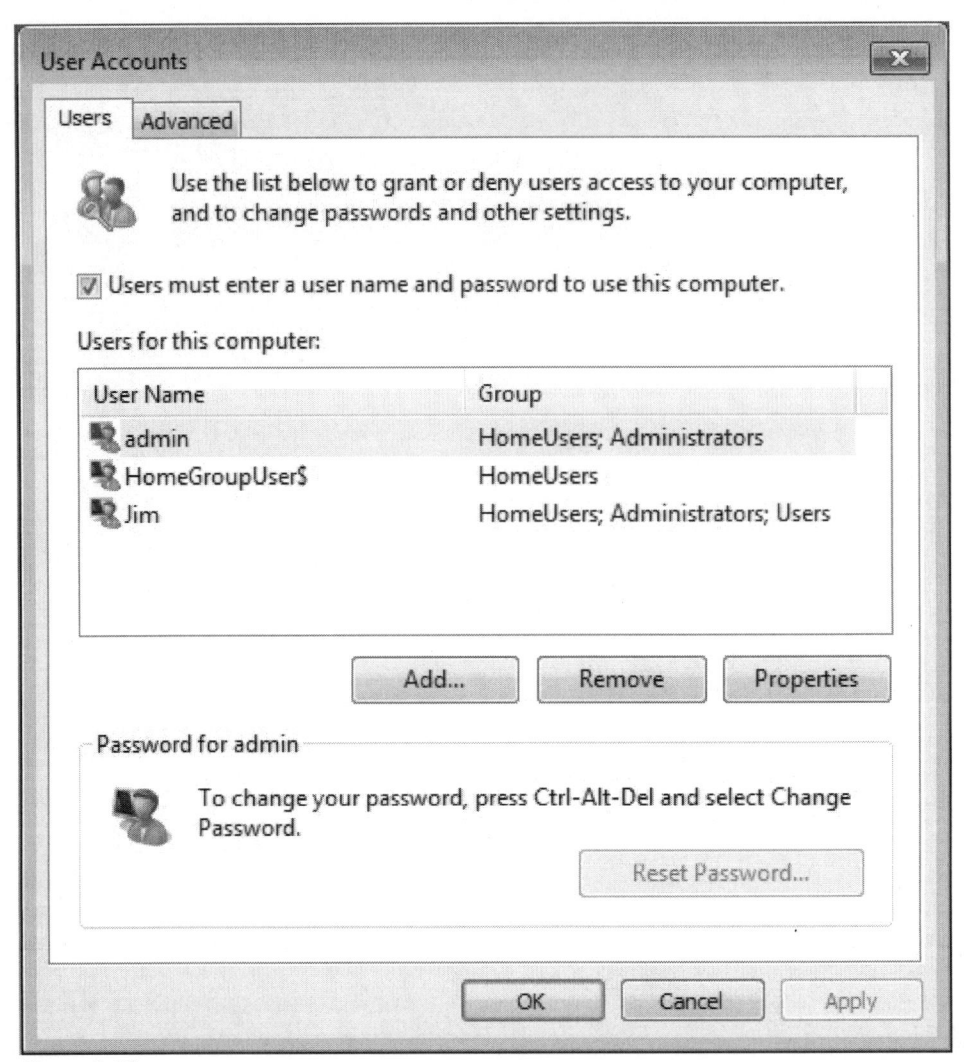

Figure 5.16

To add a new user, simply click on the *Add* button, enter the details as shown in figure 5.17, and click *Next*.

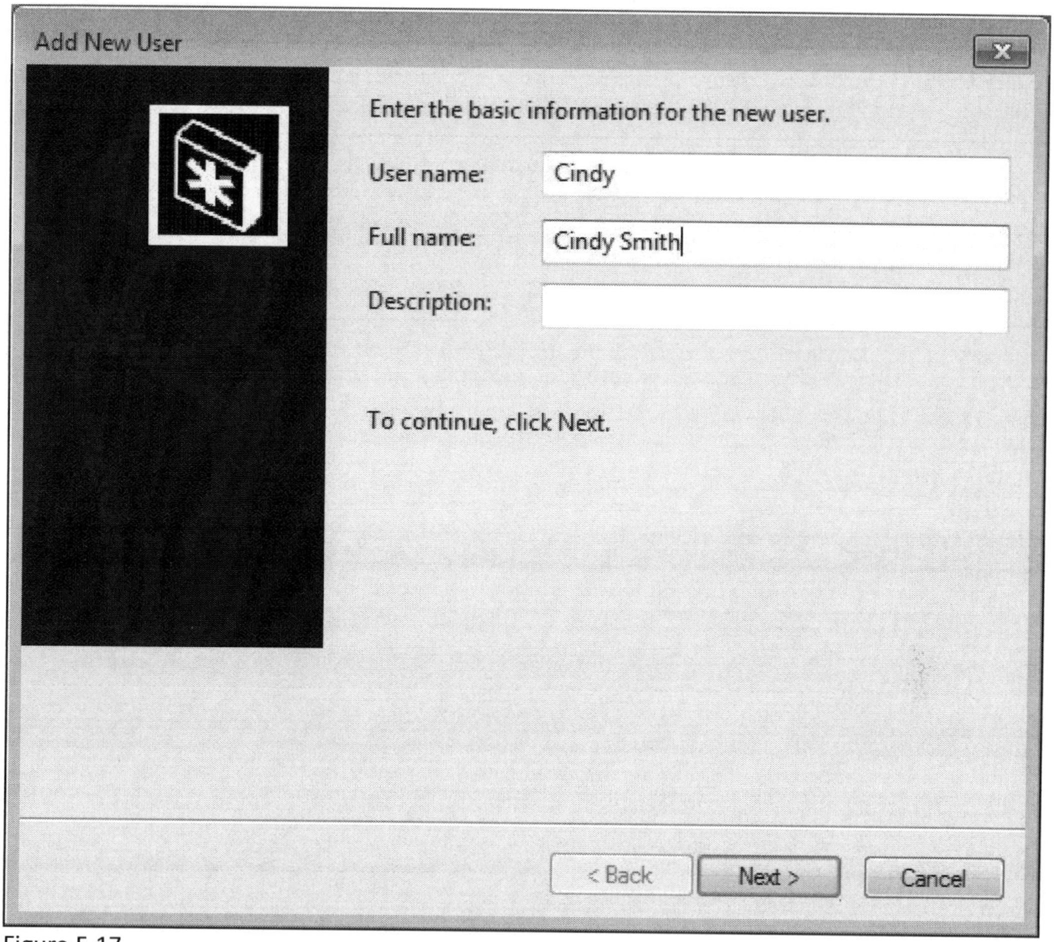

Chapter 5 – Sharing Resources

Figure 5.17

You will then be prompted to enter the password for the user and confirm it. Notice how using this method allows you to enter the password when creating the user account?

Next, you will need to choose what type of user account this should be. When using this tool, you have other options besides standard and administrator, as shown in figure 5.18. Other choices include power users, Remote Desktop users, and many other choices. You will most likely not need to worry about any of these options unless you are planning on adding a very specific user type.

91

Chapter 5 – Sharing Resources

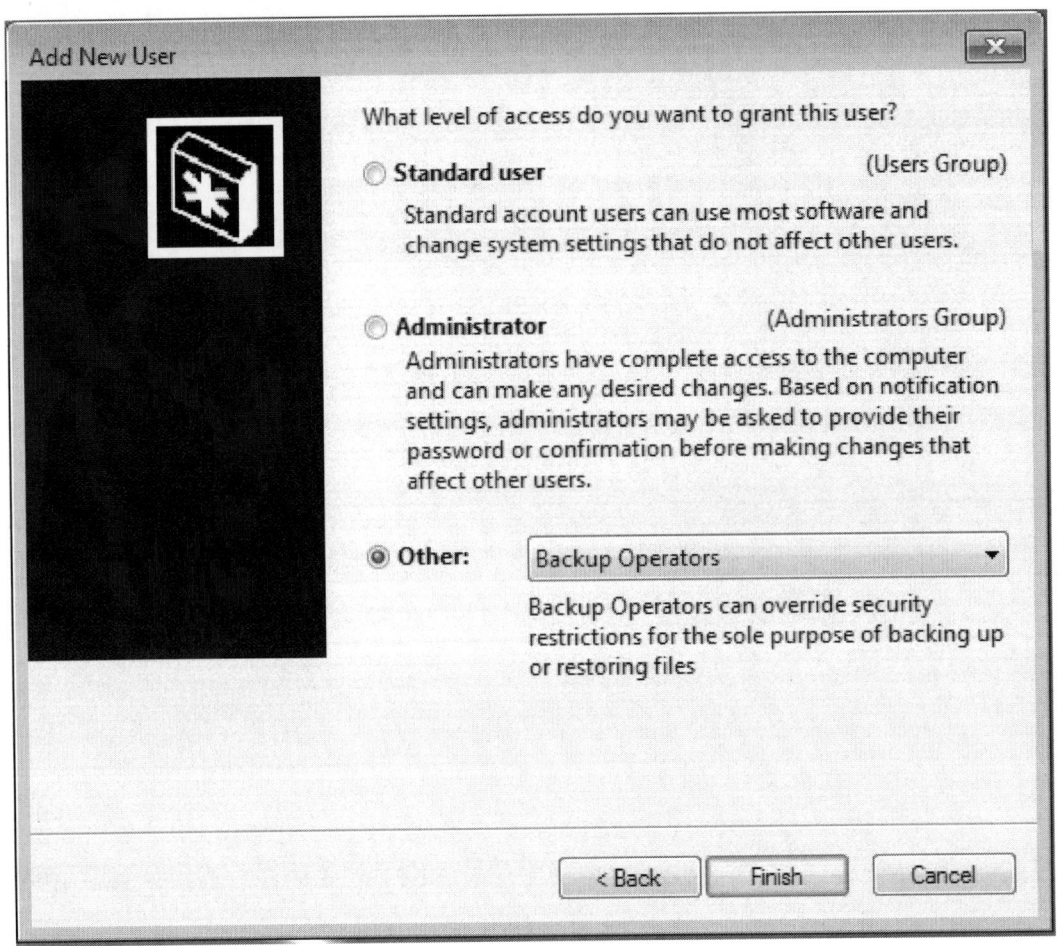

Figure 5.18

Once you click on *Finish,* you will be brought back to the main users window, where you can then click on any of the users and perform other tasks such as resetting their password and changing their access group type.

There are a couple of security measures I want to mention that you can access from this utility. If you look back at figure 5.16, you will notice a checkbox at the top that says "Users must enter a name and password to use this computer". If you uncheck this box for a user, then you can log into the computer without a password, which, of course, is a security issue. Plus, when you do this, you will have to choose which user will be logged in automatically since you won't be prompted to log in at startup.

The other thing I want to mention is on the *Advanced* tab at the bottom under *Secure logon,* where it has a checkbox that requires users to press **Ctrl+Alt+Delete** before logging on (figure 5.19). This is unchecked by default, so it's up to you if you want to make your network a little more secure by using this option.

Chapter 5 – Sharing Resources

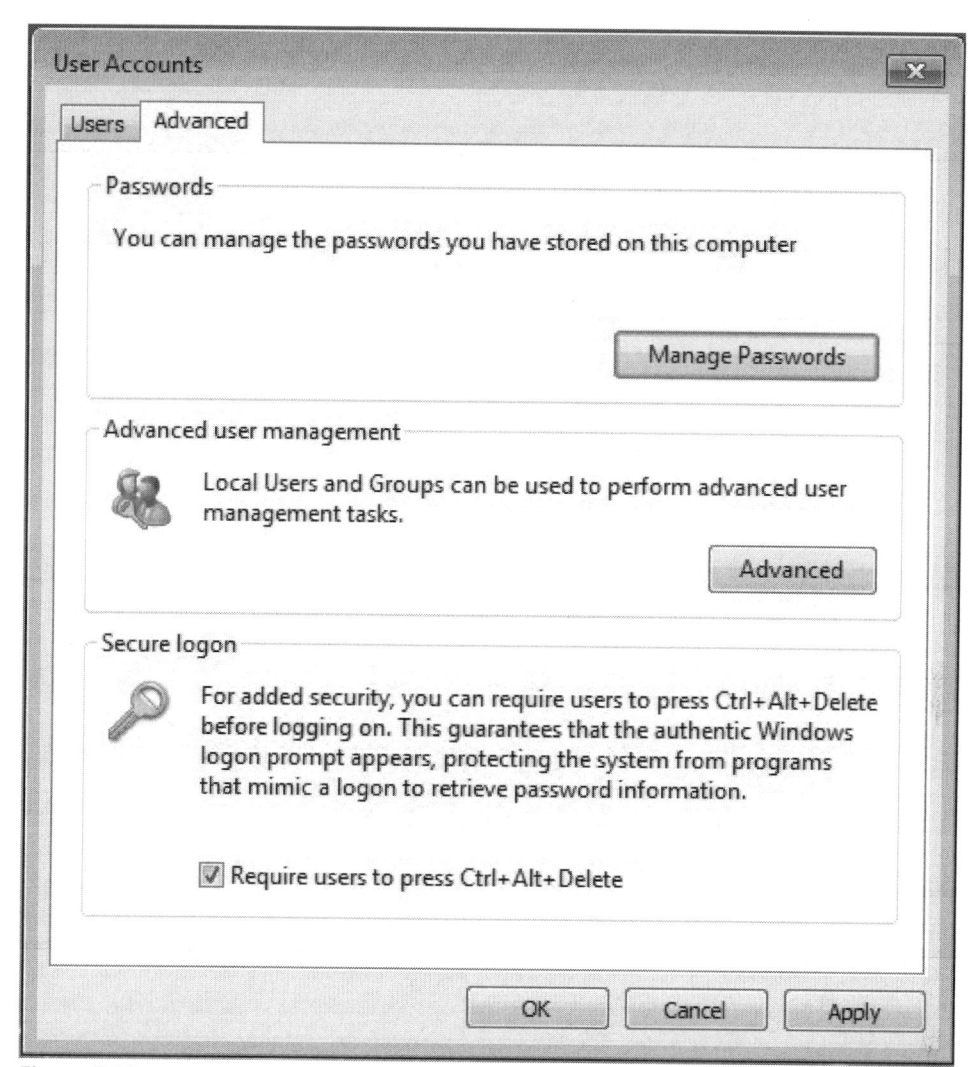

Figure 5.19

So remember that you can't use this interface to create a user account in Windows 10, but you can use it to manage your user accounts.

The final method that I will mention (again) to create a user account only applies to Windows 10. This method is done from the Windows 10 PC Setting by going to *Accounts*. Next, you will go to the section that says *Family & other people* and add the account from there. (For more specific details, go back to Chapter 4 where I went over this process step by step.)

Now that I have my user accounts created, I will first make sure that my computers are properly set up for sharing before creating some files and folders to share between all of my users. To view my sharing settings, I will go to the Windows PC Settings, and then to *Network & Internet*. From there I will double click on the name

Chapter 5 – Sharing Resources

of my network connection in the *Ethernet* section. As you can see in figure 5.20, mine is called BUDDY-5G.

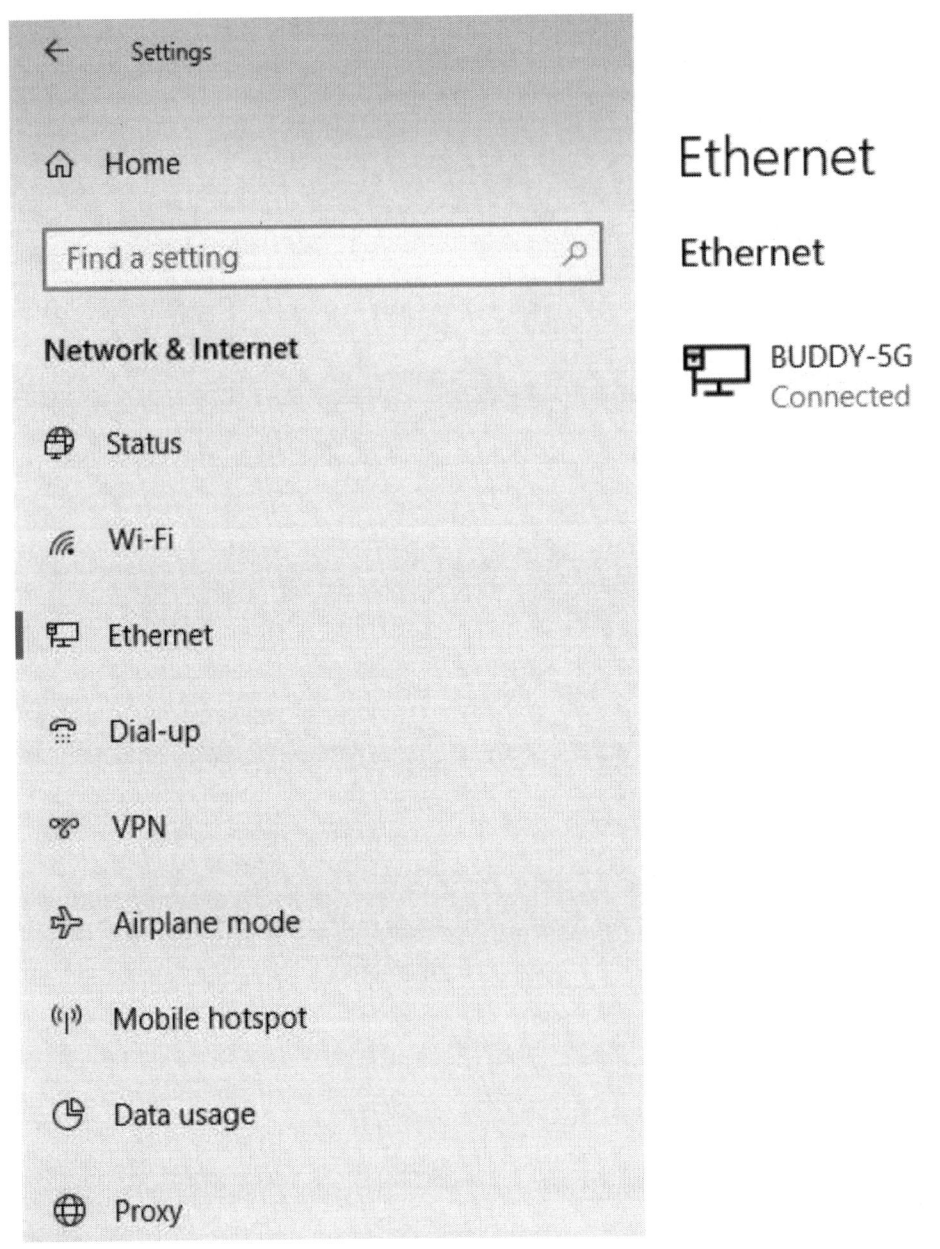

Figure 5.20

When I double click my connection, it will bring up the network profile for that connection (figure 5.21).

94

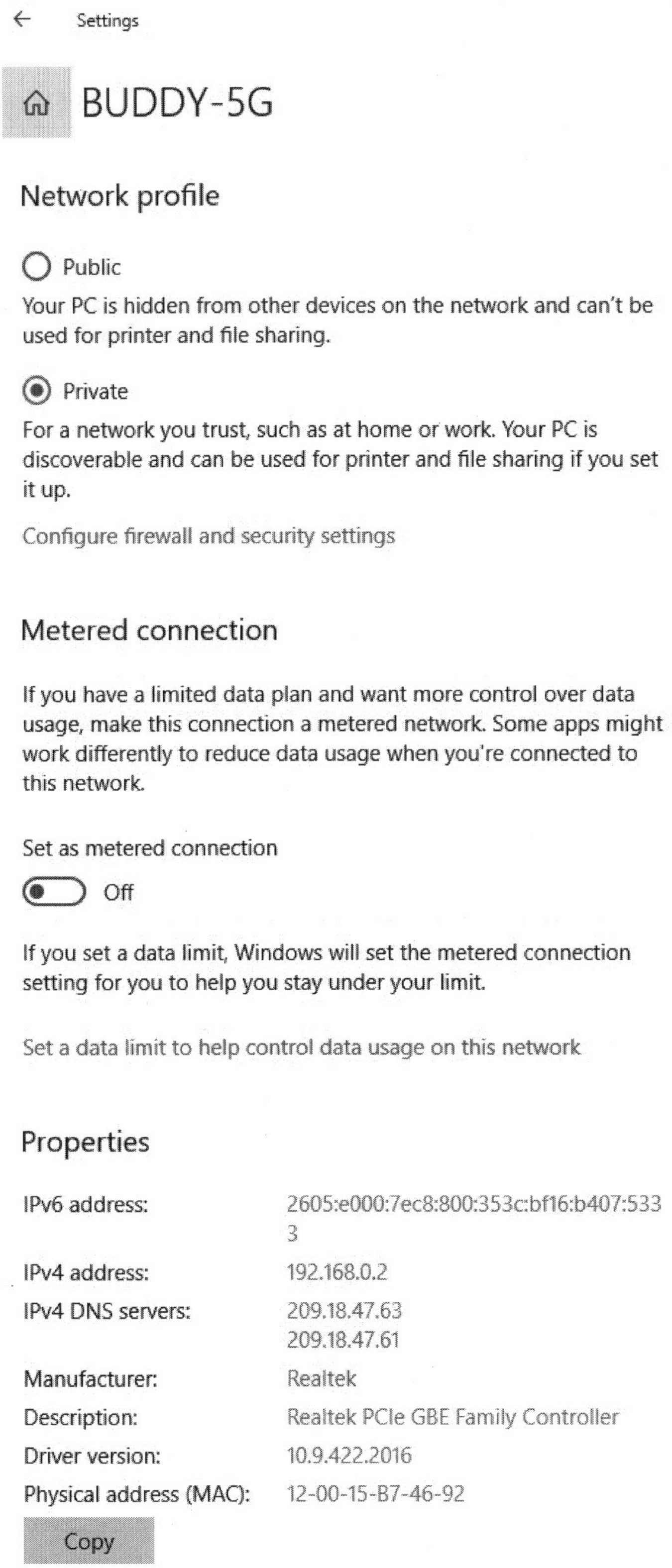

Chapter 5 – Sharing Resources

← Settings

⌂ **BUDDY-5G**

Network profile

○ Public
Your PC is hidden from other devices on the network and can't be used for printer and file sharing.

◉ Private
For a network you trust, such as at home or work. Your PC is discoverable and can be used for printer and file sharing if you set it up.

Configure firewall and security settings

Metered connection

If you have a limited data plan and want more control over data usage, make this connection a metered network. Some apps might work differently to reduce data usage when you're connected to this network.

Set as metered connection
◉◯ Off

If you set a data limit, Windows will set the metered connection setting for you to help you stay under your limit.

Set a data limit to help control data usage on this network

Properties

IPv6 address:	2605:e000:7ec8:800:353c:bf16:b407:5333
IPv4 address:	192.168.0.2
IPv4 DNS servers:	209.18.47.63
	209.18.47.61
Manufacturer:	Realtek
Description:	Realtek PCIe GBE Family Controller
Driver version:	10.9.422.2016
Physical address (MAC):	12-00-15-B7-46-92

Copy

Figure 5.21

Chapter 5 – Sharing Resources

Here you can see various information about this connection such as its IP address, DNS servers, MAC address, and so on. The section we want to look at is at the top of figure 5.14, where it says *Network profile* and has a choice for either *Public* or *Private*. You will want to make sure yours is set to Private.

For Windows 7, you can go to *Control Panel* and then to *Network and Sharing Center* and look at your network profile (as seen in figure 5.22). In this example, it's using a profile called *Home network,* but if you click on the link, you will have an option to change it to *Work network* or *Public network* (as seen in figure 5.23).

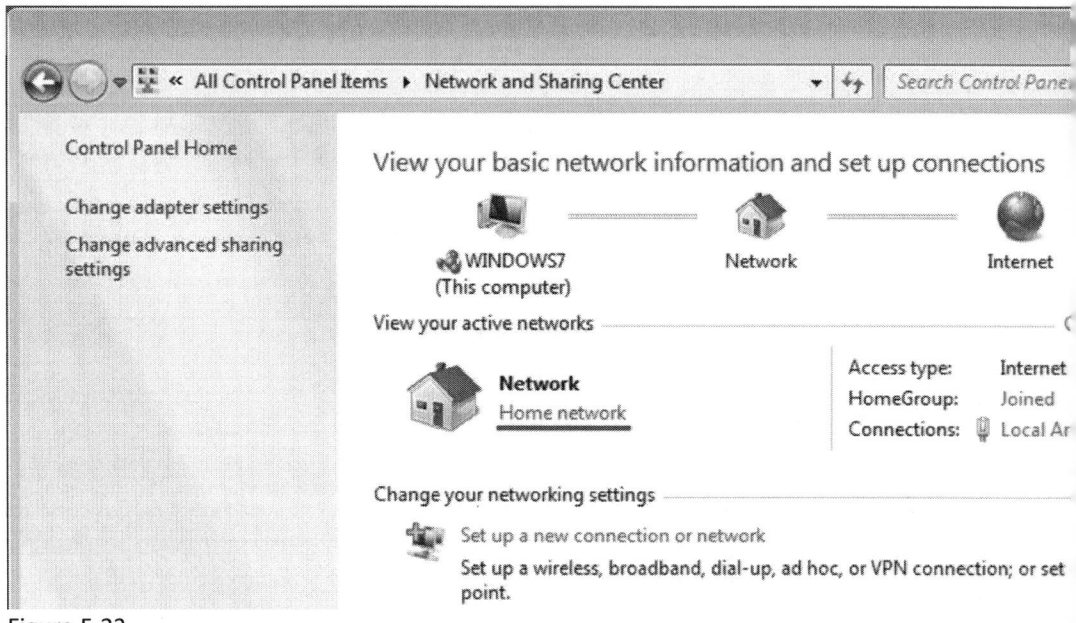

Figure 5.22

96

Chapter 5 – Sharing Resources

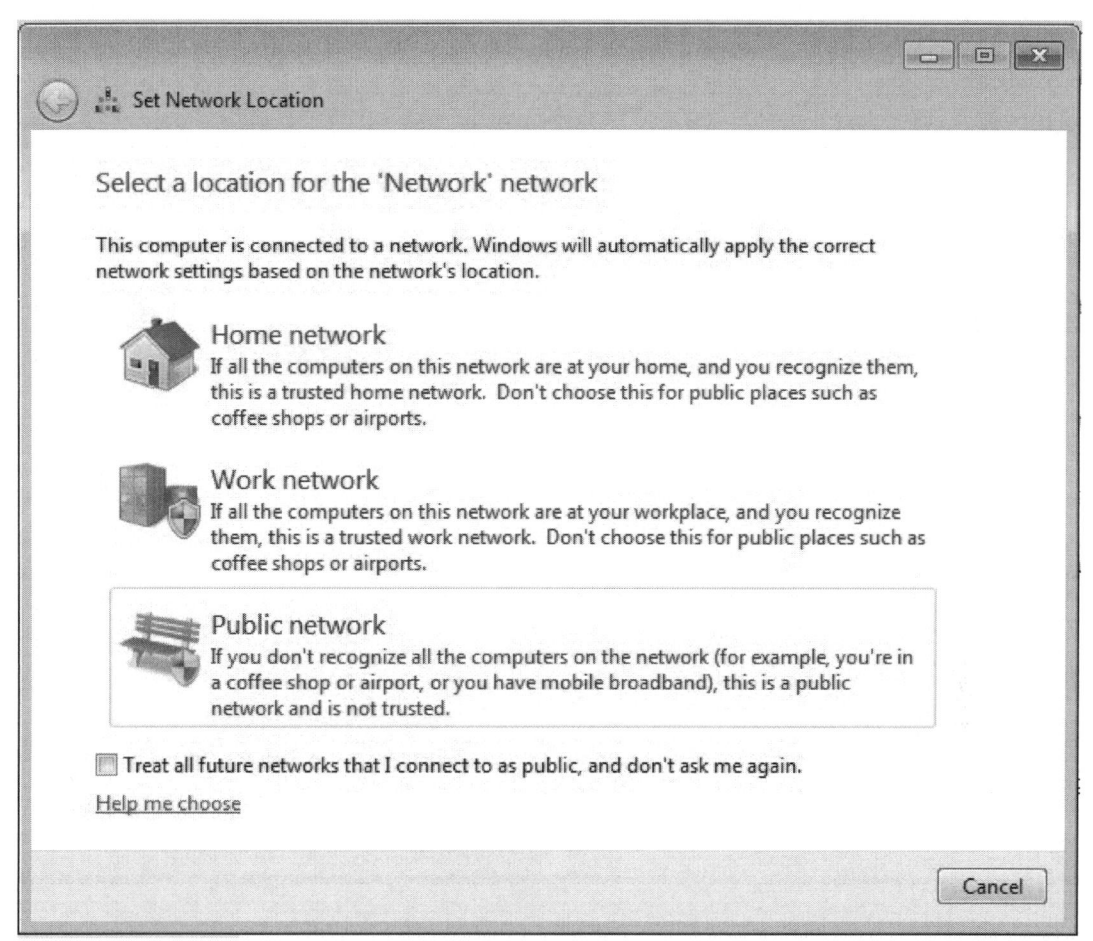

Figure 5.23

You should be fine with either Home or Work network, and the main difference is that using the Work network won't allow you to create or join a HomeGroup, which you can't use in Windows 10 anymore anyway (even though I have seen it appear in the right click menu when you share a folder for some reason).

While you are in the Windows Network and Sharing Center (either version of Windows), you will see a link that says *Change advanced sharing settings* (figure 5.24). Here you can see what sharing settings are applied to the network type you are using (figure 5.25).

Chapter 5 – Sharing Resources

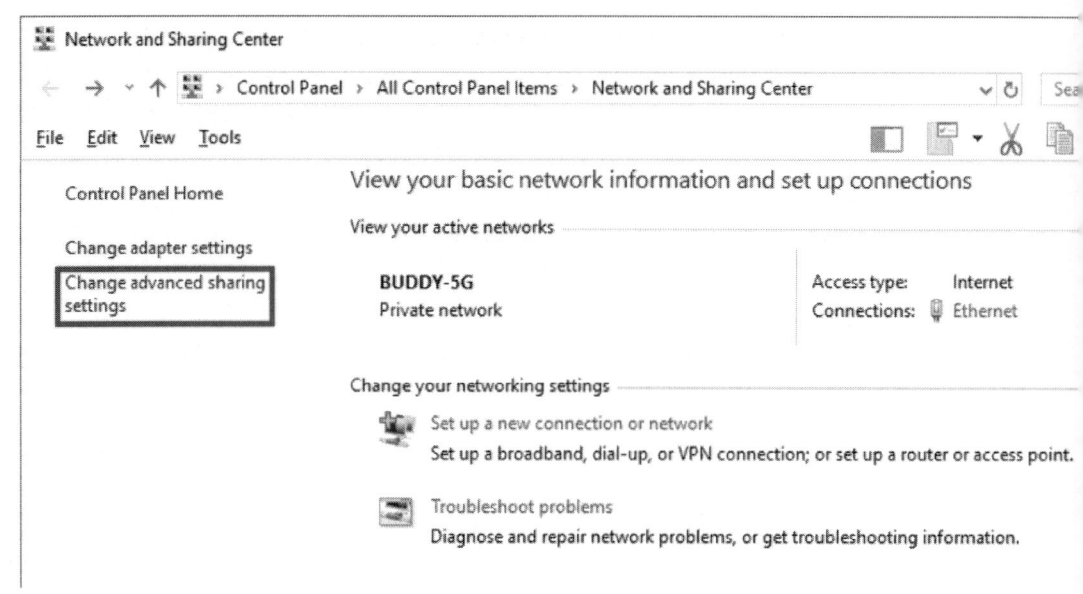

Figure 5.24

Figure 5.25

Chapter 5 – Sharing Resources

Make sure that you have *Network Discovery* turned on if you are going to want to be able to browse your network to find computers so you don't have to know their exact name and type in to connect to them. If you plan on sharing files and\or printers, then make sure the option for *Turn on file and printer sharing* is enabled as well.

Now it's finally time to start sharing some files and folders and seeing if we can connect to them and access these shared resources. I am going to open a Windows Explorer (sometimes referred to as File Explorer) window and type in the UNC path (discussed earlier) for Computer2 and see what I get. As you can see in figure 5.26, I typed in **\\computer2** (not case sensitive) just to see what showed up, and I don't get anything. This is because nothing has been shared yet, but it does tell me that my user account has access to Computer2, otherwise I would get an access denied message.

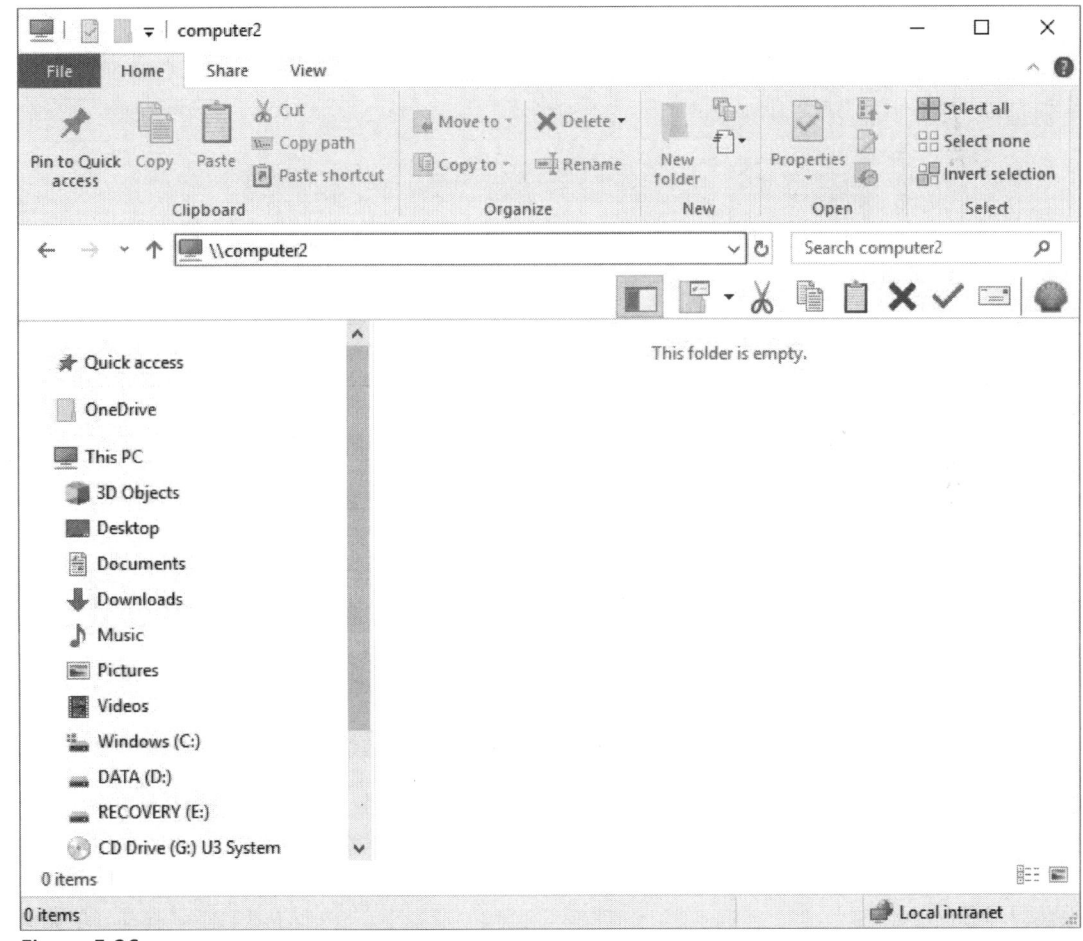

Figure 5.26

Now I will go over to Computer2 and create a shared folder, set the access permissions on it, and then add some files to that folder and see what happens. To

99

Chapter 5 – Sharing Resources

begin, I went to the root of the C drive and created a new folder called Sales Files (figure 5.27). When I say root of the C drive, that means I went to the top level of that drive and I can't go any higher in the folder level tree.

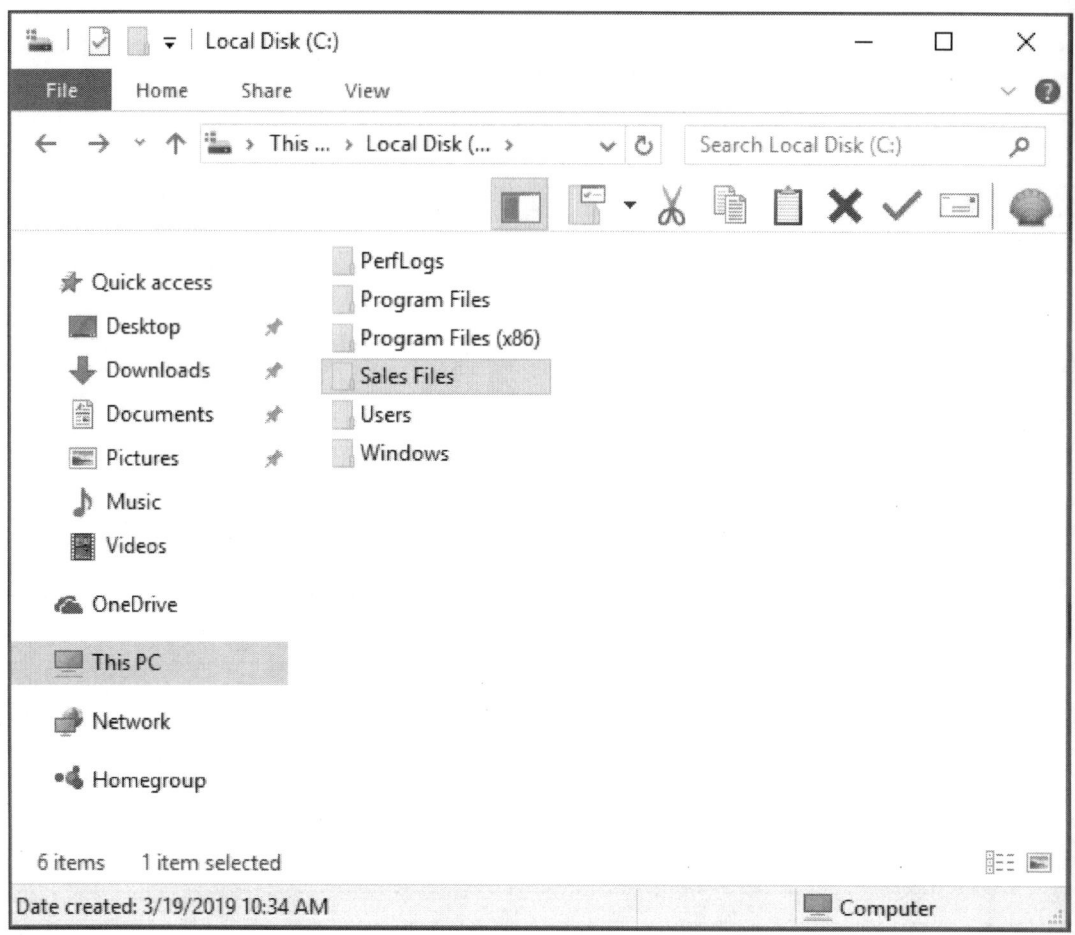

Figure 5.27

> **Tip:** If you want to be a successful Windows administrator, or even a successful Windows user, then learning file management skills is essential to that success. Once you know how to navigate the Windows file system, then everything about using your computer becomes easier.

There are several ways to configure sharing on my Sales Files folder, and I will go over two of them, which include the *Give access to* option and the *Advanced Sharing* option (which I prefer to use). By the way, in Windows 10, the *Give access to* option

Chapter 5 – Sharing Resources

was previously called *Share With,* so this is an example of how Microsoft is always changing things around for no reason except to confuse us!

Let's begin with the Give access to option, and to do so I will right click on my Sales Files folder and choose Give access to. It will give me some suggestions based on what users I have configured on the computer. In this case, I will choose Jim, since that's who I'm logged in as on my computer and that's where I want to be able to access the shared files from. Notice in figure 5.28 there are still leftover choices to create a Homegroup, which was removed from Windows 10, so who knows why it's still an option.

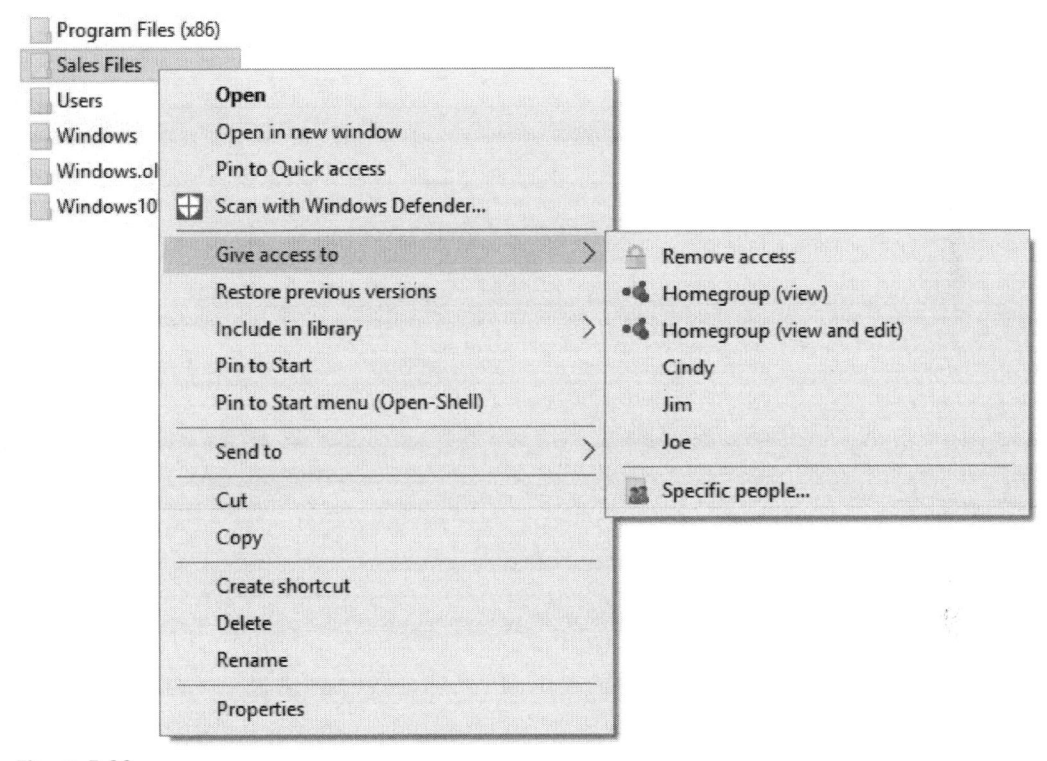

Figure 5.28

Next, it will ask me if I'm sure I want to share the selected item, to which I will click on *Yes, share the items.*

Chapter 5 – Sharing Resources

[Screenshot of a "Network access" dialog asking "Do you want to share the selected items?" with options "Yes, share the items." and "No, don't share the items."]

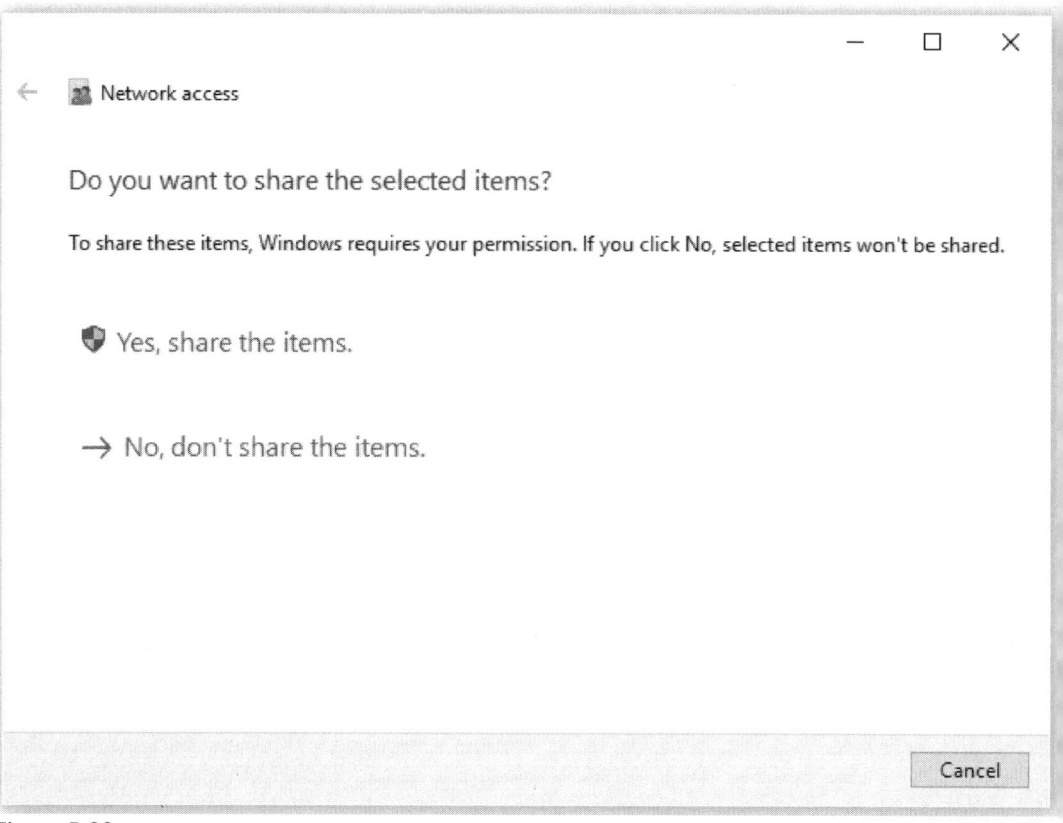

Figure 5.29

After the folder is shared it won't give you any indication that anything has changed. In older versions of Windows, you would see a hand icon holding the folder, indicating it was shared, which really came in handy.

If I were to choose *Specific people* from the options (seen in figure 5.28), I would get other options where I could fine-tune my sharing settings (figure 5.30). As you can see, the Jim user is there, and notice how just clicking my name from the suggested options only gave me *read* access. If you were to click on the dropdown arrow from the top box, it would give you the names of the other users on the computer that you could add, as well as the option to add a new user right from there.

Chapter 5 – Sharing Resources

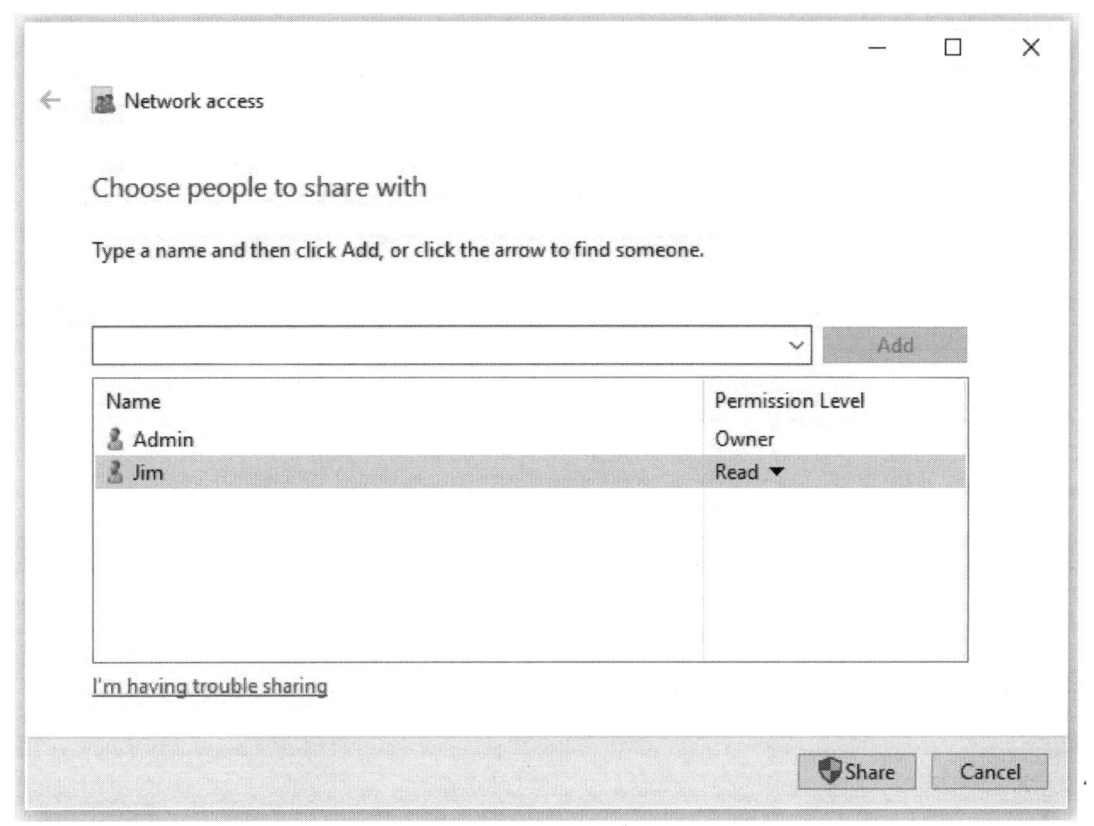

Figure 5.30

Next, I will change my access level from *read* to *read and write* by clicking the down arrow next to *read*, change it to *Read/Write,* and then click on *Share*. Then it will give me a summary of what I have done with options to send an email to people about the new share, or to copy and paste a link to the share in another app (figure 5.31). On the bottom of figure 5.31 there is a link to show all the network shares on the computer, which can come in really handy if you aren't sure what you have shared.

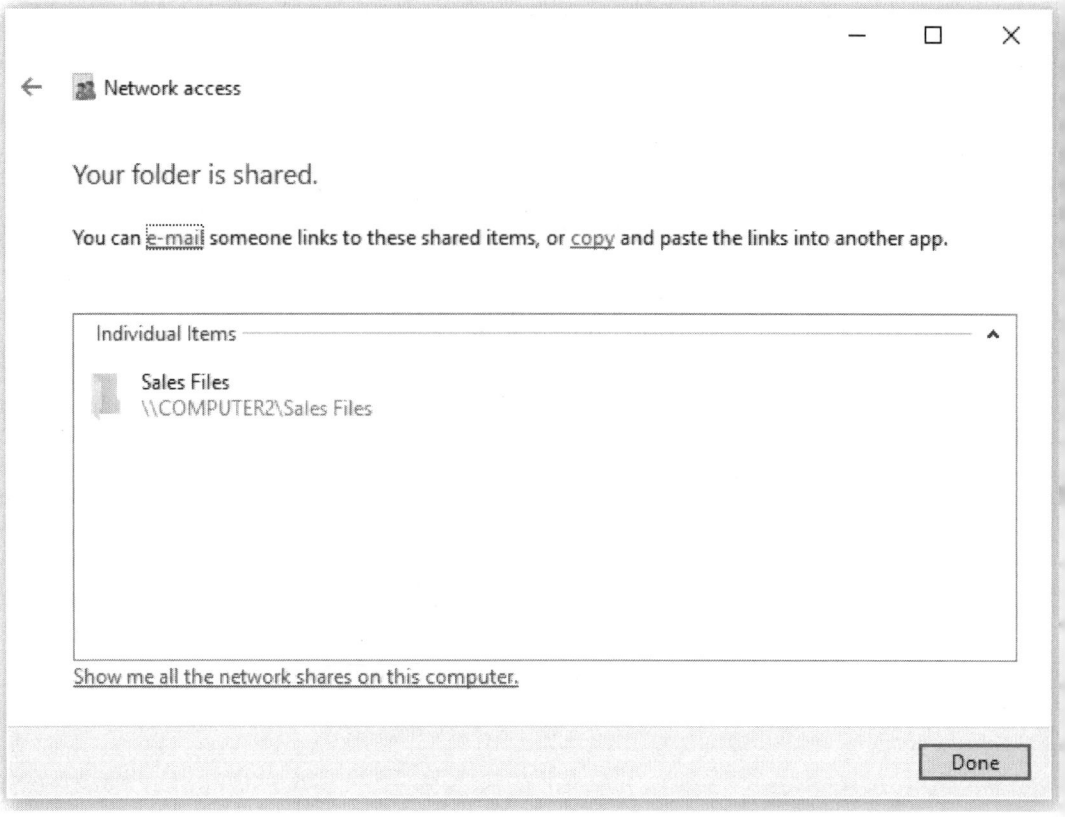

Figure 5.31

Now I am going to share the same Sales Files folder with Cindy, but I am going to use the sharing options from the right click-Properties method (also known as Advanced sharing). When I right click on the Sales Files folder and choose *Properties,* I get a Window like the one shown in figure 5.32 that has several tabs on the top.

Before I add Cindy to the folder, I want to take a minute to discuss the difference between the *Sharing* tab and the *Security* tab.

Sharing a folder (or file) makes it available to be seen by other users besides the owner or creator of that folder. You can assign different levels of permission to a share such as *Read*, *Change,* and *Full control*. Clicking on the Share button will bring you to the same screen as seen in figure 5.30. Clicking on the Advanced Sharing button will bring you to a screen similar to figure 5.33.

Chapter 5 – Sharing Resources

Figure 5.32

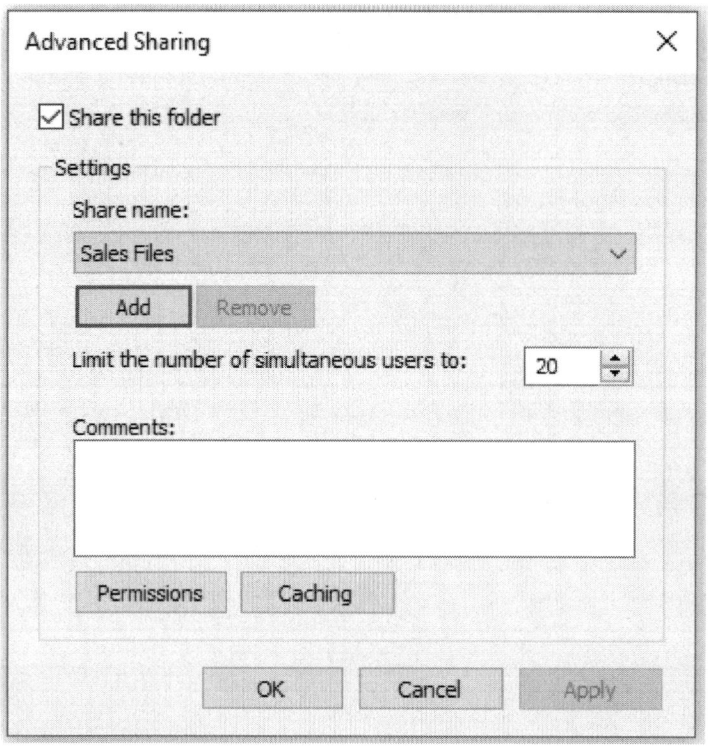

Chapter 5 – Sharing Resources

Figure 5.33

From here you can click on the *Permissions* button to determine if you want to set this share with read, change, or full control permissions (figure 5.34). Shares apply to network users as well as local users, so even if you log on to this computer as a user with read share access to a folder, that's all you will be able to do with it.

106

Chapter 5 – Sharing Resources

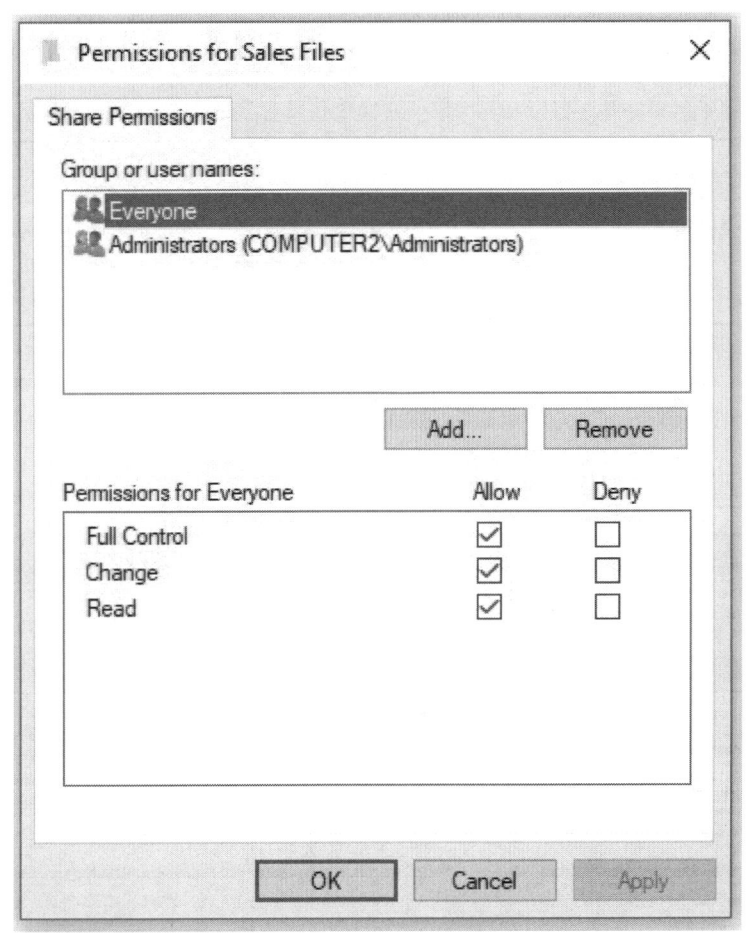

Figure 5.34

By default, the Everyone group has full control access to a share when you create it, and you usually tighten things down by using what they call NTFS permissions (or security permissions, as they are also called). So think of share permissions as what gets to you the folder, and NTFS permissions as what you can do when you get there.

You can change the share level for the Everyone group if needed, but keep in mind it will make your sharing a little more complicated since share permissions and NTFS permissions can supersede each other.

> **Tip:** Deny permissions will always take precedence over any type of allow permission, so be careful when using the deny permission level to avoid blocking access to people you don't mean to block.

Chapter 5 – Sharing Resources

Another thing to take note of from figure 5.34 is that the Jim user is not on this list. That is because when I added my user from the Give access to method, it added it to the NTFS or security permissions, which I will go over next.

One other thing I want to mention from figure 5.33 is the *Limit the number of simultaneous users to* setting. This controls how many users can access that share at one time. So, if you have network bandwidth issues, you can lower this number, but you might risk having people being blocked from accessing your share when they really need to get in there.

Now it's time to get back to adding Cindy using the advanced sharing method, which is my preferred method. If you take a look at figure 5.35, you will see that I am now on the *Security* tab. Notice how the Jim user I added earlier shows up there and has all the options checked under the Allow column except for *Special permissions* (not shown).

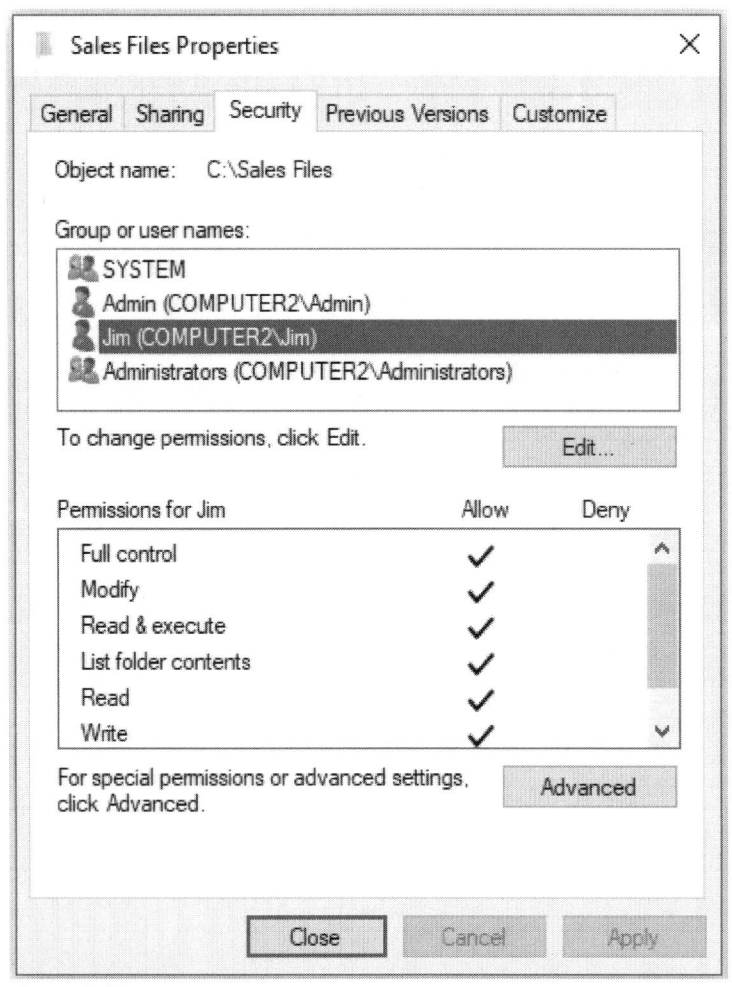

Figure 5.35

Chapter 5 – Sharing Resources

Most of the time you will not want to give your users full control like this by default (unless you *really* trust all the users on your network). For a home network or small office network, this might actually be the case, but make sure before doing so.

To add Cindy to the Sales File share I will click on the *Edit* button (as seen in figure 5.35), and then on the Add button (as seen in figure 5.36). Also notice in figure 5.36 how I have the options to change the permission levels by checking and unchecking the boxes next to each level. (Just be sure you have the right user highlighted before doing this!)

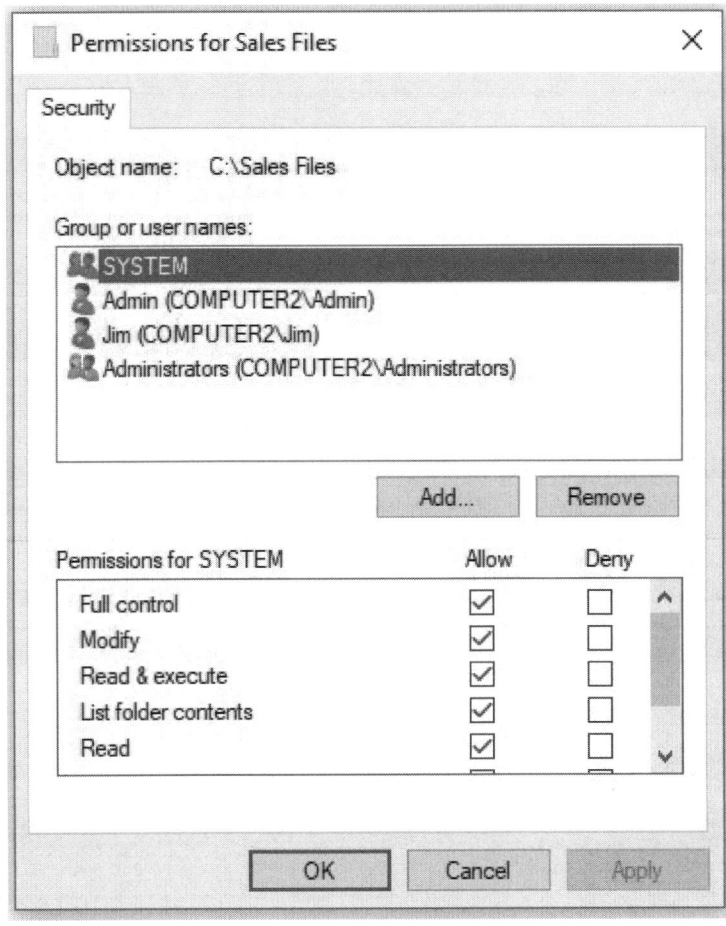

Figure 5.36

Now I will click on the *Add* button, type in Cindy, and then click on the *Check Names* button to confirm I typed it correctly. You know you did it right when it changes from the user name to the *computername\username* format as seen in figure 5.37.

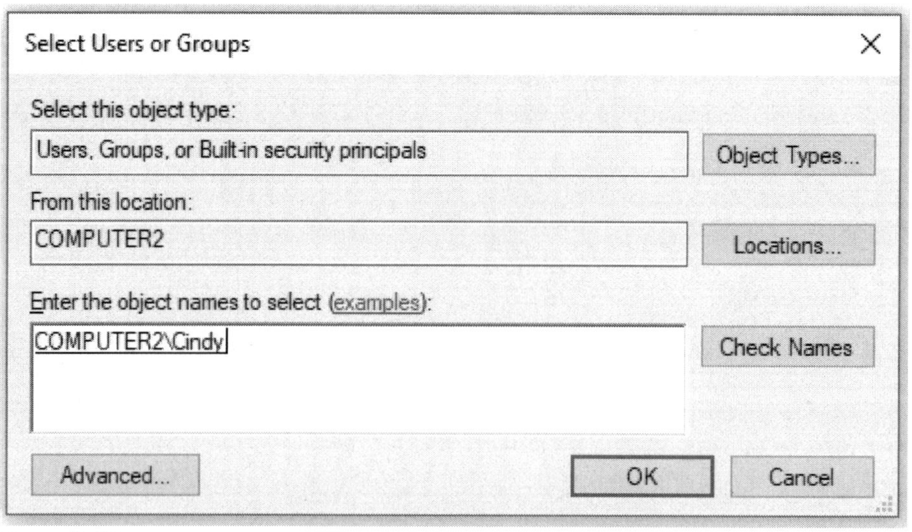

Chapter 5 – Sharing Resources

Figure 5.37

If you don't know the actual user name, you can click the *Advanced* button and then on the *Find now* button to have Windows bring up a listing of users based on your location, which in my case is Computer2 (the one I'm on). As you can see in figure 5.38, Cindy is in the list, so all I need to do is click on her name and then on the *OK* button, and OK again at the next screen, which will look just like figure 5.37.

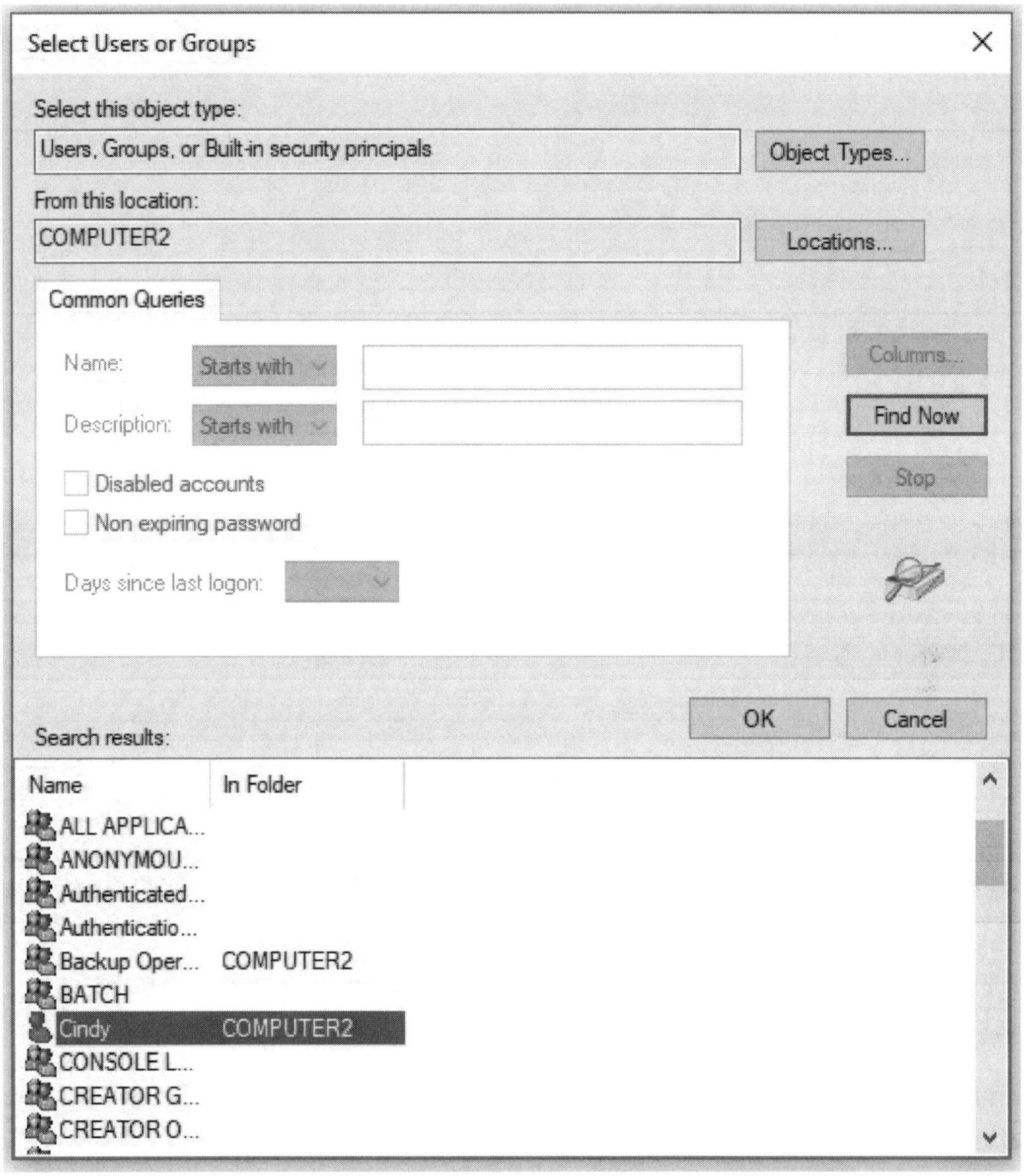

Chapter 5 – Sharing Resources

Figure 5.38

Now when I go back to my user list under the Share tab, I see Cindy's name there. Notice that this time she only has *Read & execute*, *List folder contents,* and *read* permissions compared to *Full control* like my user account had from the other sharing method.

111

Chapter 5 – Sharing Resources

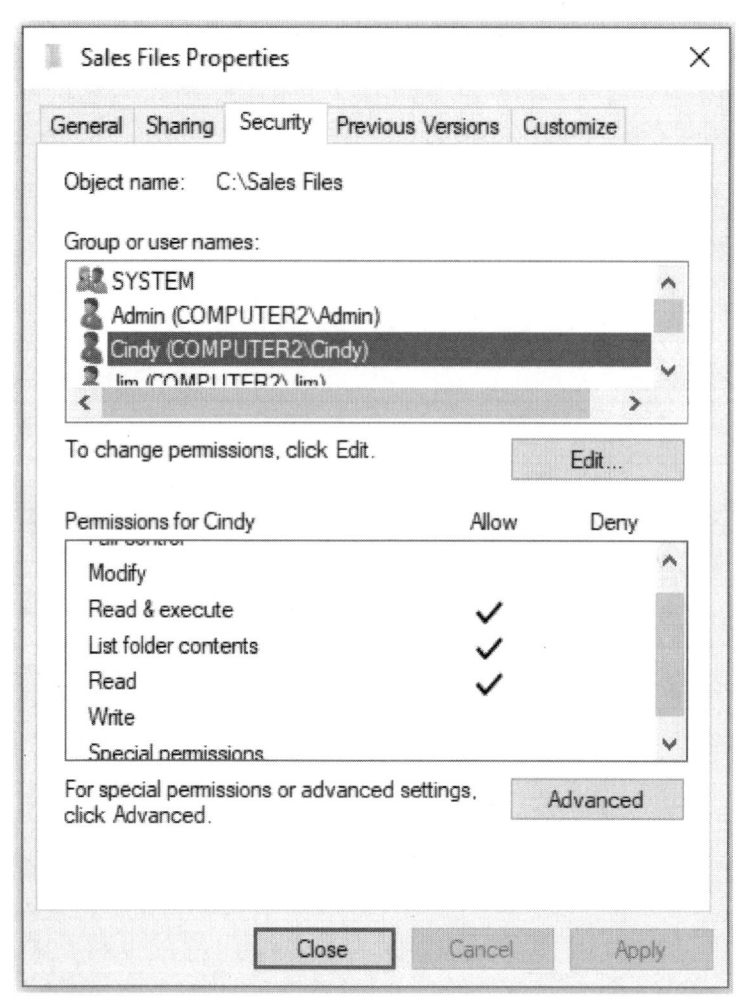

Figure 5.39

So this is the process you would use to share all of your folders, and yes, it's a little tedious if you have a lot of folders to share and a lot of users. This is why Microsoft has Domains for larger companies to centralize this type of management in one place.

I mentioned Groups in Chapter 4, but wanted to show you an example of how you can create one in this situation to save yourself some work in the future. So, going back to the process of running **lusrmgr.msc** from a command prompt, we get a window similar to figure 5.40 that shows all of the groups configured on this computer (Computer2).

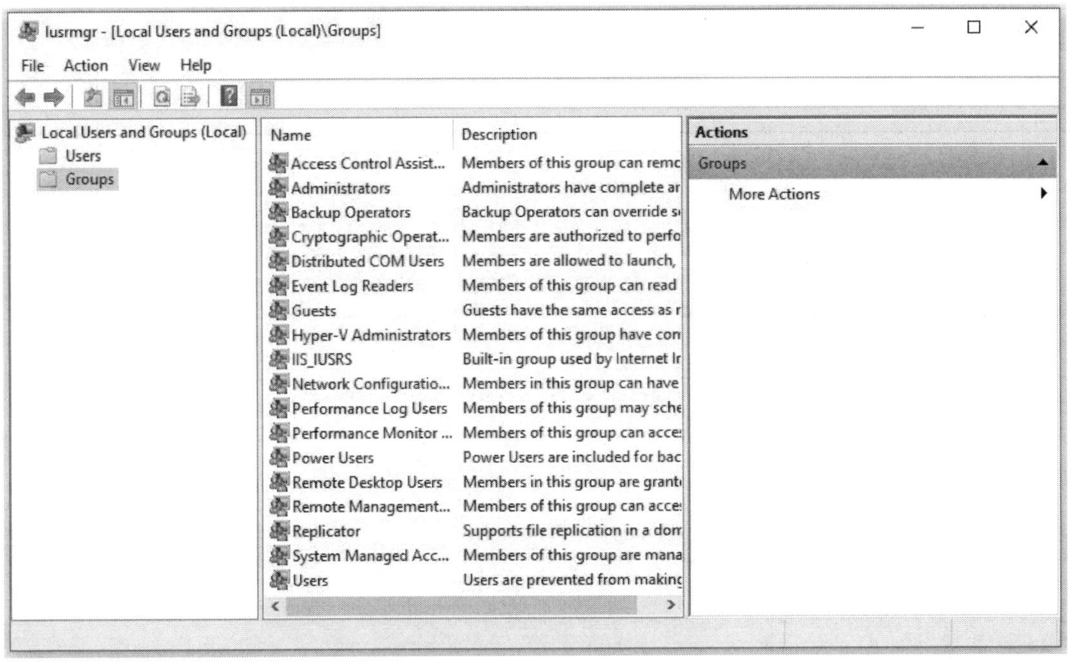
lusrmgr - [Local Users and Groups (Local)\Groups]
File Action View Help
Local Users and Groups (Local)
Users
Groups
Name
Description
Access Control Assist...
Members of this group can remc
Administrators
Administrators have complete ar
Backup Operators
Backup Operators can override s
Cryptographic Operat...
Members are authorized to perfo
Distributed COM Users
Members are allowed to launch,
Event Log Readers
Members of this group can read
Guests
Guests have the same access as r
Hyper-V Administrators
Members of this group have con
IIS_IUSRS
Built-in group used by Internet Ir
Network Configuratio...
Members in this group can have
Performance Log Users
Members of this group may sche
Performance Monitor ...
Members of this group can acce
Power Users
Power Users are included for bac
Remote Desktop Users
Members in this group are grant
Remote Management...
Members of this group can acce
Replicator
Supports file replication in a dom
System Managed Acc...
Members of this group are mana
Users
Users are prevented from makinc
Actions
Groups
More Actions
Figure 5.40

Now I will go to the *Action* menu, select *New Group,* type in *Sales Users* for the name of my group, and then click on the Add button to add Jim, Cindy, and Joe as members of this group. The results can be seen in figure 5.41.

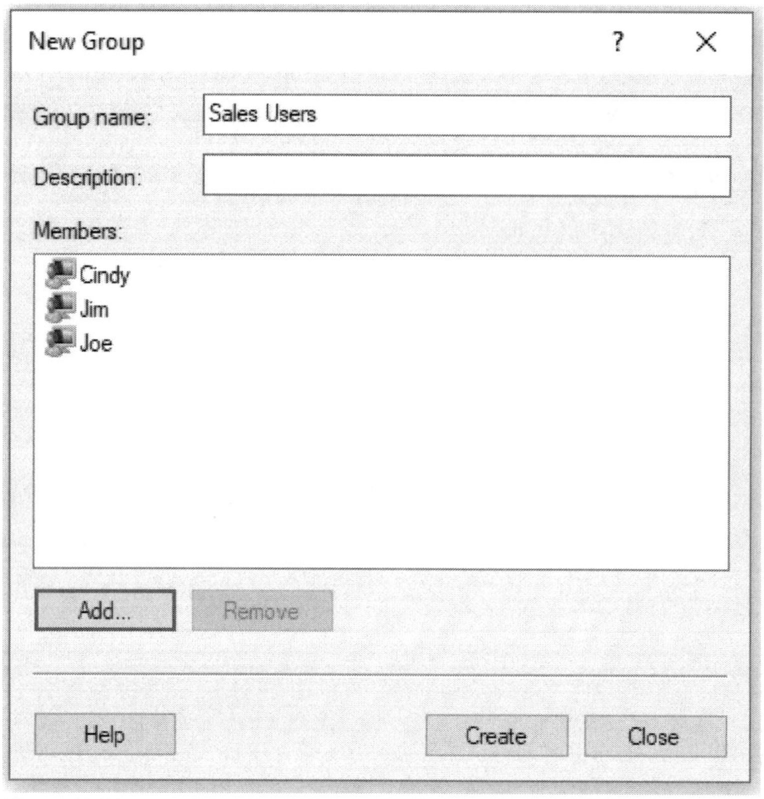

Chapter 5 – Sharing Resources

Figure 5.41

Then I will click the *Create* button and my new group will be listed along with my other groups.

Now when I go to share a folder, I will have an option to share it with the Sales Users group and not have to put in each user individually. So, if you have a bunch of users, this can save you a lot of time not having to add users manually, but rather just add the group to the share (figure 5.42). When you give share permission to a group, it gives it to everyone in that group.

Chapter 5 – Sharing Resources

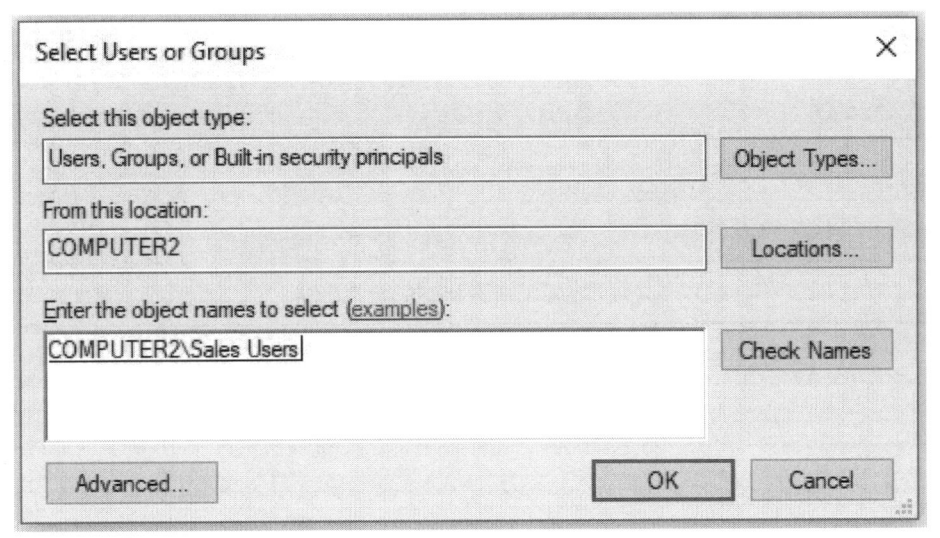

Figure 5.42

> **Tip:** If you give a group permission to a share but an individual or individuals in that group have the deny permission applied to that share for their specific account, they will still be denied access to the share.

Now that I have the Sales File share created, I can go back to my computer and type in the UNC path for Computer2 (**\\computer2**) and will be shown the new share that I can now access. As long as you have your shares and users configured correctly, you should be able to access the share this way from any computer that has one of those authorized users logged in.

Chapter 5 – Sharing Resources

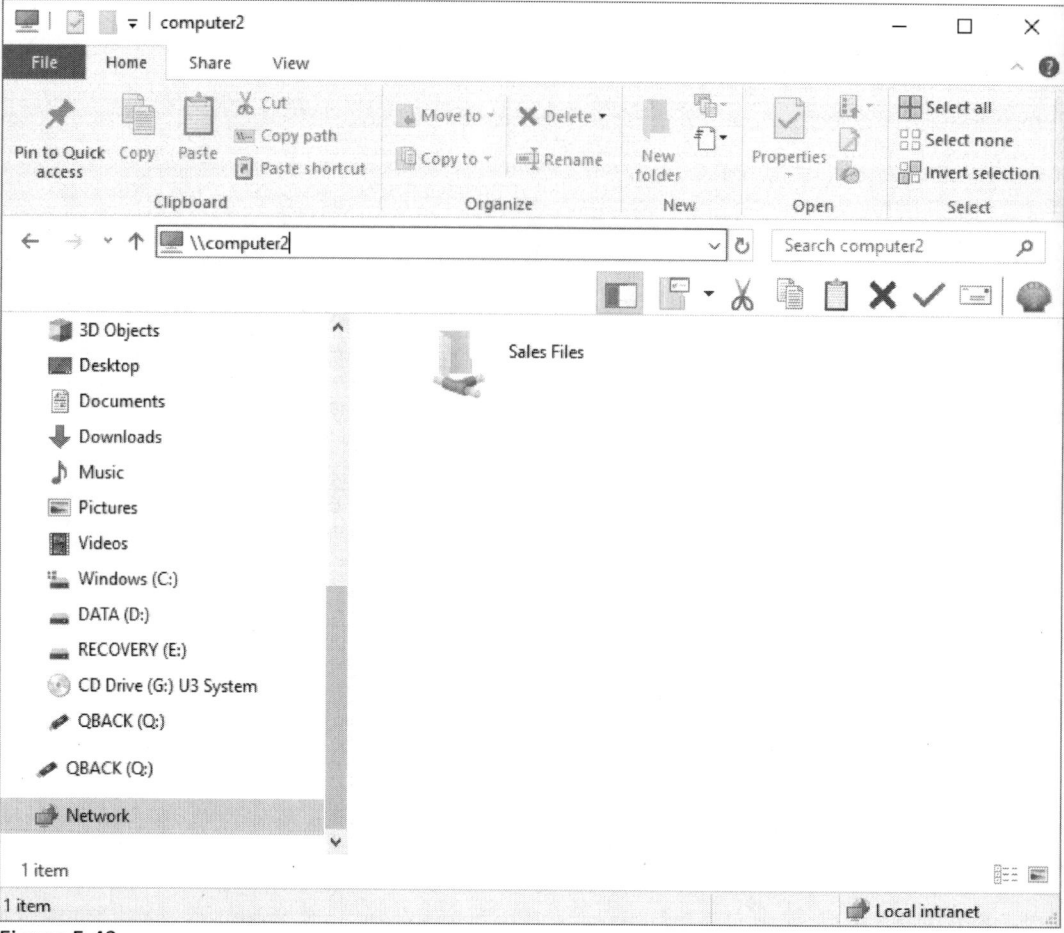

Figure 5.43

Mapping a Network Drive
I mentioned mapping a network drive earlier in this book, but now I want to show you an example of how to do it. Before doing so, I want to create a subfolder within the Sales Files share on Computer2. I will make a folder called *Reports* within the Sales Files folder and add a file named **Sales Reports**. As you can see in figure 5.44, if I use the UNC path **\\computer2\sales files\Reports**, it will take me right into that Reports folder where I can see the Sales Reports file.

Chapter 5 – Sharing Resources

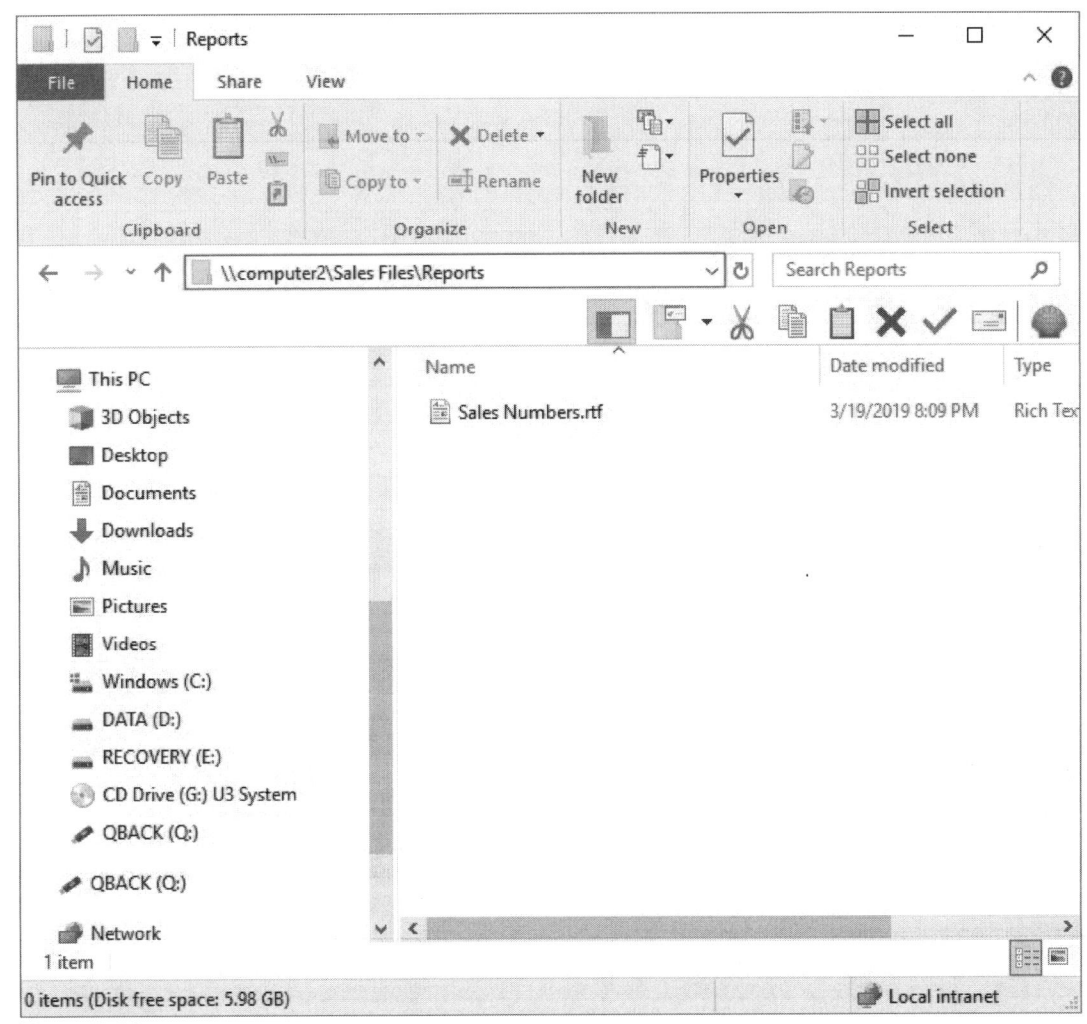

Figure 5.44

Now let's say I wanted to have quick access to this Reports folder without having to type in that UNC path or even have to worry about remembering what it actually is. This is where mapping a network drive can help you out. When you map a drive it will create another drive letter on your computer that points to the exact location that you configure it with.

To map a drive, simply open Windows Explorer and click on *This PC* on the left. Then you will see a tab named Computer with a *Map network drive* option (figure 5.45). From there click on the Map network drive button, choose Map network drive again, and you will be presented with a screen similar to figure 5.46.

Chapter 5 – Sharing Resources

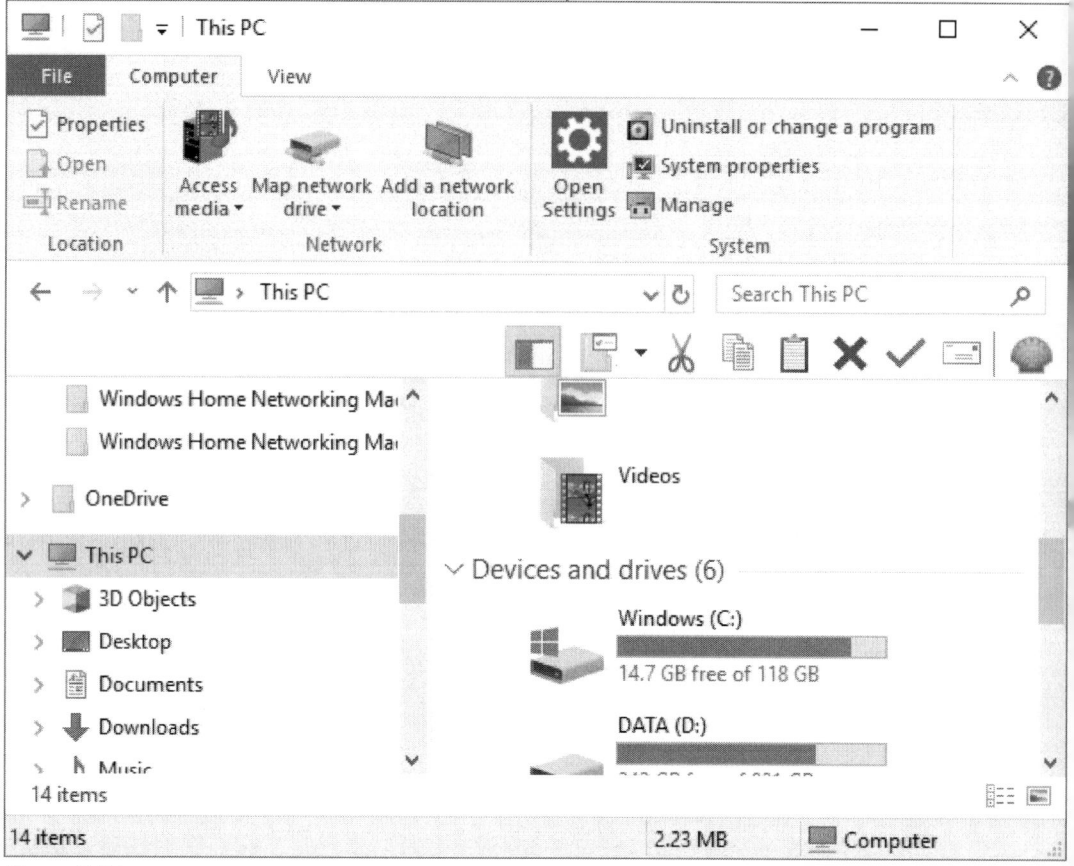

Figure 5.45

Then you can choose any available drive letter from the Drive dropdown. In my case, I will choose the R drive for Reports, and enter the UNC path of **\\computer2\sales files\Reports**. If you want this drive to stay connected when you reboot your computer, then make sure the *Reconnect at sign-in* box is checked. Then click *Finish*, and you will now have your new drive show up with your other drives (as seen in figure 5.47). To disconnect the drive, simply right click it and choose *Disconnect*.

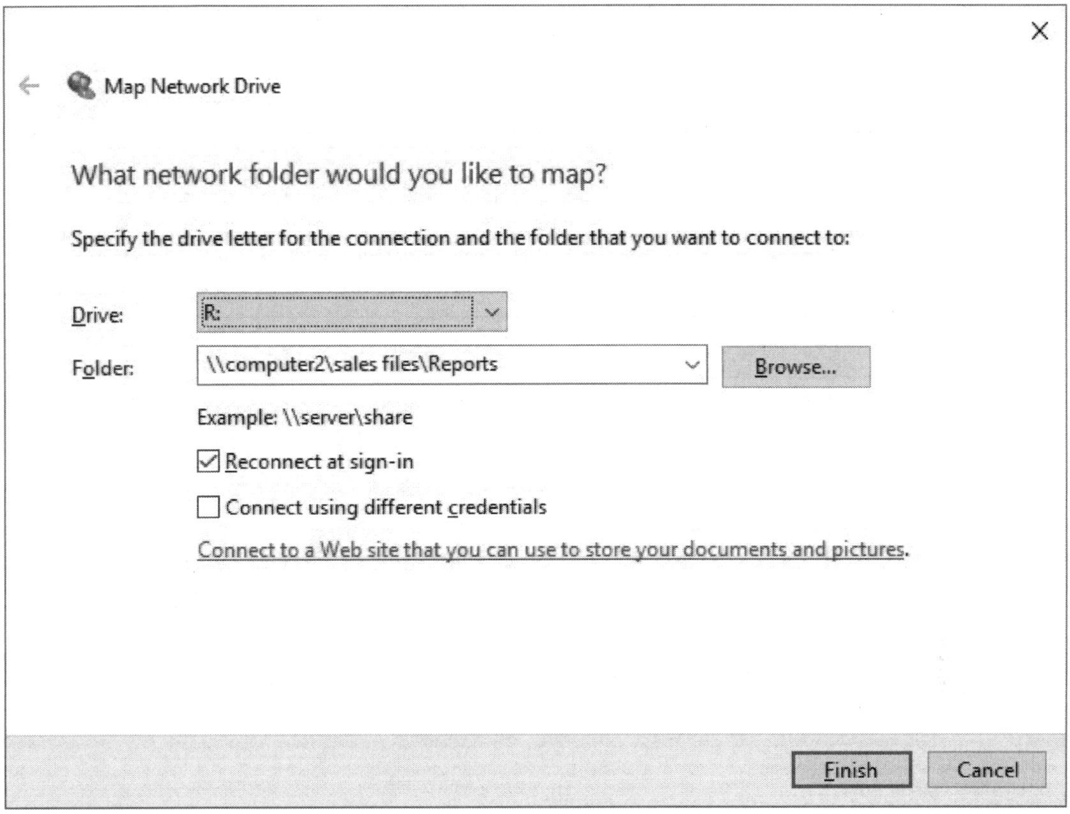

Chapter 5 – Sharing Resources

Figure 5.46

Chapter 5 – Sharing Resources

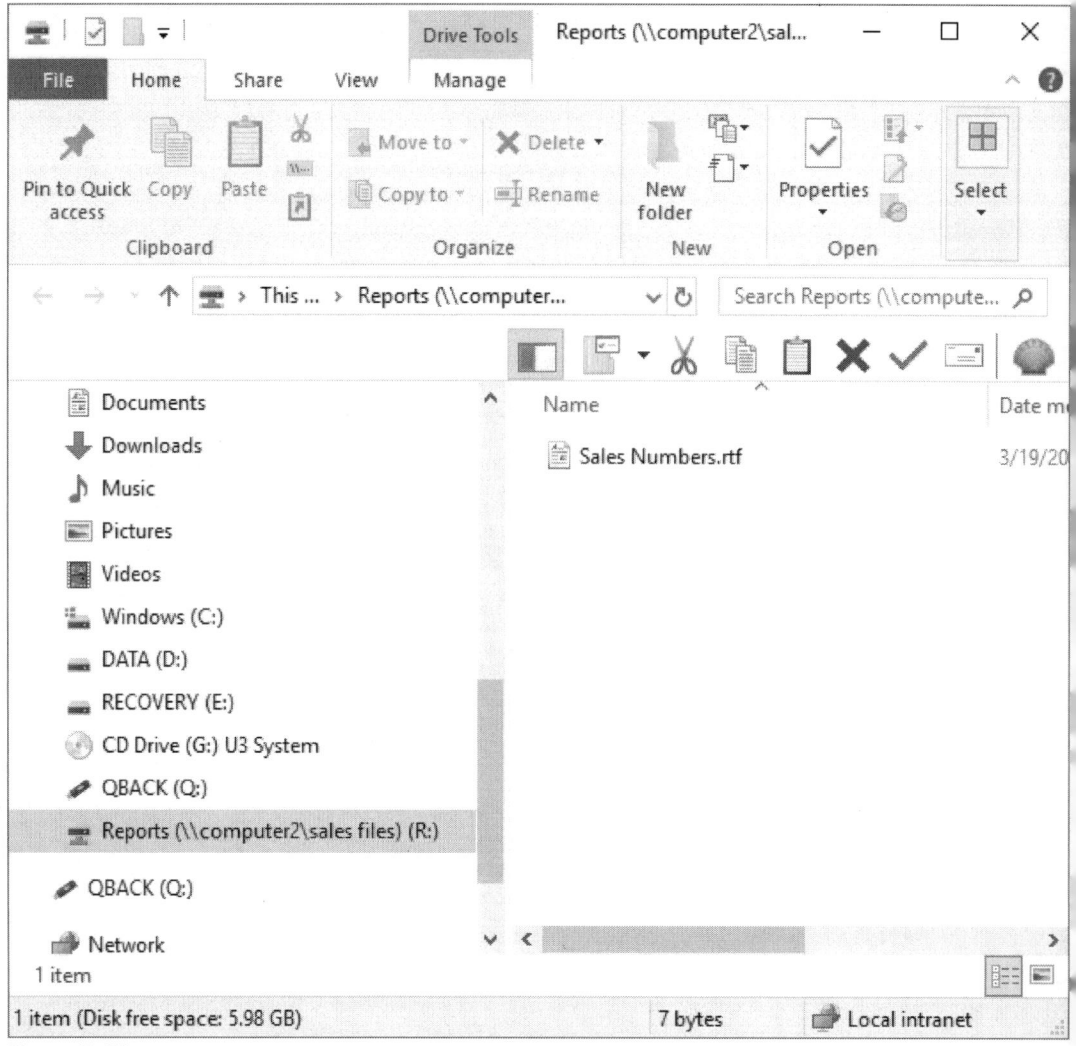

Figure 5.47

Administrative Shares
There is one other type of share that I wanted to mention that you should know about. In addition to the manual folder shares that you set up, Windows also has built in *administrative shares*. These shares are used to access other files and folders on a remote computer that have not been manually shared on that remote computer, but are hidden by default. So, if you have administrative permissions on a remote computer and need to access, let's say, the C drive or any other drive on that computer, you can do so using this type of share. Keep in mind that administrative shares are not available on the Home versions of Windows.

To access these shares, you will need to type in the UNC path just like you did for regular shares, but you will use a **$** to tell Windows that you are accessing an admin

Chapter 5 – Sharing Resources

share. To access the administrative share for the C drive on a remote computer, you would use the UNC path of **\\ComputerName\C$**. So, in my case it would be **\\computer2\c$** (as shown in figure 5.48).

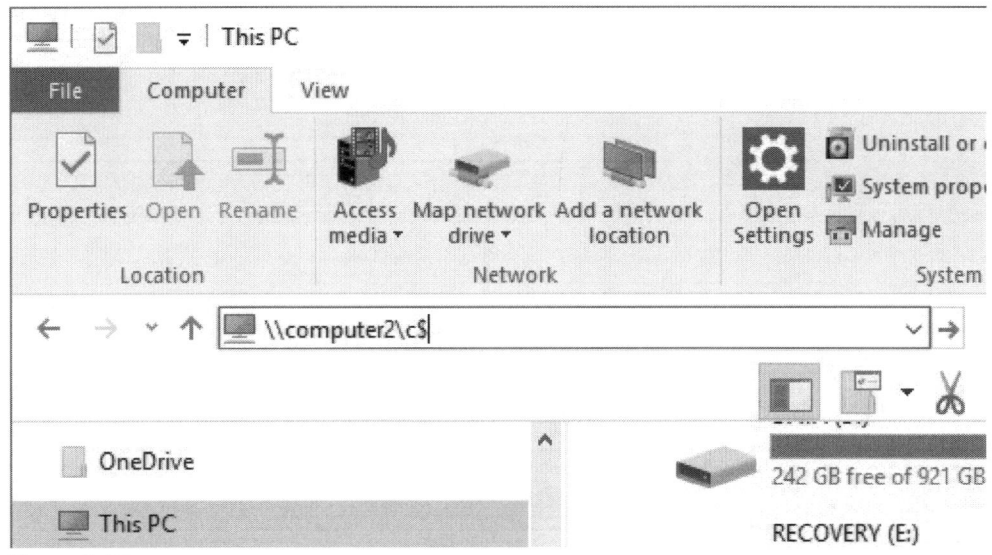

Figure 5.48

Depending on how you have your accounts configured, you might be prompted for a username and password (like shown in figure 5.49). Here you will enter a username and password for a user that has administrator access on that remote computer. Don't put in the username and password for the account you are using on your local computer unless it has admin access on the remote computer as well. In my example I will use the admin user that I have created on the remote computer (Computer2).

When typing in the username, you will need to enter it in the format of **computername\username** (as seen in figure 5.49). You can also use the IP address instead of *computername* if that works better for you, or if you are having name resolution problems.

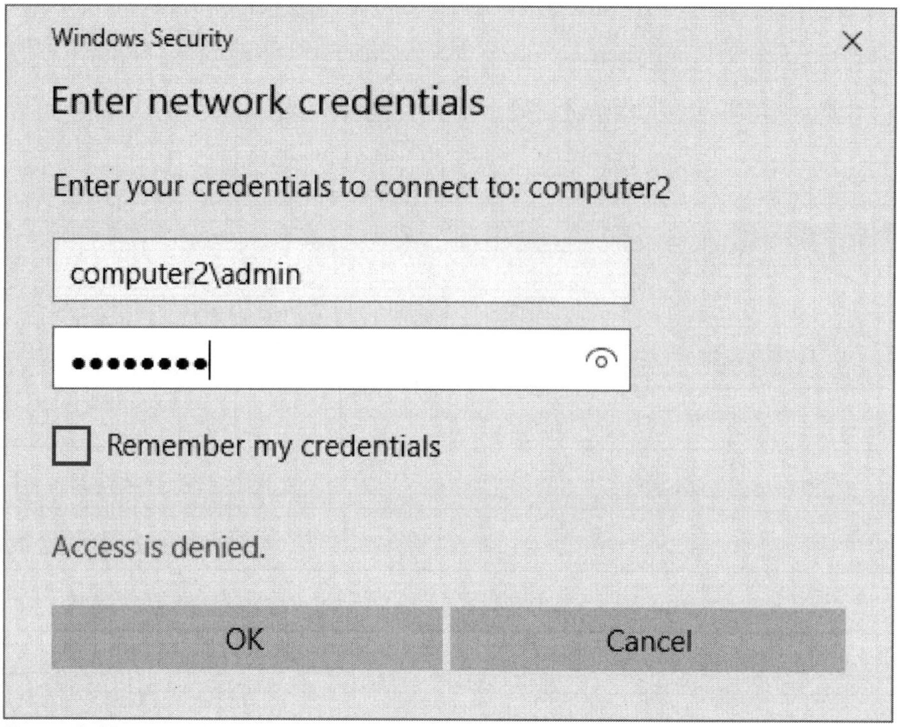

Chapter 5 – Sharing Resources

[Windows Security dialog: Enter network credentials — Enter your credentials to connect to: computer2 — computer2\admin — ●●●●●●●● — Remember my credentials — Access is denied. — OK / Cancel]

Figure 5.49

Assuming you have the correct permissions to access the remote admin share, then you will see the contents of the entire C drive (as shown in figure 5.50). If you wanted to access a different drive, such as the D drive (assuming you have a D drive), then you would type in **\\computername\D$**. Now we can see all of the folders on the C drive and not just the ones that are shared.

Chapter 5 – Sharing Resources

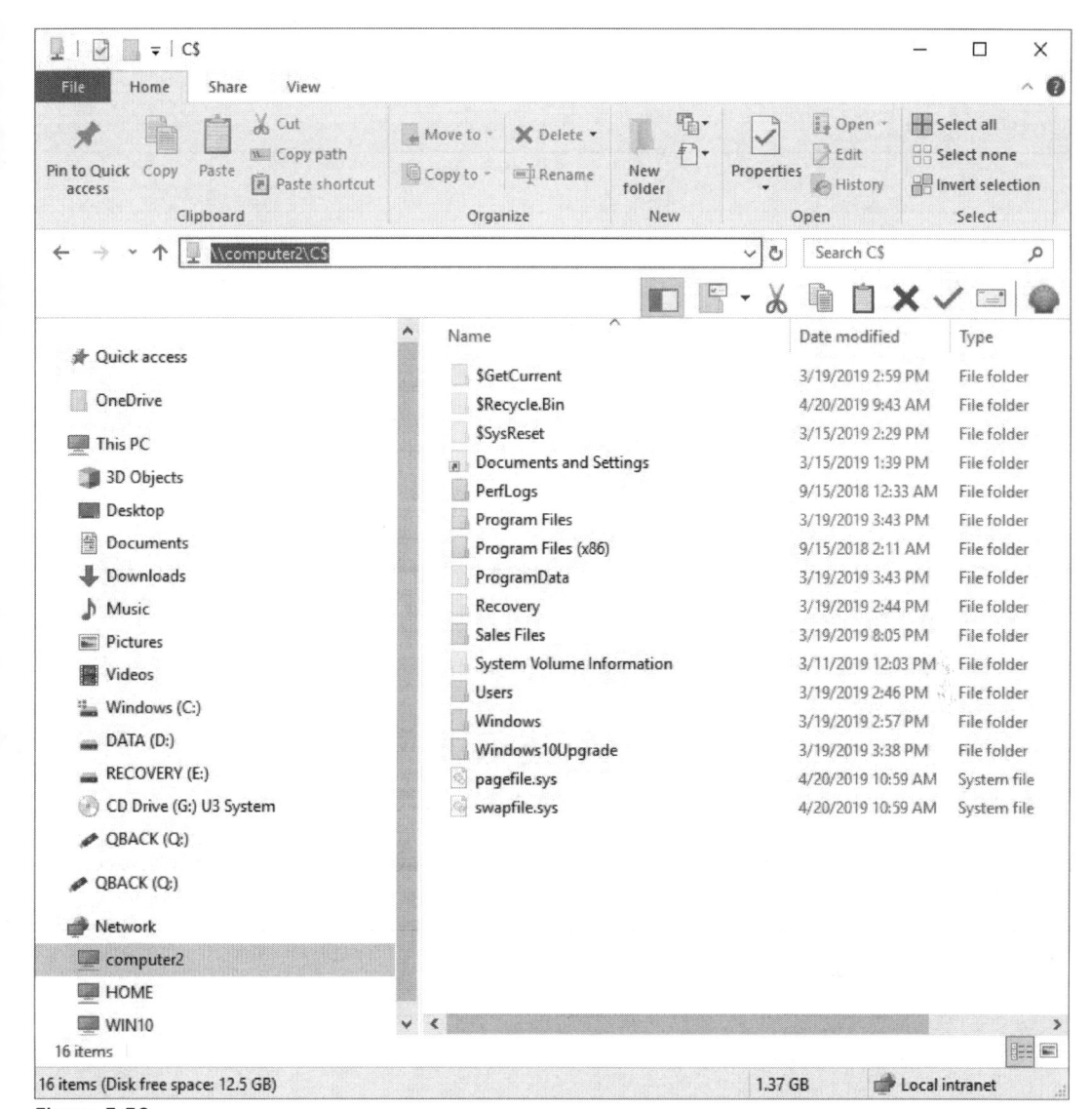

Figure 5.50

There is also another type of administrative share that might come in handy, and that is the **admin$** share. This share will show you the contents of the Windows folder on that remote computer (figure 5.51). To access this type of share, simply use the same format and type in **\\computername\admin$**.

Chapter 5 – Sharing Resources

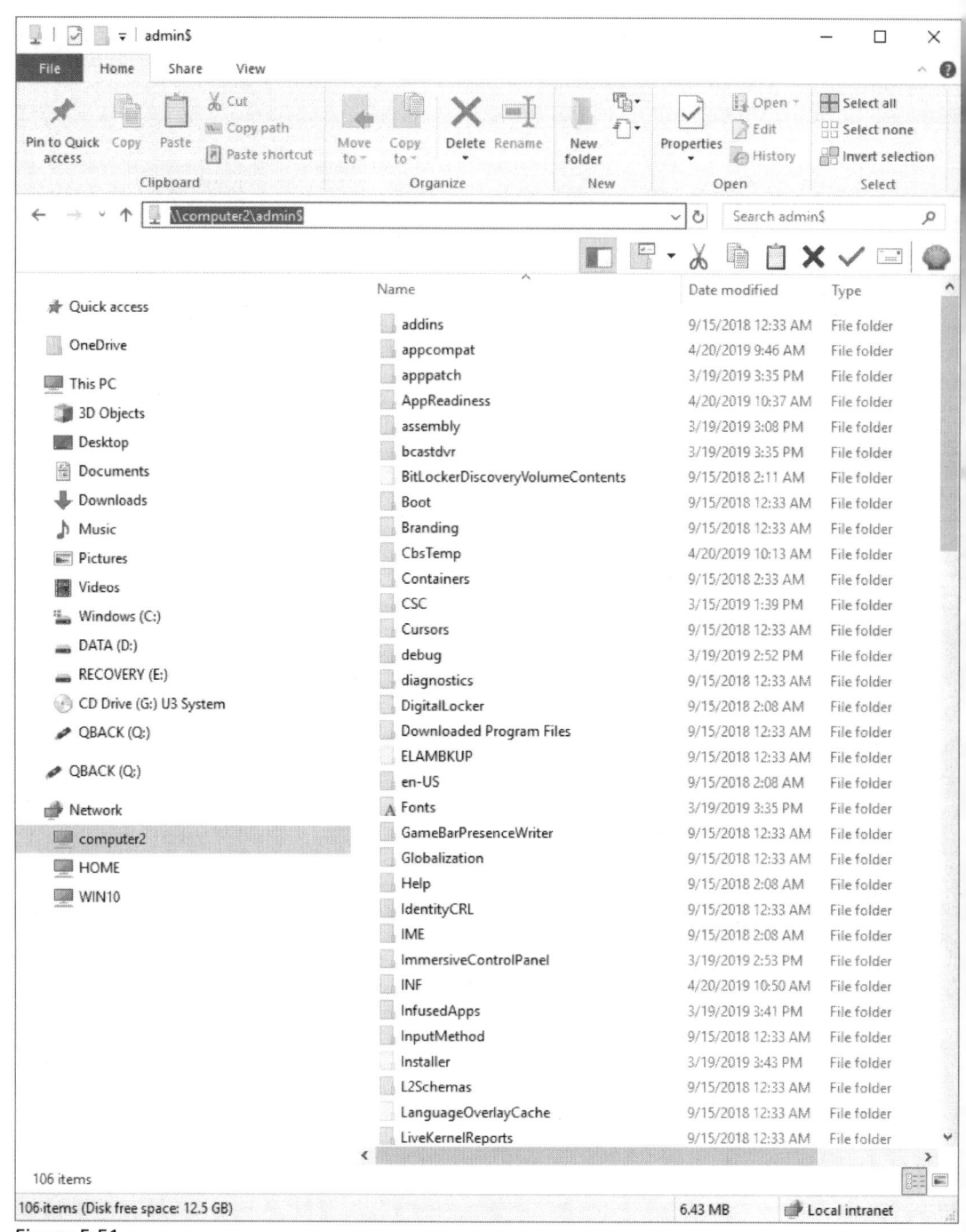

Figure 5.51

Depending on which version and\or build of Windows you're using, you might have problems accessing these administrative shares since Microsoft has been trying to secure their operating systems more and more lately. If you keep getting an access denied type message, there is a fix that involves a registry change you can make on your computer to allow these admin shares to work properly.

Chapter 5 – Sharing Resources

On the computer that you want to be able to access with the admin shares, open the registry editor by typing in **regedit** in the run box or Cortana search box. Then you will need to navigate to:

HKEY_LOCAL_MACHINE\SOFTWARE\Microsoft\Windows\CurrentVersion\Policies\System.

Then right click on any blank space and choose New>DWORD (32-bit) Value (figure 5.52), and type in **LocalAccountTokenFilterPolicy** exactly as shown, and you should end up with something that looks like figure 5.53.

Chapter 5 – Sharing Resources

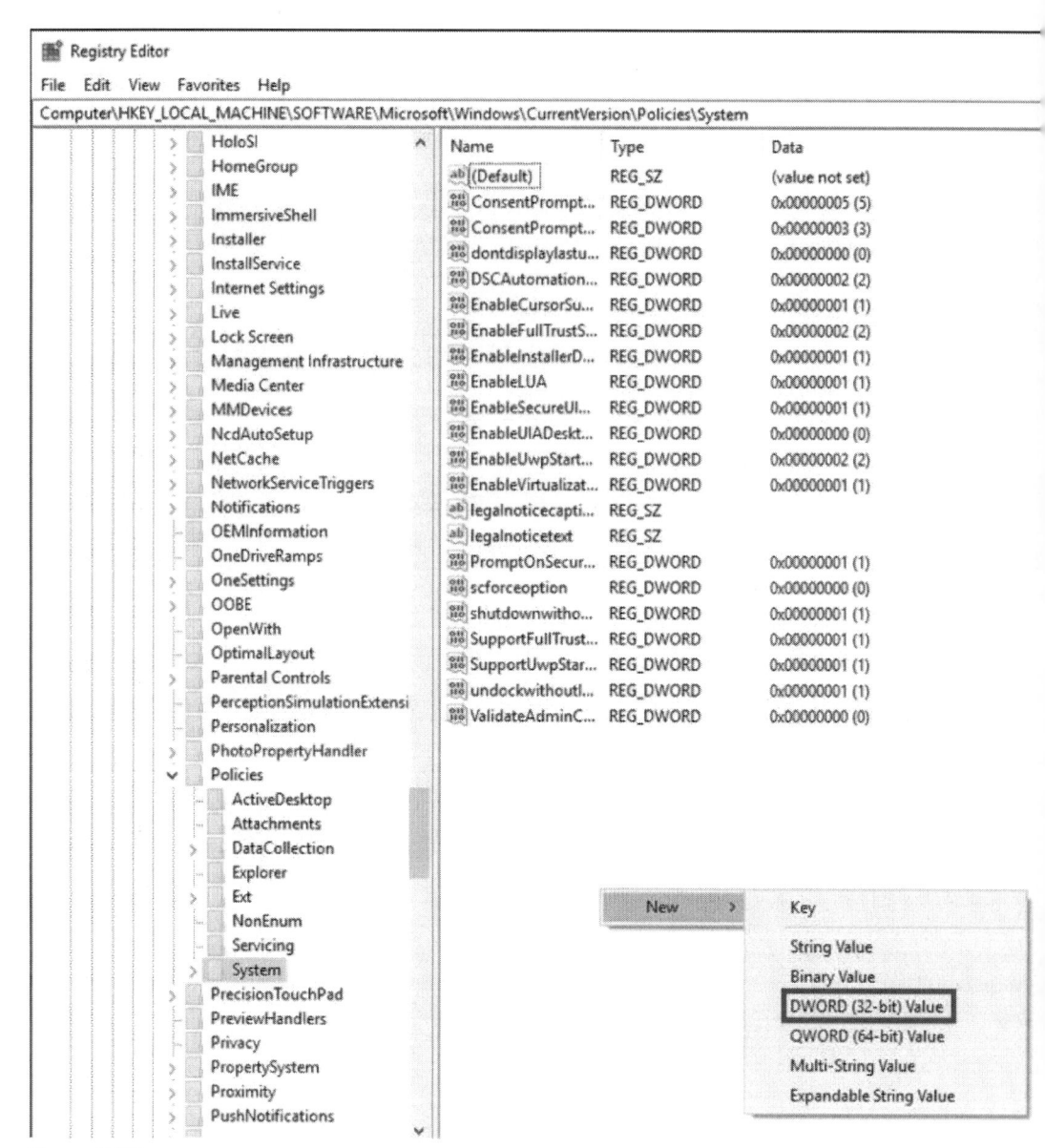

Figure 5.52

Chapter 5 – Sharing Resources

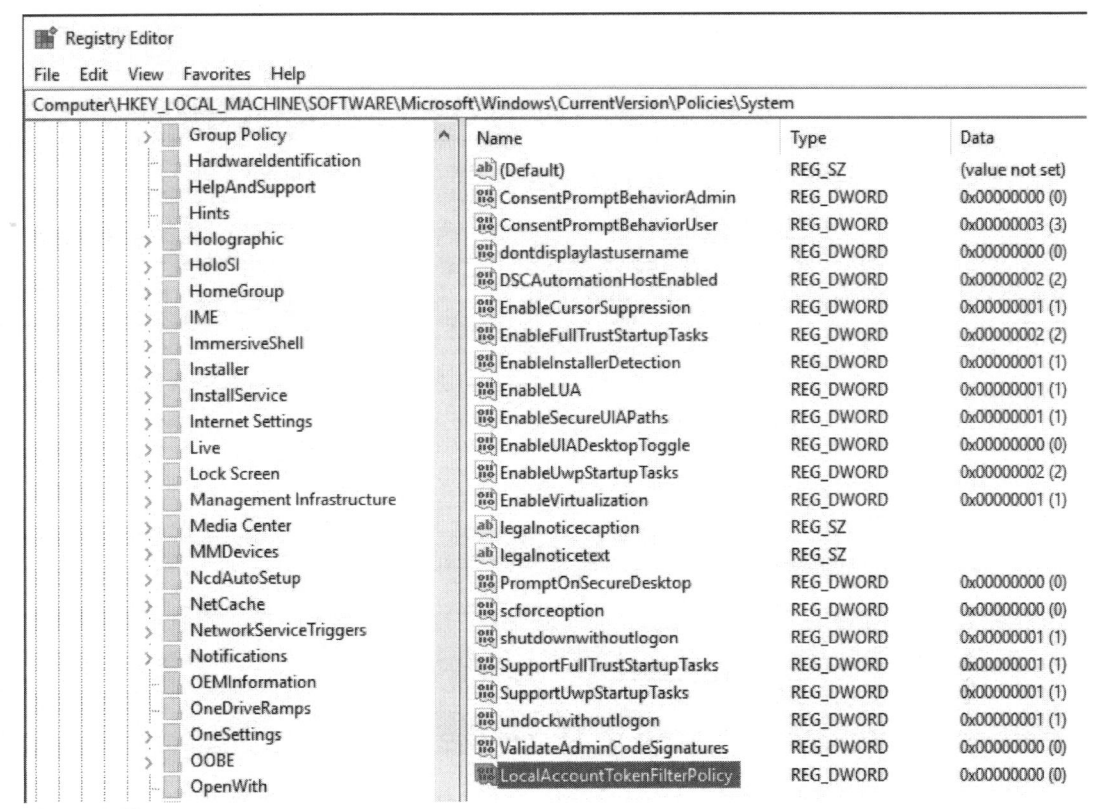

Figure 5.53

Now you will need to edit the value for this new item you just created. Simply double click on it and change the Value data from 0 to 1, click OK, and reboot the computer.

Figure 5.54

If you want a faster way to do this process, then you can type in the following data into your Run box and press enter:

127

Chapter 5 – Sharing Resources

reg add HKLM\SOFTWARE\Microsoft\Windows\CurrentVersion\Policies\system /v LocalAccountTokenFilterPolicy /t REG_DWORD /d 1 /f

Viewing Shares

If you get to a point where you have created a bunch of shares and are starting to lose track of what folders you have shared, then there's an easy way to see them all in one place and even manage them if needed.

To view your shares, you will need to open up Computer Management on the computer with the shared folders, or connect to that computer using your local Computer Management interface. To open the Computer Management console, simply right click on *This PC* and choose *Manage*, or type in *Computer Management* in the Run box or Cortana.

Once the Computer Management console opens, navigate to *Shared Folders* and then *Shares* (as seen in figure 5.55). All of your shares, as well as the administrative shares I just discussed, will be shown there. You will see the path, as well as how many other clients are connected to that share at the moment.

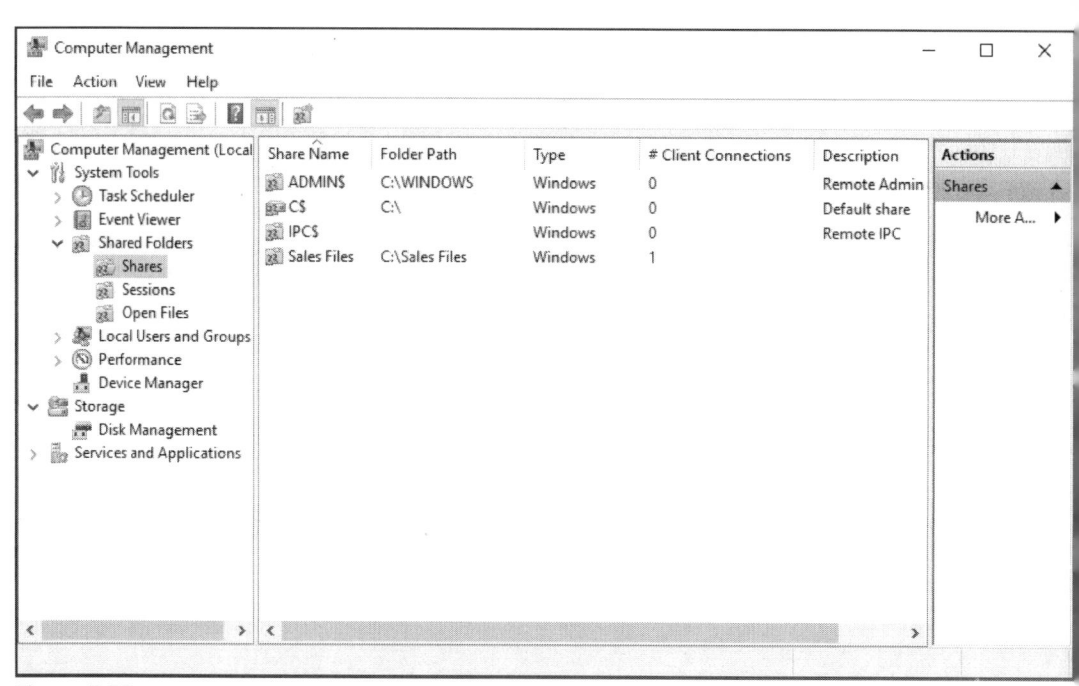

Figure 5.55

You can do things such as stop sharing a folder and edit shares from here by right clicking on a particular share and choosing the appropriate option. You can even

Chapter 5 – Sharing Resources

create new shares from the Action menu, or by right clicking a blank area and choosing *New Share*.

If you click on the *Sessions* item on the left, then you will be able to see who is currently connected to that computer remotely (figure 5.56). Here you can see the username of the person connected, as well as the computer name that they are making the connection from. You can also see how long they have been connected and how many files they have open. You can even close out their connection by right clicking on it and choosing *Close Session*.

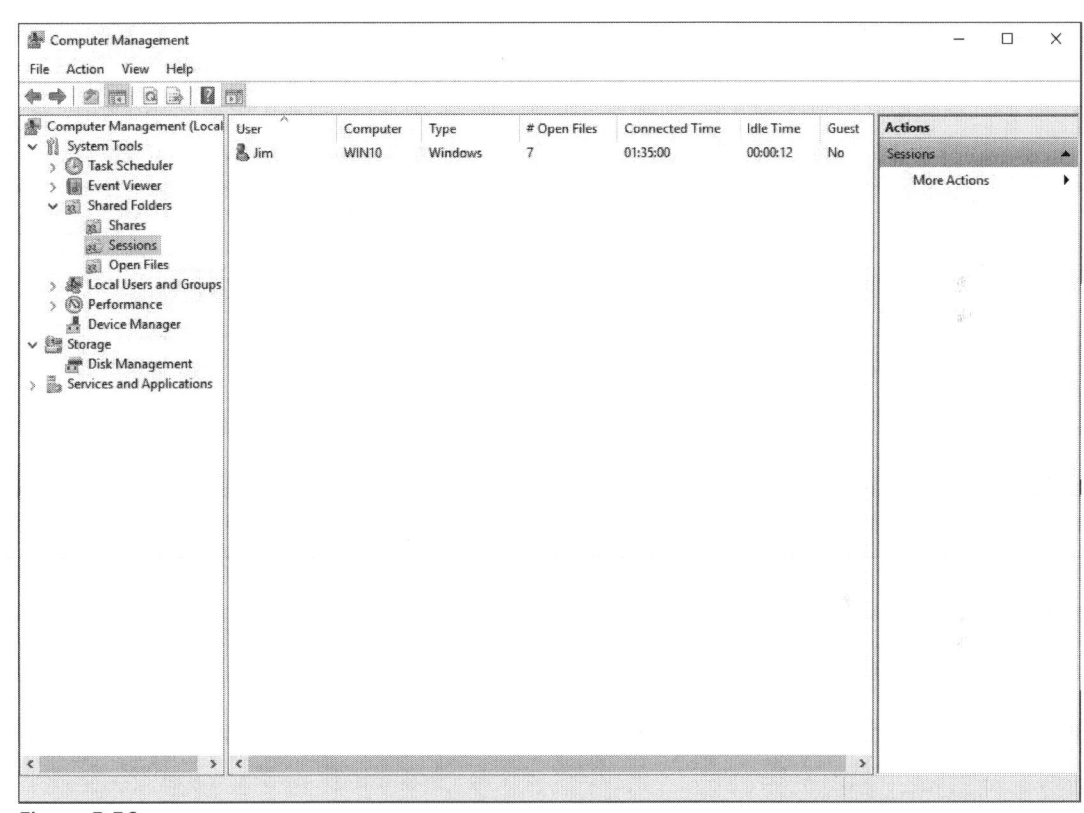

Figure 5.56

The *Open Files* area will show you what files and folders the connected users are accessing (figure 5.57). Right clicking on a file will give you an option to close that open file.

Chapter 5 – Sharing Resources

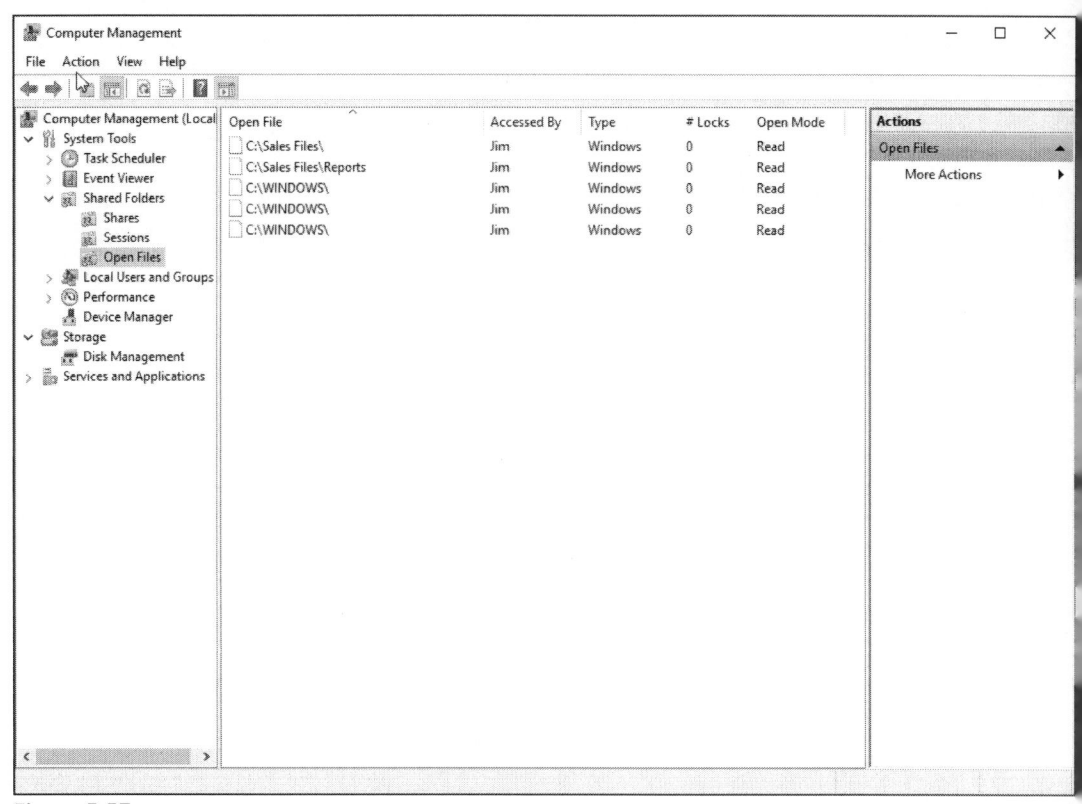

Figure 5.57

If you would like to view shared information on a remote computer from your local computer, then you can open Computer Management locally, right click on Computer Management at the top left, choose Connect to another computer, and type in the name of that remote computer. Then you will be able to perform the same tasks you were able to do while logged in locally to that same computer.

Chapter 5 – Sharing Resources

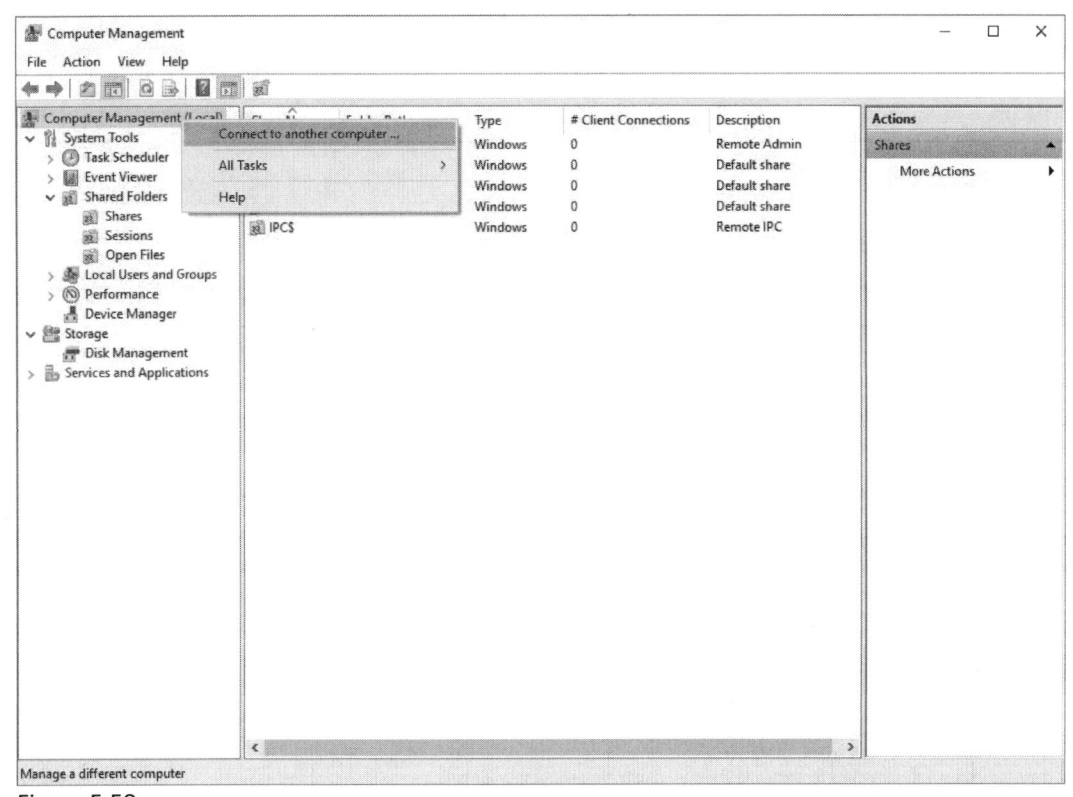

Figure 5.58

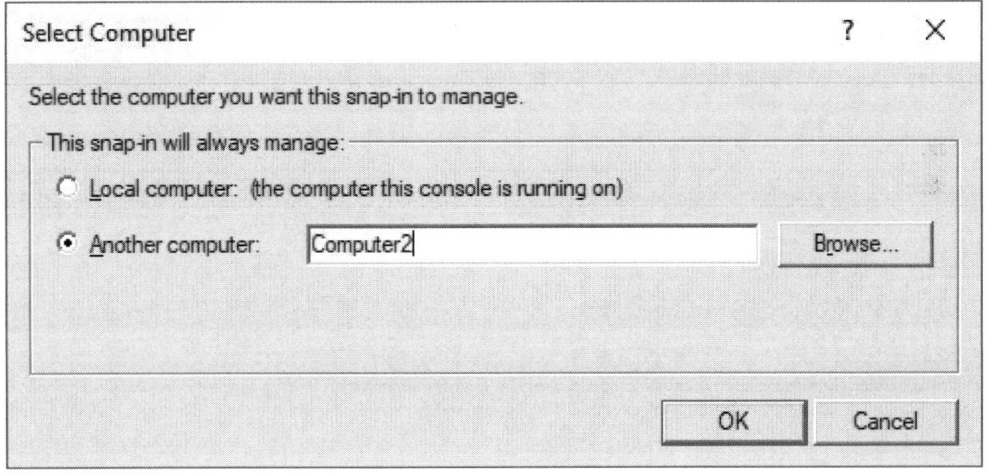

Figure 5.59

Sharing Printers

Another benefit of having your computers networked at home or at the office is the ability to share printers between them. By sharing a printer on your computer, it will allow other computers on your network to print to that printer without having to be plugged into it so you don't need to buy a separate printer for each computer. Sure

Chapter 5 – Sharing Resources

most home printers have wireless capabilities now, allowing you to connect multiple computers to them, but if you are using a computer without a Wi-Fi adapter, then you won't be able to connect to it this way. Or, if you are using a printer that doesn't have wireless capabilities (such as a larger laser printer that might not have built-in wireless), then you will need to use a different method to access that printer if it's not connected directly to your computer.

Keep in mind that there *is* a difference between being connected to a shared printer, and connecting to a network printer, and I will go over both in this section. First I will discuss how to share a locally attached printer on your computer so that other users on your network can connect to it from their own computers.

To share your local printer on your network, all you need to do is go to your printers within Windows, which is located under *Devices and Printers*. Once you are there, find the printer you want to share, right click on it, choose *Printer Properties,* and then click on the Sharing tab.

Chapter 5 – Sharing Resources

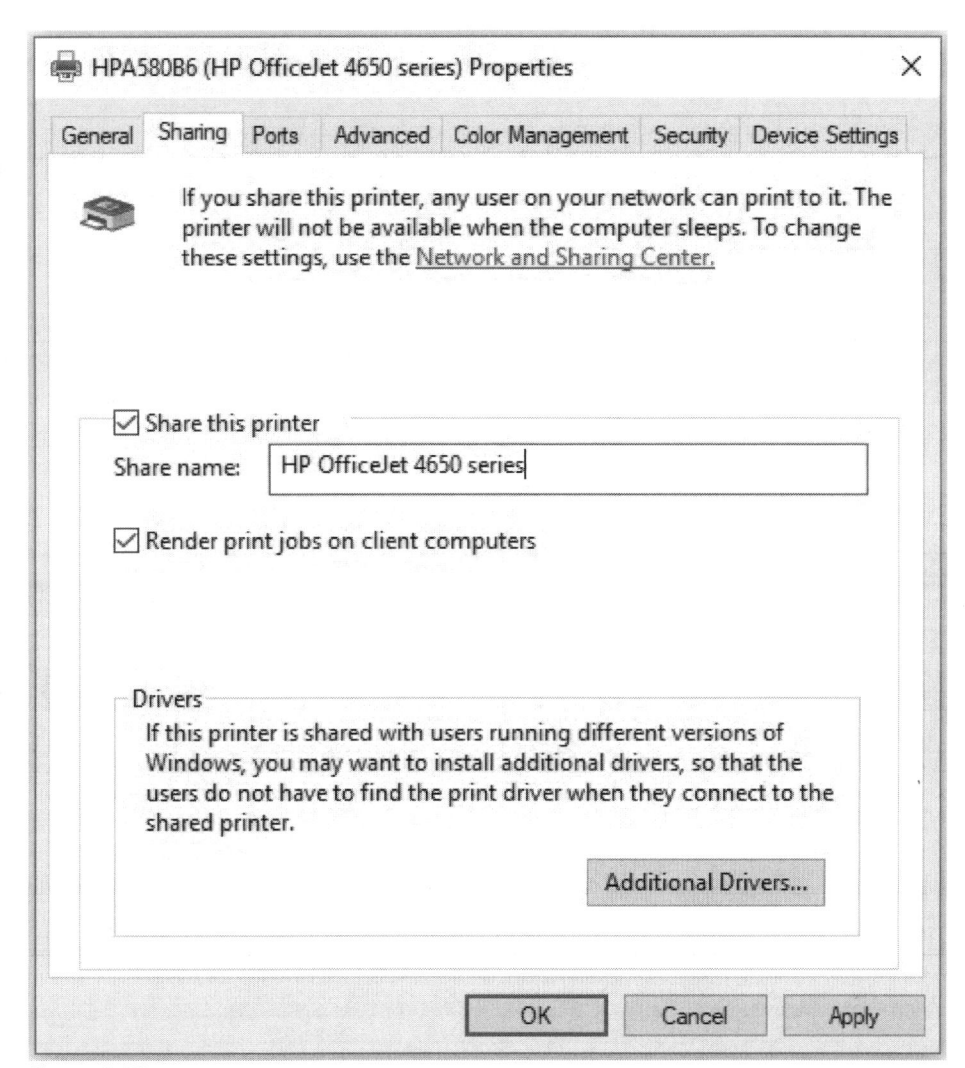

Figure 5.60

Next, you will check the box that says *Share this printer* and either use the name it chooses for you based on the printer name, or type in a name of your own. The box that says *Render print jobs on client computers* is checked by default, and this means that the processing of the print jobs will be done on the computer that is doing the printing rather than the computer that has the printer installed on it.

The next step is optional, for the most part, but if you want to fine-tune your security settings, then you can click on the Security tab to do so. As you can see in figure 5.61, the *Everyone* group has the Print permission applied to them, which means they can print to the printer, but not do things such as manage the printer or other user's print jobs.

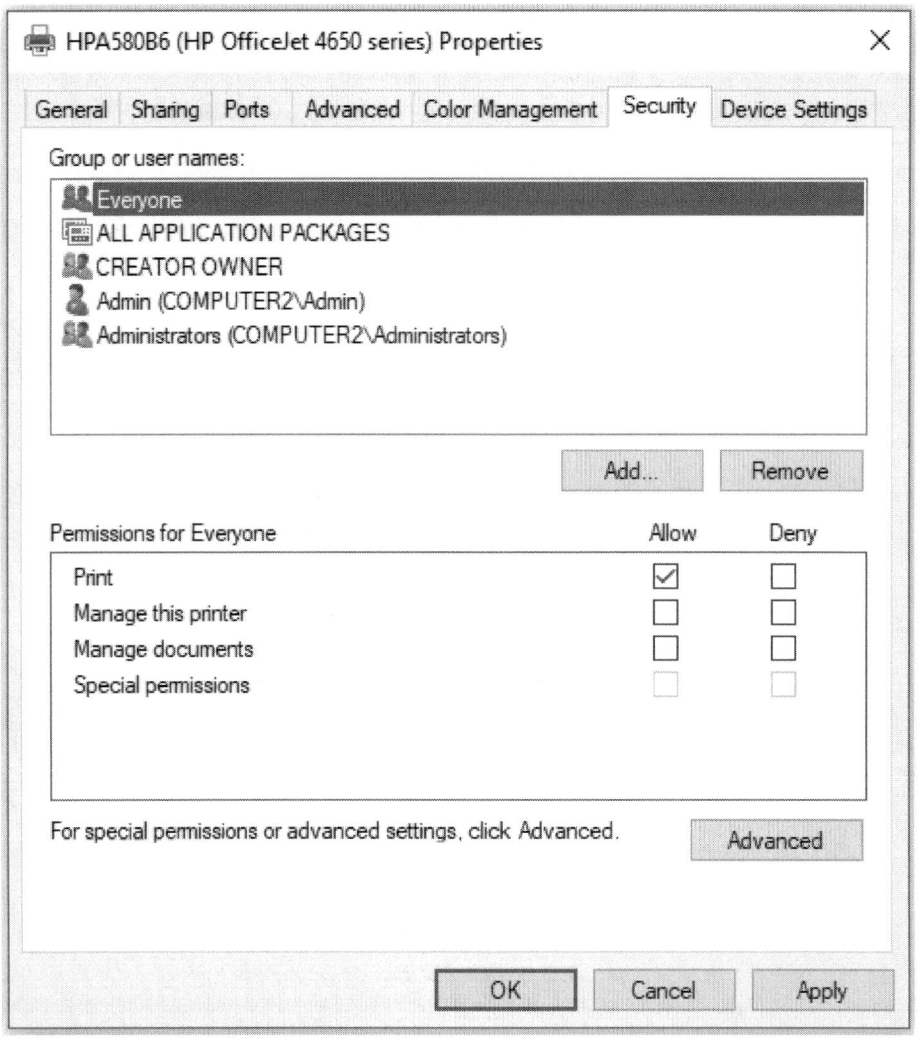

Chapter 5 – Sharing Resources

Figure 5.61

If you want to add a specific user to this list to give them special access, then you can simply click on the *Add* button like you would do to add a user to a shared folder and select the user you want to give the specific permission to.

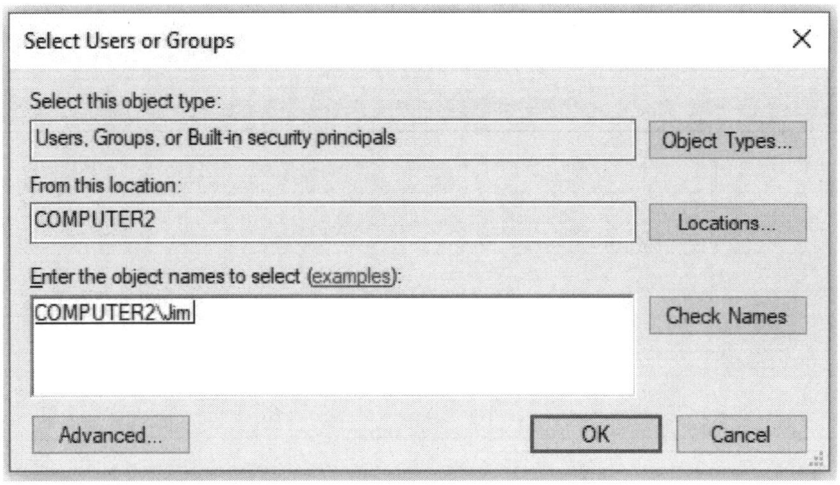

Chapter 5 – Sharing Resources

Figure 5.62

Then you would check the boxes next to the required permission and click OK. Just remember that the Deny permission will *always* overwrite the Allow permission.

Chapter 5 – Sharing Resources

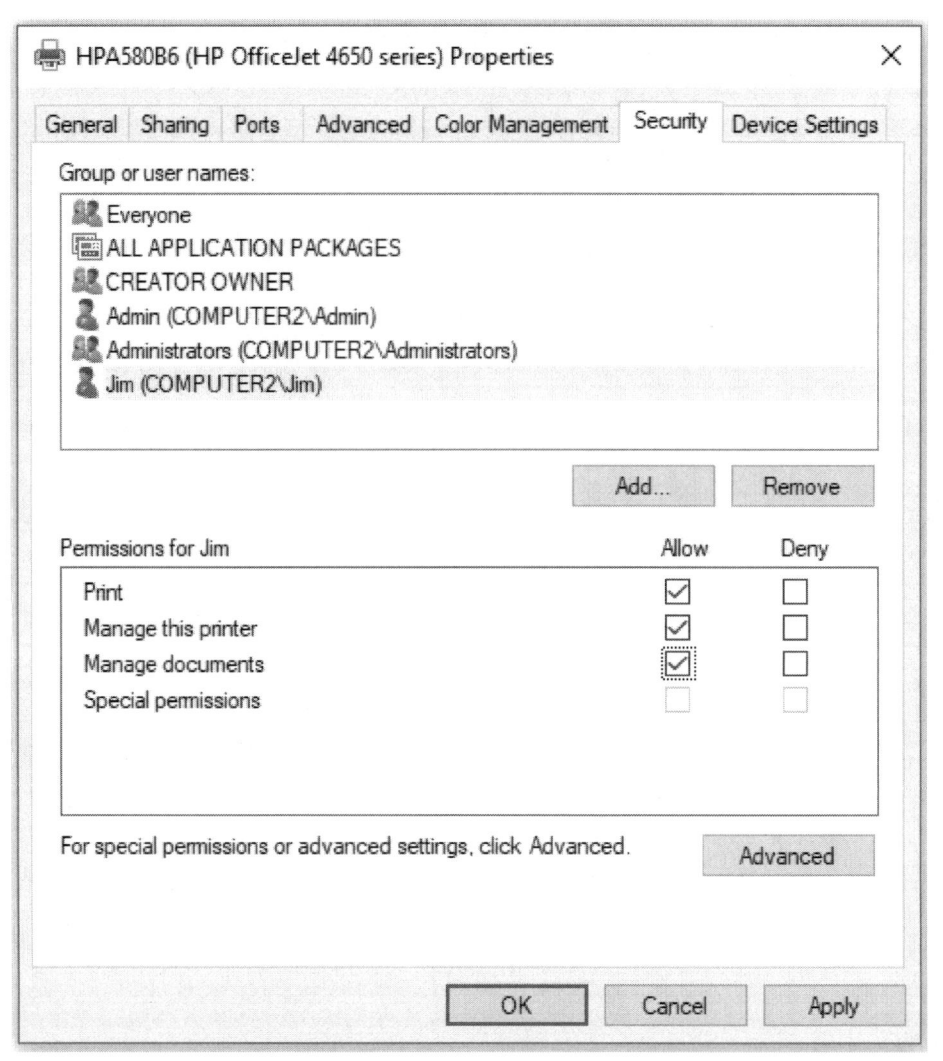

Figure 5.63

Now that I have shared my printer, when I go back to Devices and Printers it will have a small icon next to the shared printer indicating it has been shared.

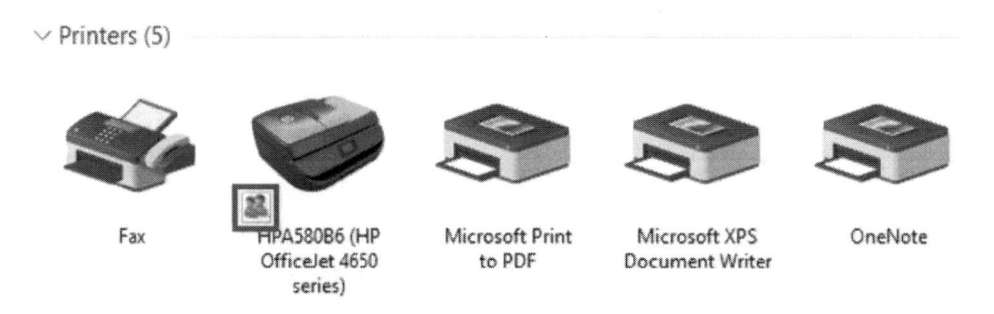

Figure 5.64

Chapter 5 – Sharing Resources

If I type in the UNC path for the computer that has the shared printer, you will see that the printer shows up, along with the shared folders from that networked computer. If I want to install that shared printer on my local computer, then all I need to do is double click on it and follow the prompts to have it configured for me to use.

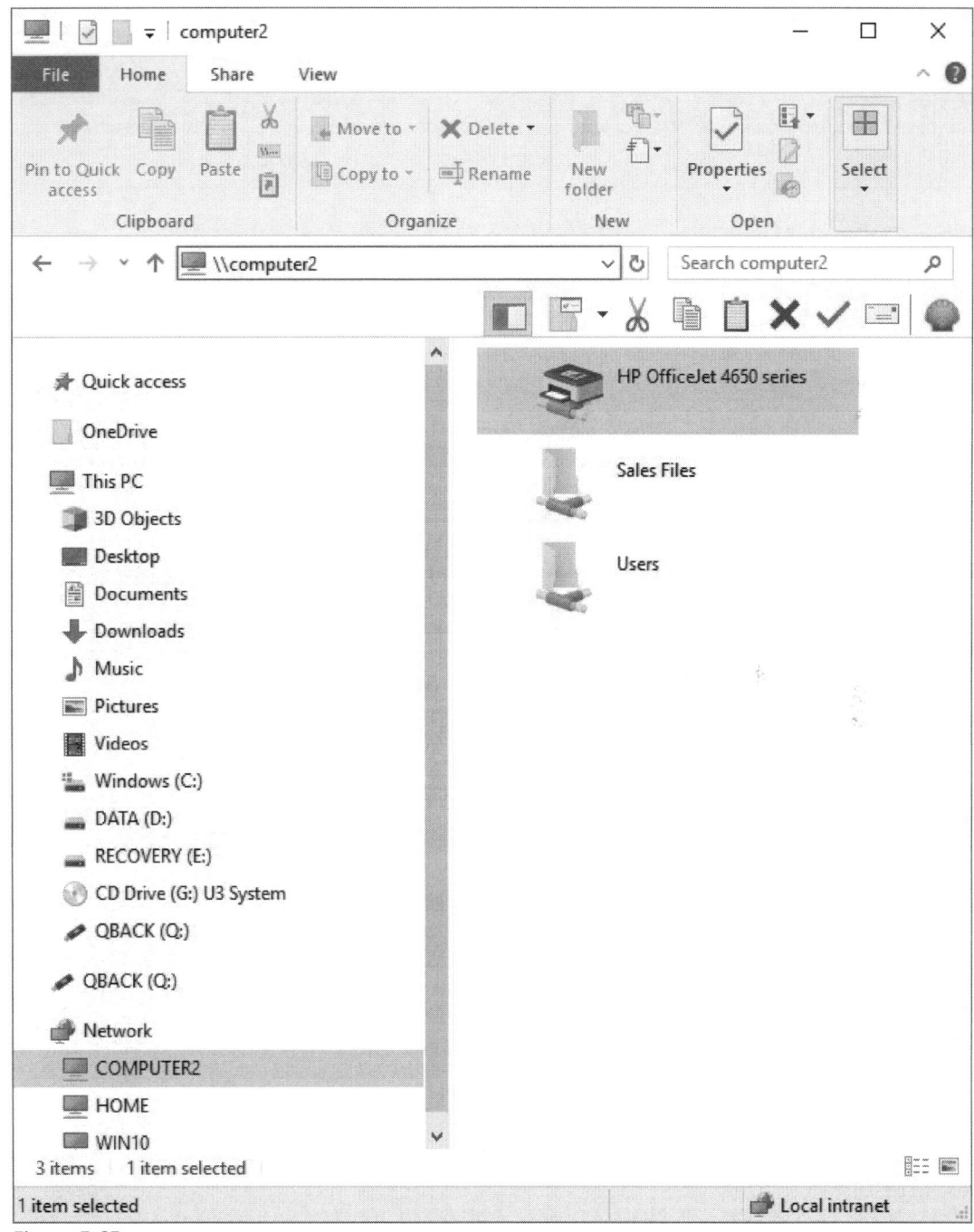

Figure 5.65

Chapter 5 – Sharing Resources

After installing the shared printer, I will be able to see it listed with my other printers on my local computer and use it as if it were installed locally.

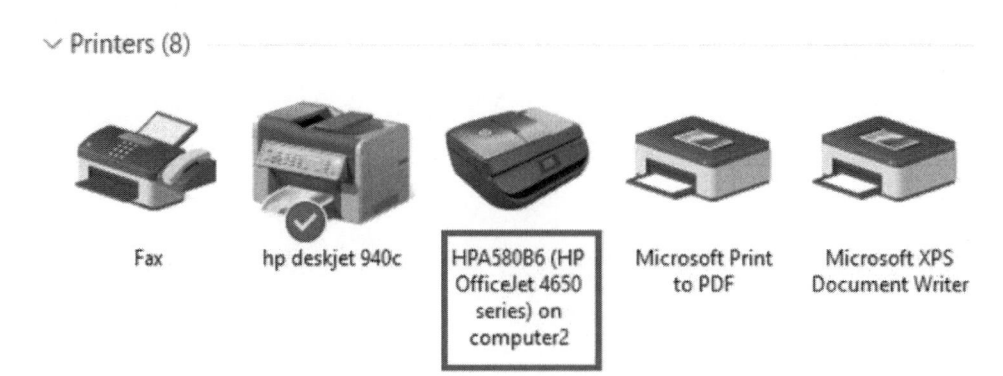

∨ Printers (8)

| Fax | hp deskjet 940c | HPA580B6 (HP OfficeJet 4650 series) on computer2 | Microsoft Print to PDF | Microsoft XPS Document Writer |

Figure 5.66

> **Tip:** When it comes to shared printers, one important thing to remember is that if the computer that is sharing the printer is not on or not available on the network, you will *not* be able to print to that shared printer.

Networked Printers
The other type of printer that I want to go over is what is called a *networked printer*. The difference between a networked printer and a shared printer is that a networked printer has its own network card and can be accessed directly over the network without having to rely on another computer to share it.

In order to attach to a networked printer, you will need to know its configuration so you can configure it on your computer. Most of the time you connect to these types of printers by their IP address, so you will need to know that. Sometimes you can also use their hostname as well. And, of course, the printer itself will need to be configured properly with an IP address that is on the same network as the computers that need to access it are. Figure 5.67 shows an example of an IP configuration page for an HP printer. You might have noticed how it's configured the same way as the network card on your computer.

Chapter 5 – Sharing Resources

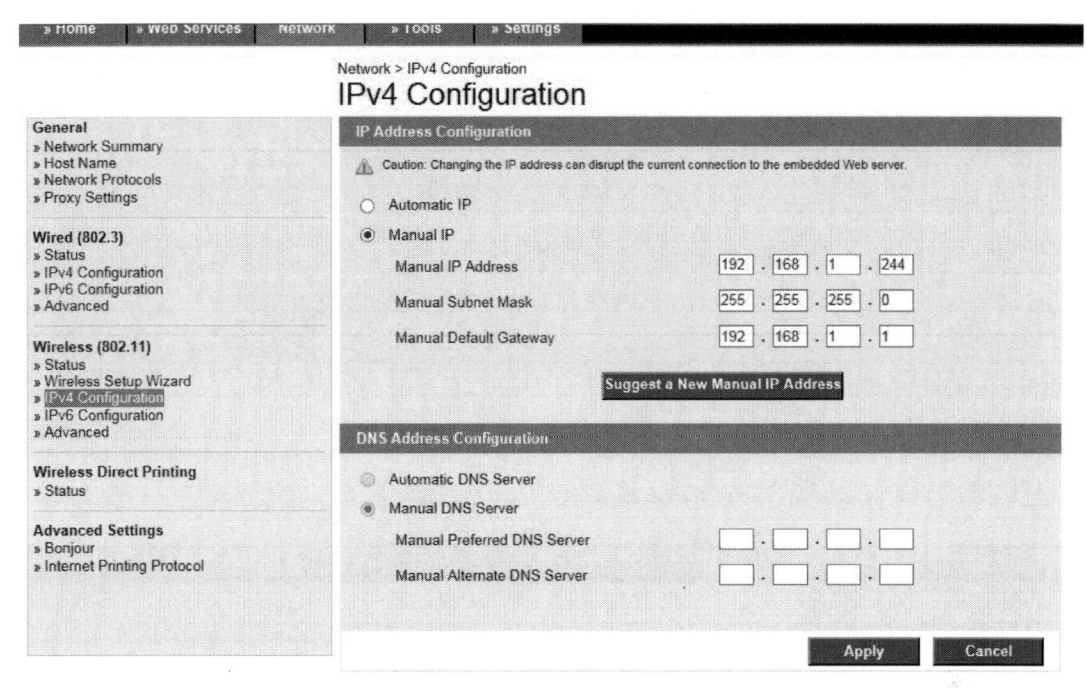

Figure 5.67

Once you have your networked printer configured, then you can add that printer to your computer from the same place you add other printers (Devices and Printers). From here you can choose the *Add a printer using a TCP/IP address or hostname* option, or even the *Add a local printer or network printer with manual settings* option.

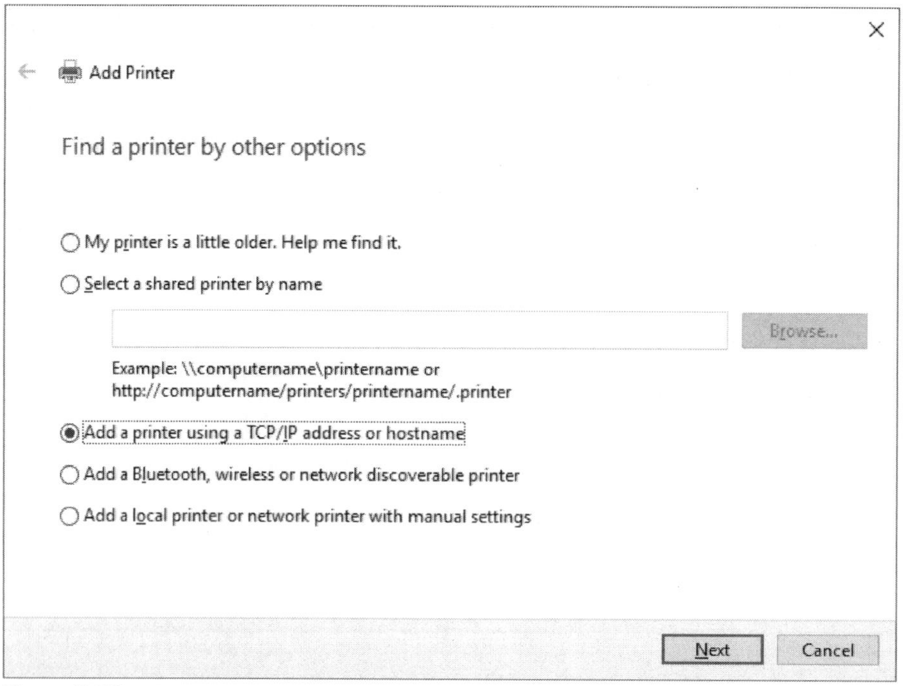

Chapter 5 – Sharing Resources

Figure 5.68

In my example, I will add a printer using its IP address. When doing this, it's best to set up your printer with a static IP address so it doesn't change and cut off your ability to use the printer without reconfiguring the printer settings on your local computer.

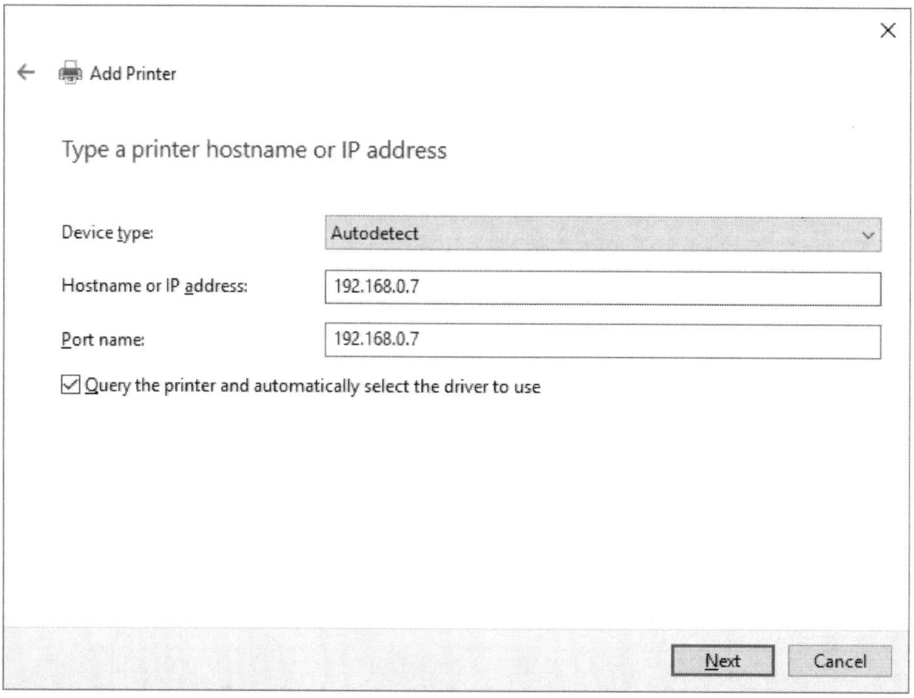

Figure 5.69

Chapter 5 – Sharing Resources

I will give my printer a name, and also add the IP address to the name to help out with troubleshooting if needed in the future.

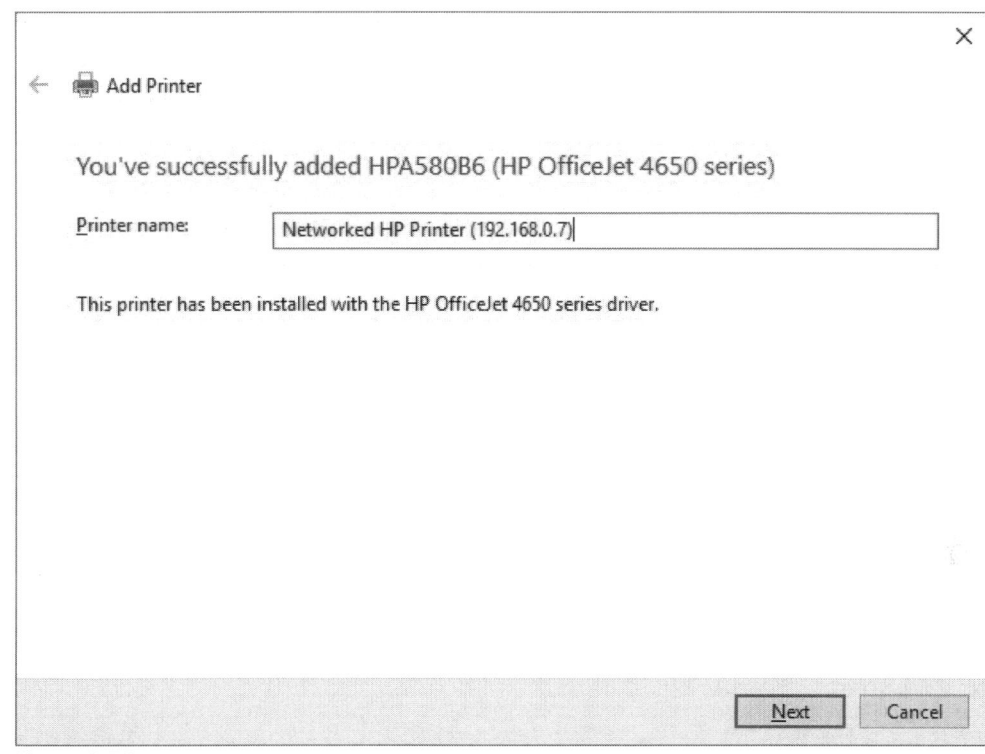

Figure 5.70

Then I will be prompted to share the printer, which I will not do in this case. When everything is complete, my networked printer will show up along with my other printers and will be ready for use.

Remote Connections
There will most likely come a time where you will want to use another computer on your network besides the one you are sitting at. If the computer is in the same room, then it's easy enough to go over to that other computer, log in, and get to work. But if the computer is not nearby, or maybe even running in a server closet with no attached monitor, then using it might not be so easy to do.

For Windows users, one common way to connect to a remote computer over the network is to use a Remote Desktop connection. Remote Desktop is Microsoft's built-in remote access client that allows you to log into a remote computer and use it as if you were sitting right in front of it.

Chapter 5 – Sharing Resources

The Remote Desktop client is built into Windows, and all you need to do to open it is to find it on your Start Menu (most likely under Windows Accessories). You can do a search for it as well. Another way many people start the program is by typing **mstsc.exe** in the run box.

Once the Remote Desktop client is up and running, you will need to fill in the required information needed to make the connection. All you really need is the IP address or host name of the computer you are going to connect to (figure 5.71). You can also enter the username before logging on, or wait for a login prompt to enter the username and password.

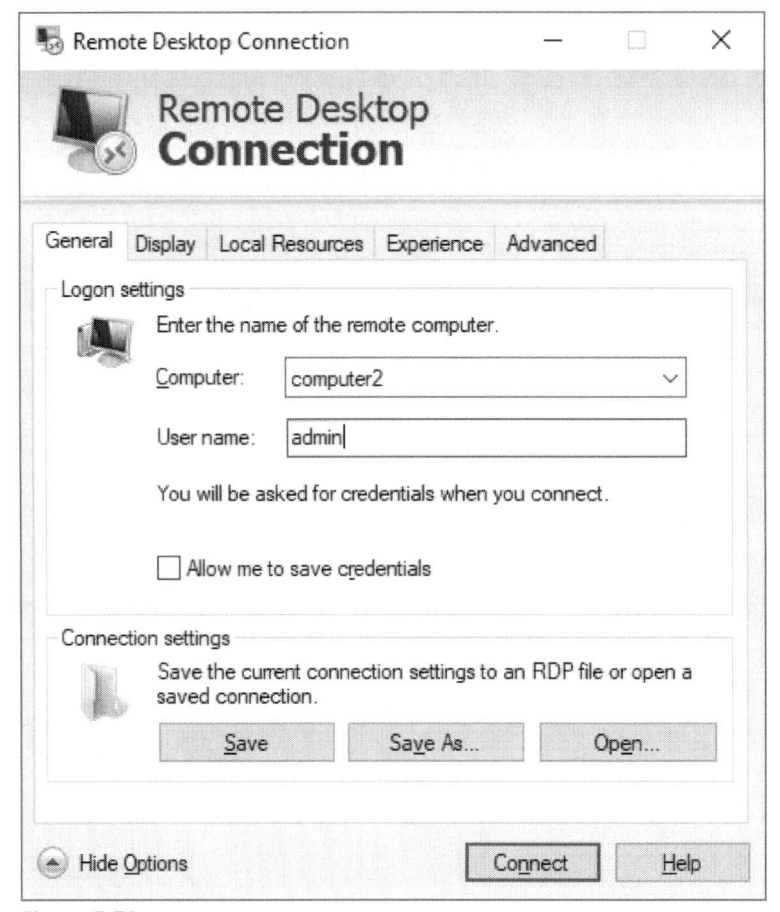

Figure 5.71

As you can see in figure 5.71, there are other tabs that you can use to configure the Remote Desktop settings before you make the connection.

- **General** – Here you will enter the computer's hostname or IP address that you want to connect to, as well as the username if you like.

142

Chapter 5 – Sharing Resources

- **Display** – This is where you can set a custom screen resolution and color quality.

- **Local Resources** – If you want things like sounds from the remote computer or access to the remote computer's printer and Windows clipboard, you can enable these things here.

- **Experience** – In this section you can alter the quality of your session based on various connection speeds.

- **Advanced** – Here you can change the security settings for server authentication, as well as the Remote Desktop Gateway settings.

Under the section that says *Save the current connection settings to an RDP file or open a saved connection* is where you can save the connection settings so you won't need to manually configure them next time you want to connect to that computer or even remember its name or IP address. It will create a file that you can just double click to start the session.

> It's generally not a good idea to save credentials for any computer you access, especially if you have administrator rights on that computer. That would be the same as removing the password from your desktop and allowing anyone who walks by access to it.

Before making the connection, I will need to look on the computer that I will be connecting to and make sure that remote connections are allowed, and that my user account is allowed to make that connection. To do this, I will go to my System Settings, click on *Remote Setting* on the left (figure 5.72), and then on the *Remote* tab (as shown in figure 5.73).

Chapter 5 – Sharing Resources

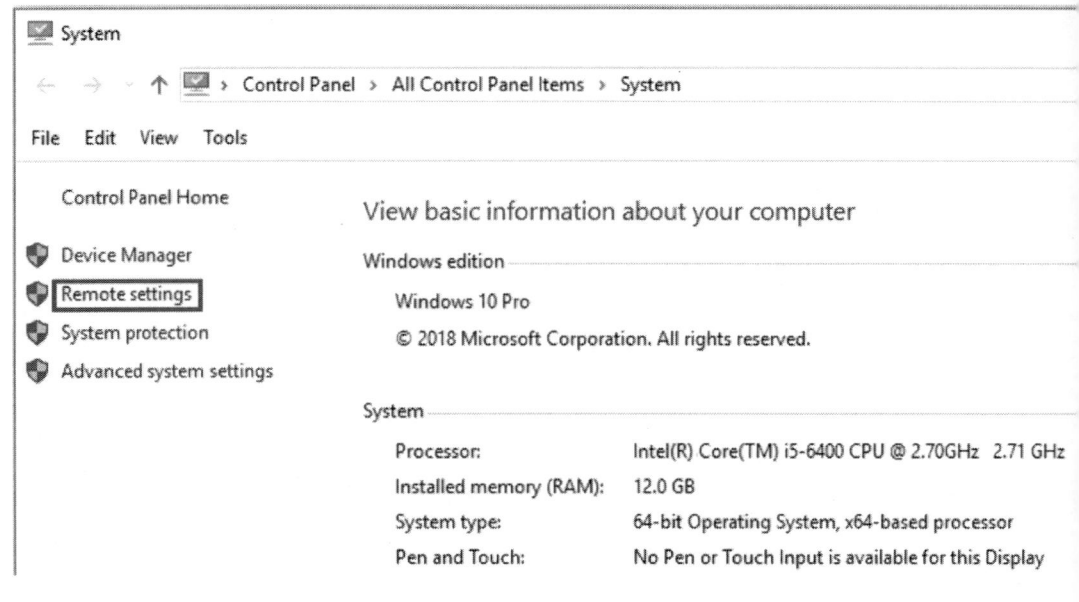

Figure 5.72

Chapter 5 – Sharing Resources

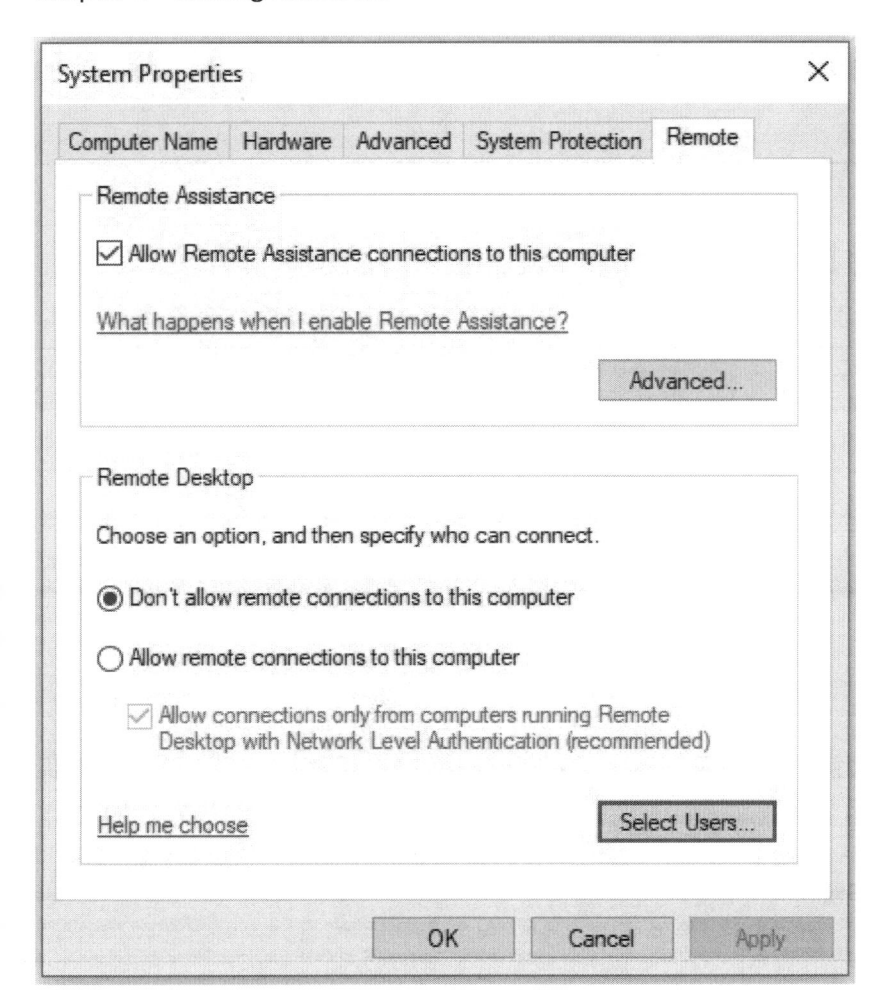

Figure 5.73

Then I will check the radio button where it says *Allow remote connections to this computer*. You might have noticed that it's set to *don't allow* by default. Under that is a checkbox that says *Allow connections only from computers running Remote Desktop with Network Level Authentication*. It's a good idea to have this checked for security reasons, and any newer version of Windows will be able to connect without any issues.

Next, I will click on the *Select Users* button to make sure that the user accounts that I want to be able to access this computer remotely are enabled. When I clicked the Select Users button, it showed me that the user named Admin already has access for remote connections, and then I clicked on *Add* and added my Jim user account to the list. You can do this for any users you like, and user accounts that are local administrators will be able to connect by default.

Chapter 5 – Sharing Resources

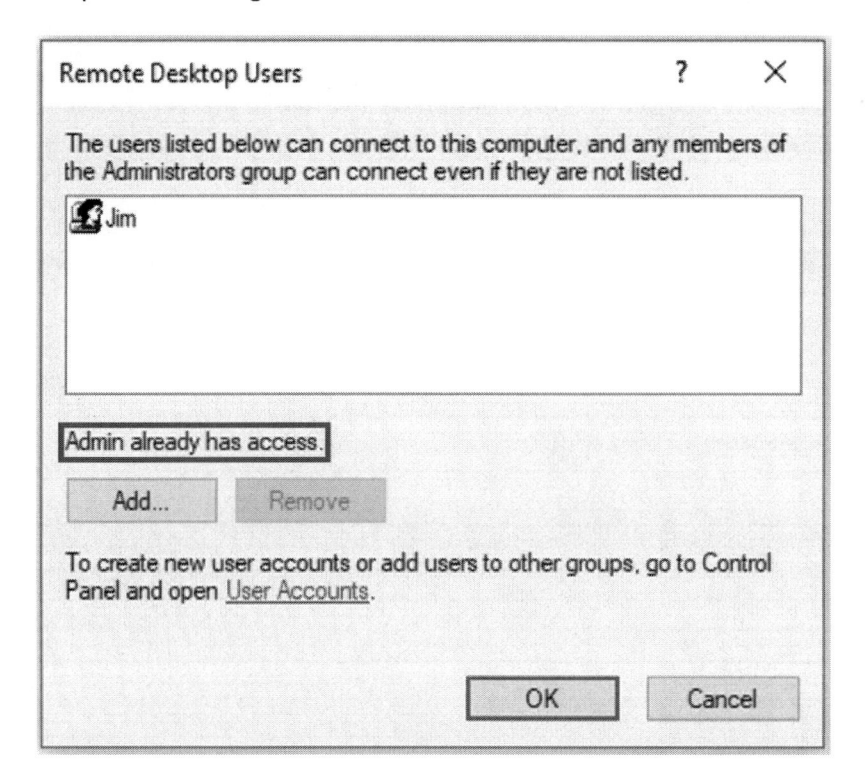

Figure 5.74

You can also configure these options from the Windows 10 settings under *System*, and then *Remote Desktop* (figure 5.75).

Chapter 5 – Sharing Resources

![Settings Remote Desktop screen]

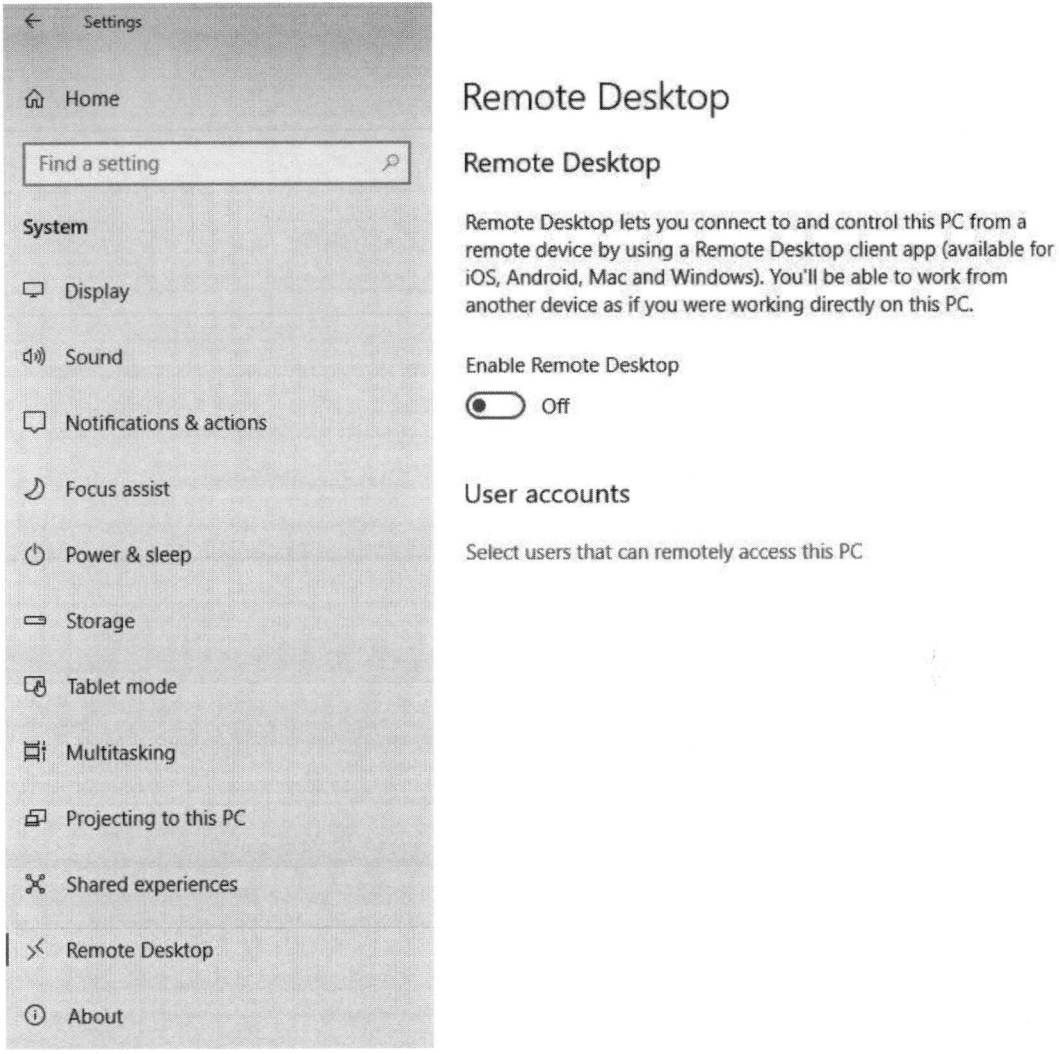

Figure 5.75

Now that I have everything configured on the remote computer, I will attempt to make a Remote Desktop connection to that computer from my computer by clicking on the Connect button.

Chapter 5 – Sharing Resources

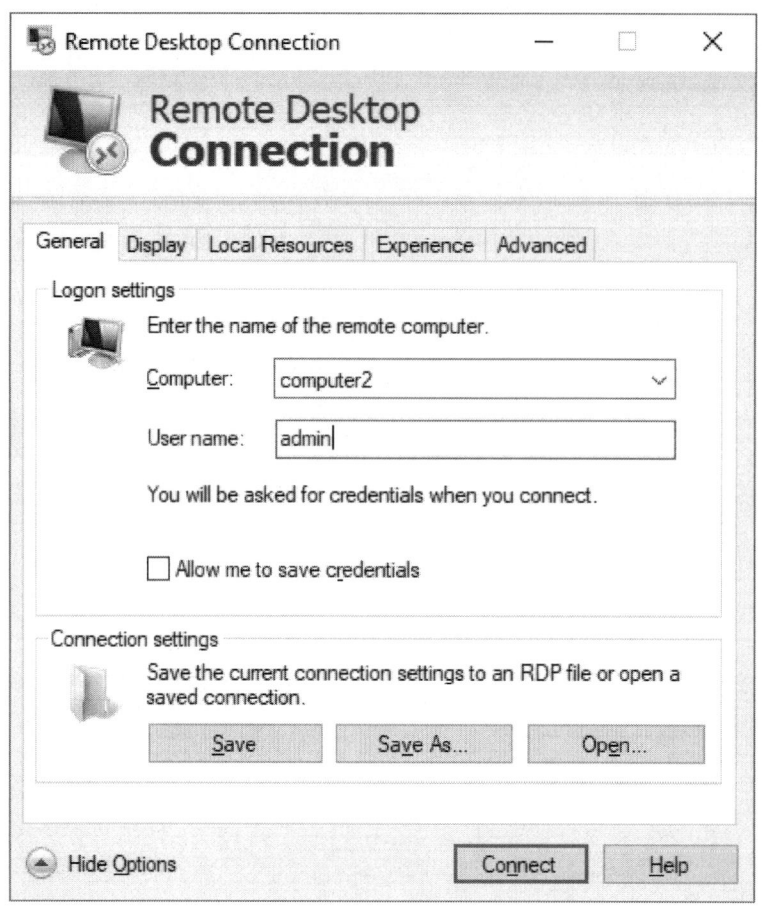

Figure 5.76

As you can see in figure 5.77, I am prompted to enter the password for the admin user that I preconfigured in the Remote Desktop settings (as seen in figure 5.76). If I didn't add that, I would be prompted for the name and password of the account I wanted to connect with.

Chapter 5 – Sharing Resources

Figure 5.77

The first time you connect to a remote computer, you will most likely get a security certificate message asking you if you trust this remote computer. For the most part, you can check the box that says *Don't ask me again for connections to this computer* if you know it's a computer on your network that you trust, and then click on *Yes*.

Figure 5.78

149

Chapter 5 – Sharing Resources

Once you make the connection, it will look just like you are sitting at the remote computer, and all of the Windows settings (such as desktop icons, mapped drives, etc.) will all be in place for you. If you want to switch back and forth between your local computer and the remote computer, all you need to do is minimize the Remote Desktop window.

> **Tip:** One thing to remember when using Remote Desktop is that when you make a connection to a computer running a desktop version of Windows (such as Windows 10), it will lock that computer so nobody can physically access it or see what you are doing. There is also a chance you can kick the local user off of their session, so pay attention to any messages when logging on.

Chapter 6 - Troubleshooting

Now that you have your network up and running and things are looking good, what do you do when something breaks and your computers are not communicating with each other anymore? That's when you need to put on your troubleshooting hat and get down to business. But where do you start? In this chapter, I am going to go over some basic troubleshooting steps you can take to see if you can get your network talking again.

Hardware Issues
First, I would like to talk about potential hardware issues you can face with your networking equipment. Trying to figure out hardware issues is the first step in determining what exactly is being affected by the current problem. Is it just one computer? Is your Internet access down? Or is it a group of devices that can't connect?

If it's just one computer that is down, then I would first check the network connection status from the operating system itself. With Windows, it's pretty simple because you will have a network connection status icon in the system tray down by the clock. If it has a yellow exclamation point or red X through it, then you know there is a network problem that is affecting Windows.

On the back of the computer where the Ethernet cable is plugged in, you can check to see if there is a green link light indicating a connection to the device on the other end of the cable. If the light is amber\orange that usually means it's running at a slower speed (such as 100Mbps), or it can sometimes mean there is a problem. There is no real standard to what color means what, so you are kind of stuck guessing. Some network cards even have two lights, one for the link connection, and one that flashes for activity. If there is no light, then there is definitely a problem with either the network card, the cable, or maybe the device it's connected to on the other end.

To see if Windows is having a problem with your network card, you should check Device Manager because it may help to give you an idea as to why it's not working. If you don't see your network card in the list of hardware under *network adapters,* then that means Windows does not recognize it and it could be dead. You may also have a problem with a driver, or conflict with another device. If that's the case, you may see a yellow question mark or exclamation point next to the device.

Chapter 6 - Troubleshooting

The easiest way to get to Device Manager is just to do a search for it from the run box at the Start menu. Then you will see a list similar to figure 6.1, but you most likely won't have as many items under network adapters unless you are using some sort of virtualization software like I am.

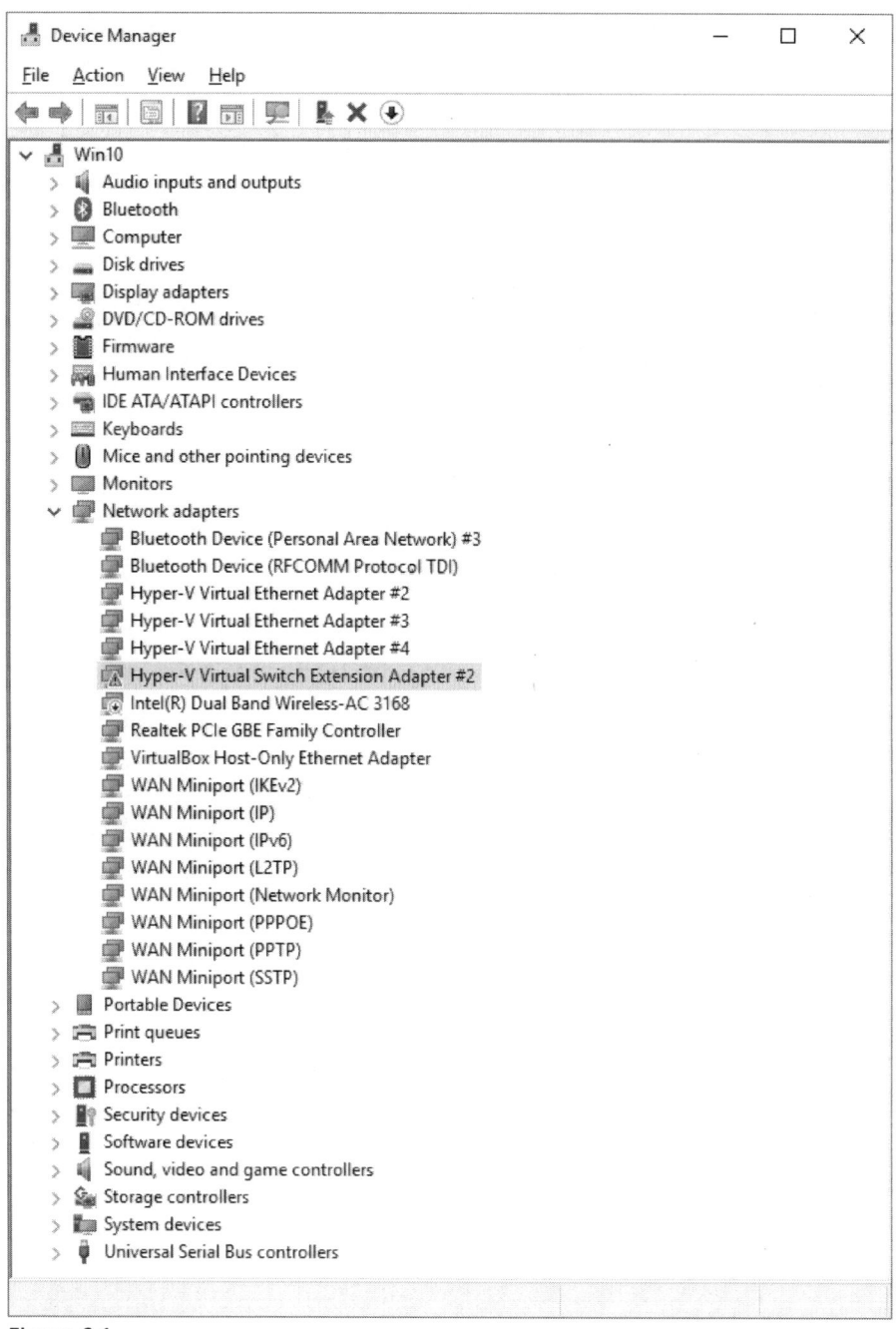

```
Device Manager                                    —    □    ×
File  Action  View  Help

∨  Win10
   >  Audio inputs and outputs
   >  Bluetooth
   >  Computer
   >  Disk drives
   >  Display adapters
   >  DVD/CD-ROM drives
   >  Firmware
   >  Human Interface Devices
   >  IDE ATA/ATAPI controllers
   >  Keyboards
   >  Mice and other pointing devices
   >  Monitors
   ∨  Network adapters
         Bluetooth Device (Personal Area Network) #3
         Bluetooth Device (RFCOMM Protocol TDI)
         Hyper-V Virtual Ethernet Adapter #2
         Hyper-V Virtual Ethernet Adapter #3
         Hyper-V Virtual Ethernet Adapter #4
         Hyper-V Virtual Switch Extension Adapter #2
         Intel(R) Dual Band Wireless-AC 3168
         Realtek PCIe GBE Family Controller
         VirtualBox Host-Only Ethernet Adapter
         WAN Miniport (IKEv2)
         WAN Miniport (IP)
         WAN Miniport (IPv6)
         WAN Miniport (L2TP)
         WAN Miniport (Network Monitor)
         WAN Miniport (PPPOE)
         WAN Miniport (PPTP)
         WAN Miniport (SSTP)
   >  Portable Devices
   >  Print queues
   >  Printers
   >  Processors
   >  Security devices
   >  Software devices
   >  Sound, video and game controllers
   >  Storage controllers
   >  System devices
   >  Universal Serial Bus controllers
```

Figure 6.1

Chapter 6 - Troubleshooting

As you can see, there is an issue with the device called Hyper-V Virtual Switch Extension Adapter #2. Right clicking the device will give you options to do things like update the driver or disable the device, as well as view its properties. As you can see in figure 6.2, the General tab of the device's properties shows that there is a code 10 error saying the device cannot start. You can use this information to start your researching into finding out what the cause might be.

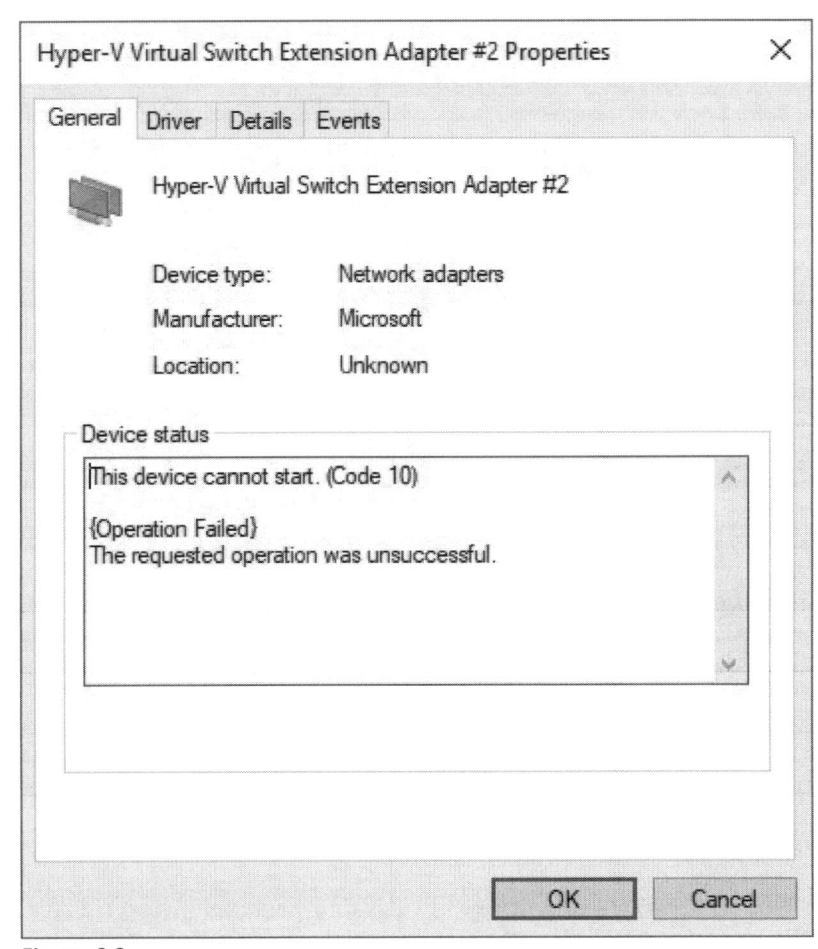

Figure 6.2

You may also want to try and download and install a newer driver for the device that is having the problem. Sometimes even uninstalling the device and rebooting the computer to make it reinstall the device will give it the kick it needs to start working again, so it's worth a shot.

So, let's say your computer is working fine, and there are no errors in Device Manager or in the device settings of whatever operating system you are using. You can then look at what device your computer is connected to. If you are connected to

Chapter 6 - Troubleshooting

a network switch, you can try another free port on the switch and see if your connection comes back. If you have another computer that is working fine that you can disconnect from the network, then you can try and use its switch port to see if your connectivity comes back. If multiple computers that are connected to the same switch are not working, then you can assume you are having a switch problem. You might get lucky and fix it with a simple switch reboot, but keep in mind that any devices that are working on that switch will go down.

If your problem only involves no Internet connection but the network is working fine, then you should look at your modem or whatever device provides your Internet connection. Check all the status lights on the modem and make sure nothing is out that shouldn't be, and nothing is flashing that shouldn't be. Even if everything looks to be in order, you can try to reboot the modem to reset it and have it try and reconnect and get its settings again. Also, be sure to check the link light on the back of the modem and the switch port it plugs into.

Cabling Issues
I'm sure you were wondering why I didn't mention checking the cables when discussing the possible hardware issues and checking link lights (etc.). That's because I wanted to do a separate section just on cabling issues.

Ethernet Cables
Network cables don't last forever, and they can get damaged from things such as rolling your chair over them and bending them too much or too far. The ends can also get damaged to where the wires inside the RJ45, plus they can lose their connection from things like tugging too hard on them.

If you are having a connection problem and everything on the computer looks okay hardware-wise, and switching ports on the switch doesn't make a difference, then you should try to replace the cable (assuming it's something you are able to access).

If it's a jack in the wall with the cabling going inside the wall and through the ceiling, then you will not be able to replace the cable to test. (Or at least it won't be an easy task.) In that case, you can use a cable tester\toner to see if the connection from the wall jack to wherever it terminates is good (figure 6.3). One end plugs into the Ethernet port, and then you take the toner wand on the other end to see if there is a proper signal going through the wire. If you don't get a tone, then there is a broken

Chapter 6 - Troubleshooting

connection somewhere in the cable, and that's where the fun part begins because you will need to track it down. You can also use these testers to test cables that you make yourself before putting them in production.

Figure 6.3

Another potential problem with cabling is if it has been run by something that is giving off electrical interference, which can be radio frequency interference (RFI) or electromagnetic interference (EMI). These can occur when things like radio frequency energy causes an electrical device to produce noise that can interfere with the function of an adjacent device. You can have cases of RFI or EMI when you run your cables too close to things like power relays, cordless phones, microwaves, air conditioning units, lights, and so on. If this is the cause of your problem, then you can either reroute your network cable, or remove the object causing the interference.

Network Configuration
The most important thing to get set up correctly when it comes to having your network function properly is its network configuration. You can have the greatest networking hardware in the world connected to top of the line workstations, servers, and printers, but if it's not configured properly, then all that high end equipment won't do you any good.

I went over IP addresses and subnet masks in Chapter 2, so this is where you want to start when trying to diagnose a network connection issue that is not hardware related. If your computer has been assigned an IP address on a different network

Chapter 6 - Troubleshooting

from the computer or printer you are trying to reach and you don't have a router to forward the traffic, then you won't be able to make the connection.

To begin, you should determine where your computer is getting its IP address from. Was it manually configured by you, or was it dynamically assigned by a DHCP server? If it was manually assigned, you should begin by going into the properties of your network adapter and double checking your work.

To do this, go to the *Network and Sharing Center* and then click on *Change adapter settings*. From there, find the adapter you are using, right click it, and choose *Properties*. If you are using IPv4 then double click on *Internet Protocol Version 4*. If you are using IPv6 then double click on Internet Protocol Version 6.

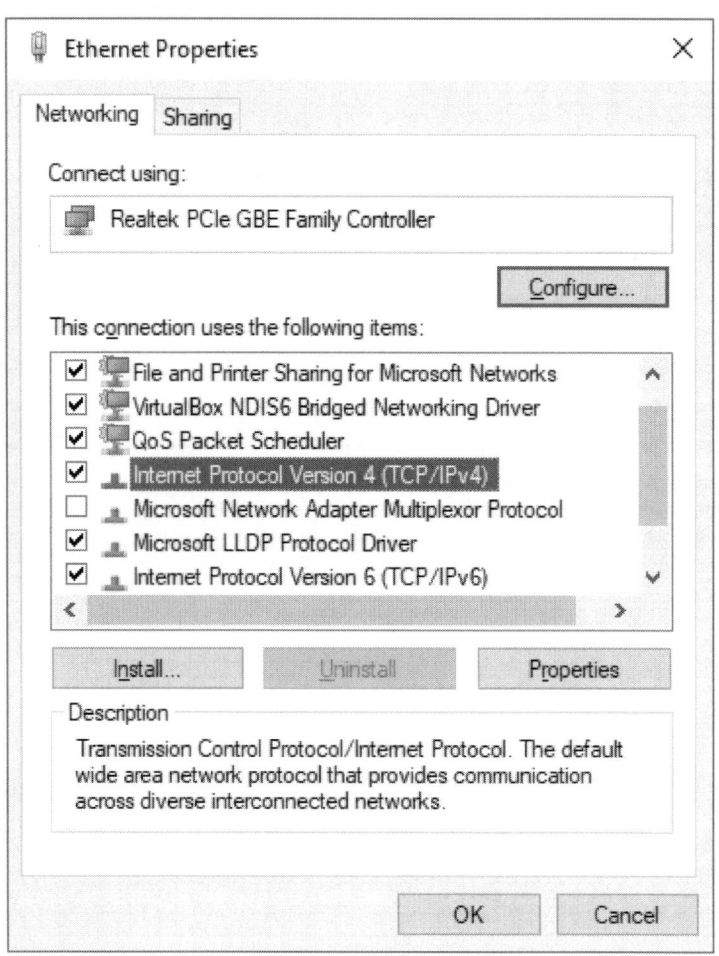

Figure 6.4

Figure 6.5 shows the information used in a typical statically assigned TCP/IP configuration. Your settings will vary based on your network configuration. Notice

Chapter 6 - Troubleshooting

how the IP address is 192.168.**2**.10 and the default gateway is 192.168.0.1? That right there tells you that there is most likely a problem with your settings. In most networks, especially small ones, the IP address and the default gateway will be on the same network. Changing the 2 to a 0 in the IP address should fix the issue in this case.

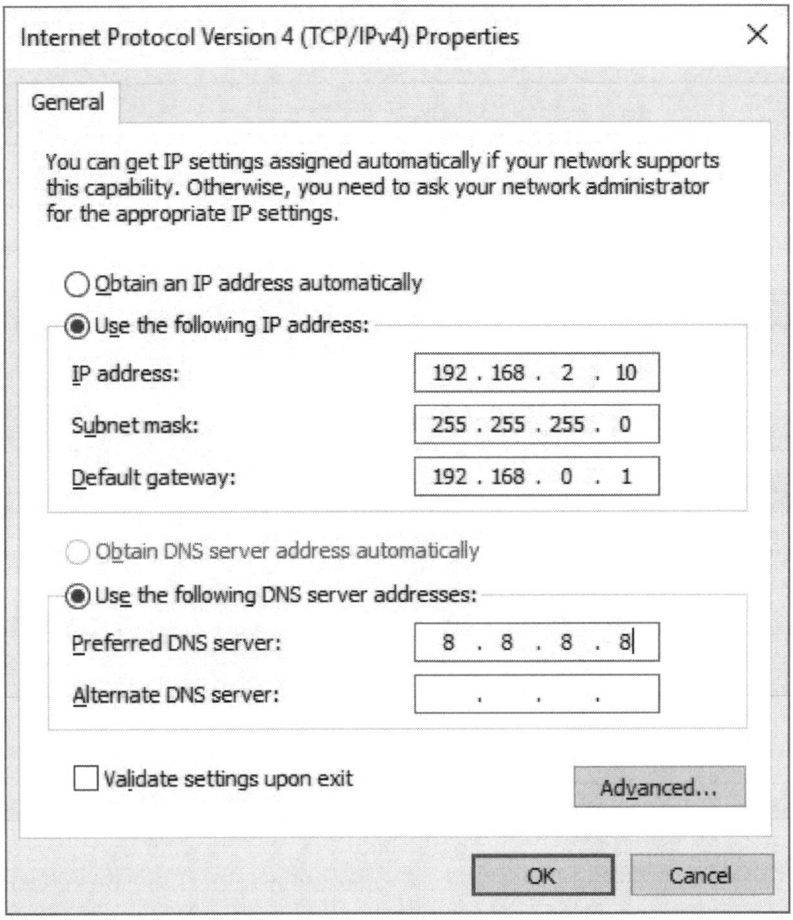

Figure 6.5

If you are using dynamic IP addressing, then you should check your DHCP server or whatever device is providing IP addresses to your computers. In many home and small office networks, the broadband modem\router is giving out the IP addresses to the clients rather than a dedicated DHCP server.

Running the **ipconfig /all** command from a command prompt will tell you if DHCP is enabled on your computer, and also the address of your DHCP server as shown in figure 6.6.

Chapter 6 - Troubleshooting

```
Command Prompt                                                    —   □   ×
(c) 2018 Microsoft Corporation. All rights reserved.

C:\Users\Admin>ipconfig /all

Windows IP Configuration

   Host Name . . . . . . . . . . . . : Computer2
   Primary Dns Suffix  . . . . . . . :
   Node Type . . . . . . . . . . . . : Hybrid
   IP Routing Enabled. . . . . . . . : No
   WINS Proxy Enabled. . . . . . . . : No

Ethernet adapter Ethernet:

   Connection-specific DNS Suffix  . :
   Description . . . . . . . . . . . : Intel(R) PRO/1000 MT Desktop Adapter
   Physical Address. . . . . . . . . : 08-00-27-02-98-FD
   DHCP Enabled. . . . . . . . . . . : Yes
   Autoconfiguration Enabled . . . . : Yes
   IPv4 Address. . . . . . . . . . . : 192.168.0.17(Preferred)
   Subnet Mask . . . . . . . . . . . : 255.255.255.0
   Lease Obtained. . . . . . . . . . : Monday, April 22, 2019 7:47:02 AM
   Lease Expires . . . . . . . . . . : Monday, April 22, 2019 9:39:23 PM
   Default Gateway . . . . . . . . . : 192.168.0.1
   DHCP Server . . . . . . . . . . . : 192.168.0.1
   DNS Servers . . . . . . . . . . . : 209.18.47.63
                                        209.18.47.61
   NetBIOS over Tcpip. . . . . . . . : Enabled

C:\Users\Admin>
```
Figure 6.6

If you know what device the IP address of your DHCP server is referring to, then you can go to that device and check its DHCP configuration settings or its logs to make sure it is working correctly. I have seen where a home router is working just fine for passing traffic, but not for giving out IP addresses to clients.

Another thing I want to mention when it comes to DHCP addressing is if you see that you are getting an IP address that starts with **169.254,** which means that your computer can't contact a valid DHCP server and is using what is called an APIPA address. APAIA (Automatic Private IP Addressing) is when Windows gives itself an IP address rather than just leaving it blank. You can use APIPA addresses on your network, but all of your computers and devices would need to be on the same address range\subnet. APIPA address can't be used to get to the Internet though, so it's not a good idea in general.

Permission Issues
If you encounter a situation where your connectivity is fine, but you are getting messages such as access denied when trying to open a file or folder, then you might be looking at permission issues. These types of issues can be difficult to diagnose because they can go several levels deep. For example, let's say we have a path to a

Chapter 6 - Troubleshooting

shared file called **expenses.xlsx** which is located in a folder named **Finance**. The UNC path to this shared file is as follows: **\\Computer2\Finance\expenses.xlsx**. But on Computer2, the actual path to the file is:
C:\AccountingData\Employees\Current\Finance\expenses.xlsx.

Notice how the actual path on the local computer is much longer than the UNC path to the shared file? This is because the Finance folder has been shared, and when you go to **\\Computer2,** you will only see the UNC share path and not the entire path to that Finance folder.

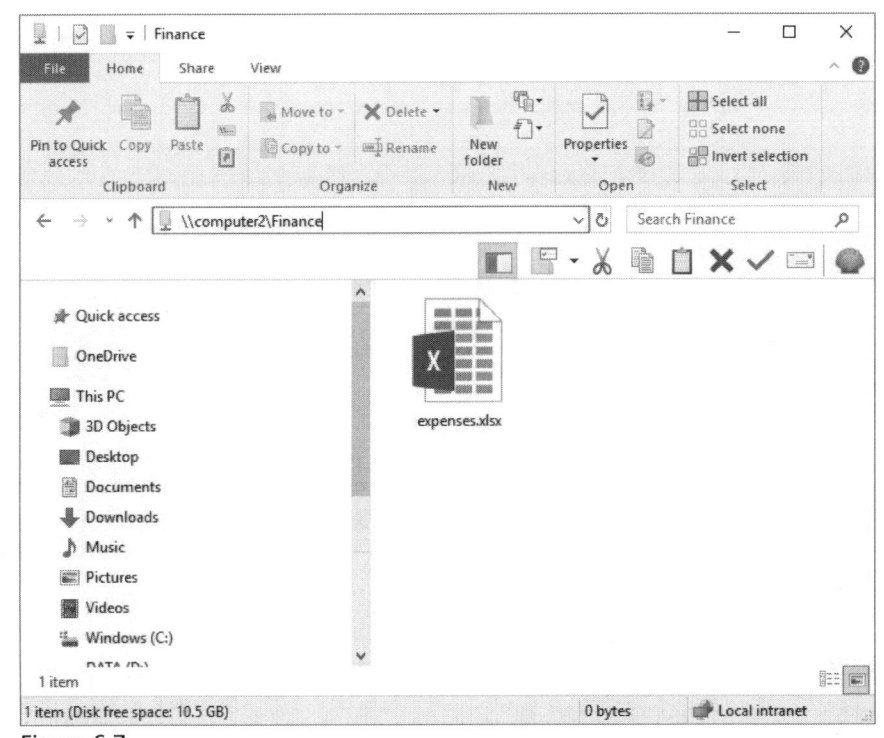

Figure 6.7

The access permissions have been set on the Finance folder, but to get to the Finance folder you need to pass through the AccountingData, Employees, and Current folders. This is called traversing a folder. So, if you are denied access at one of these upper level folders, it will affect you being able to get to the Finance folder. Figure 6.7 shows what happens when I access the **\\computer2\Finance** share. I am able to see the expenses.xlsx file just fine.

Now I will go to Computer2 locally and change the access level of the Employees folder for my account to deny as shown in figure 6.8.

159

Chapter 6 - Troubleshooting

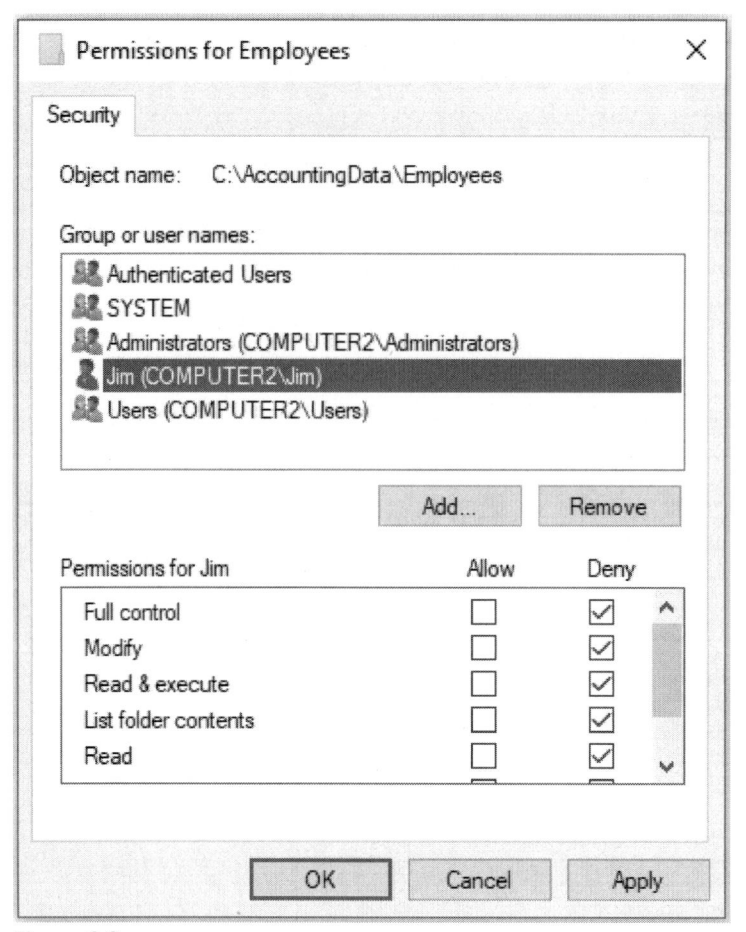

Figure 6.8

Now, when I go to access the **\\computer2\Finance** share, I get the message shown in figure 6.9.

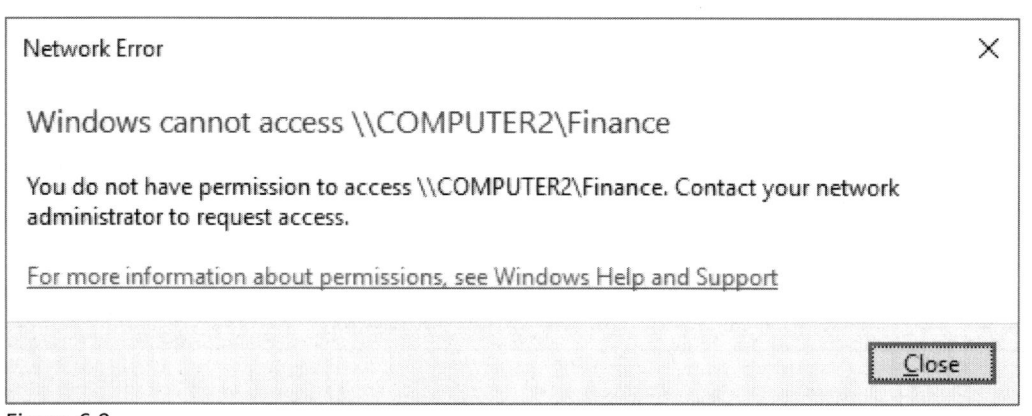

Figure 6.9

160

Chapter 6 - Troubleshooting

To fix this, I will go back to Computer2 and check the access permissions on the Finance folder, as well as folders higher up from the Finance folder because I don't know where the problem lies (even though I really do in this case).

First, I will check the Finance folder itself. When I go to the Security tab, I see that my account is showing the Deny permission for my account. Since it's greyed out and I am not able to change it, that tells me to look at a higher level folder to see if my access is being blocked from there.

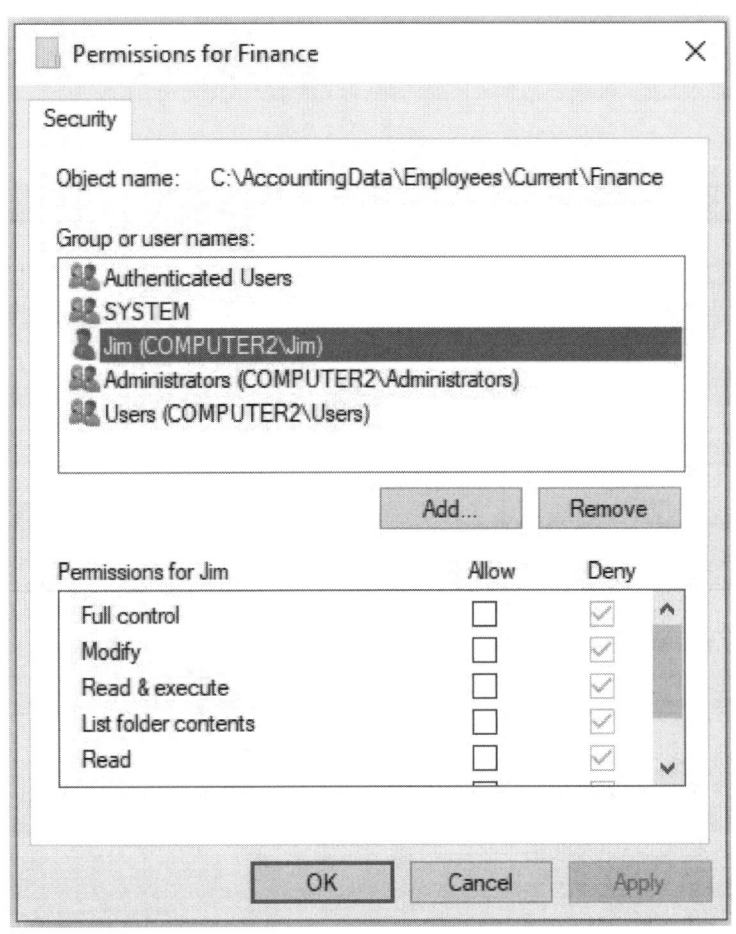

Figure 6.10

Tip: In order to change permission levels on a local computer, you will need to have the appropriate access levels assigned to the account you are using to do so. Otherwise, you will not be able to make the changes necessary to fix the problem.

Chapter 6 - Troubleshooting

Now I will go up 2 levels to the Employees folder since I know that's where the problem is and to save a step for your sake. When I look at the security permissions for my account, I can see that they are not greyed out, meaning I can change them (which I will now do).

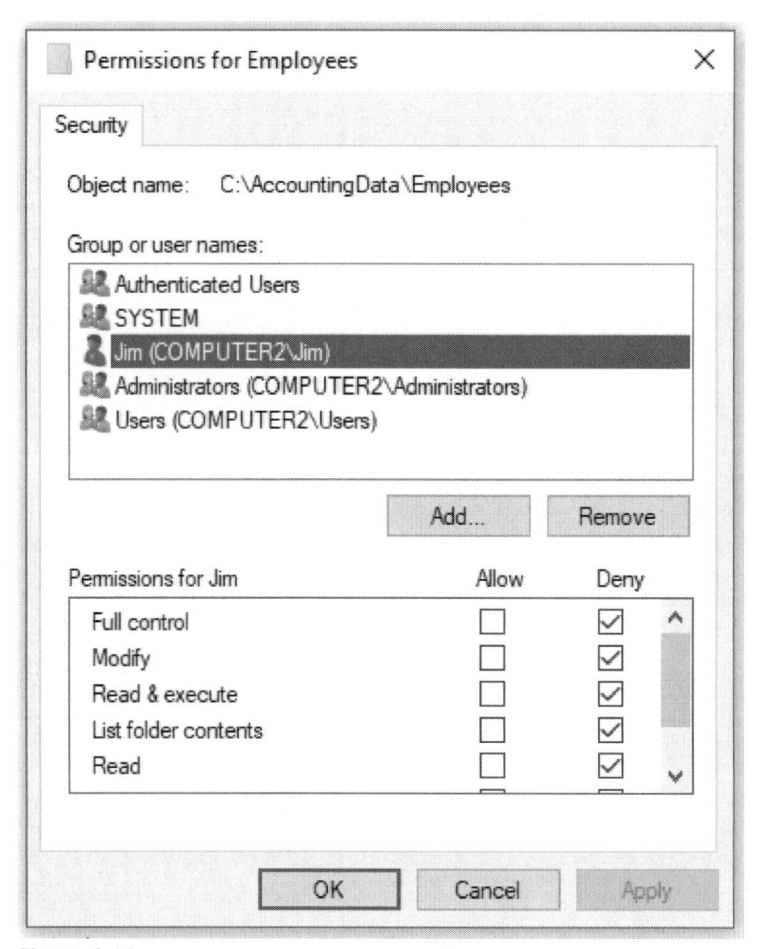

Figure 6.11

This *should* propagate the changes down through the other subfolders so I don't need to make the same change on the Current and Finance folders as well. Remember that our path on the local computer is:

C:\AccountingData\Employees\Current\Finance

The reason these changes are propagated is because *inheritance* is enabled on the folders on Computer2. To see this, you would go to the Security tab of the Employees folder and click on the *Advanced* button. Notice at the bottom left of figure 6.12 that there is a button that says *Disable inheritance*? This tells you that inheritance is

Chapter 6 - Troubleshooting

enabled, which means when you make a change on the folder it will apply that change to all the subfolders and files below it, so in our case: **\Employees\Current\Finance**.

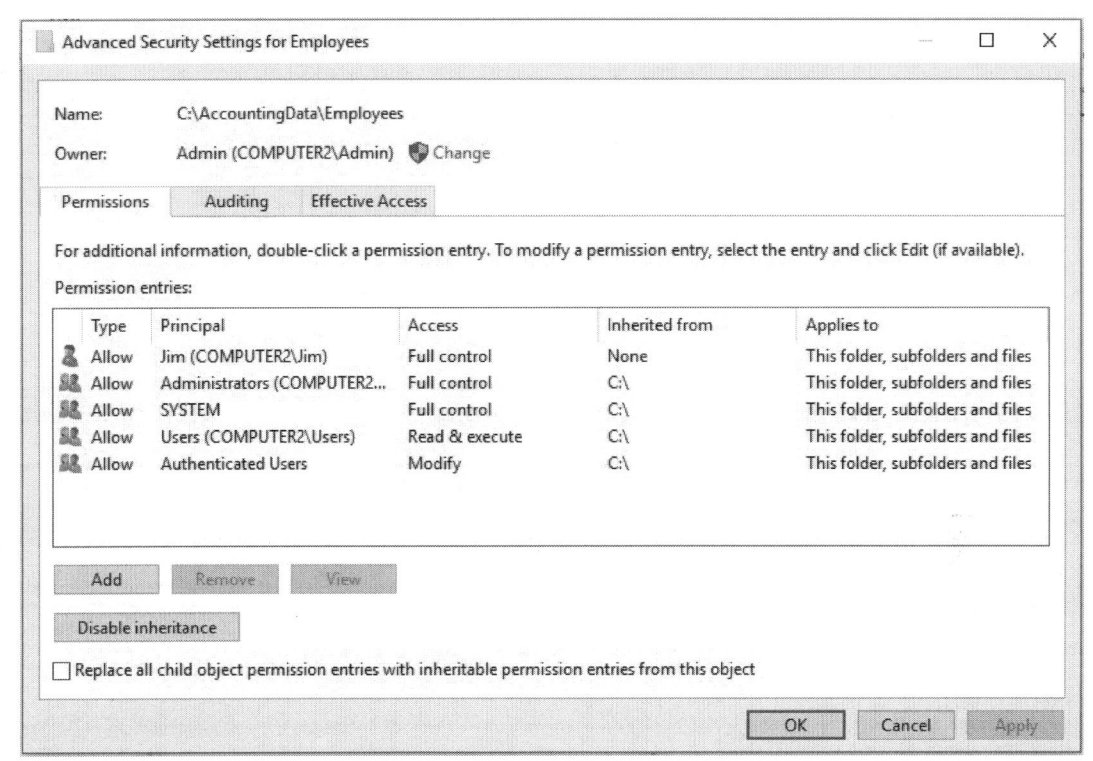

Figure 6.12

There are times when you will want to disable inheritance so a change only applies to the folder you are working on and not the subfolders, and you can do that from here when needed. Also, make note of the checkbox that says *Replace all child object permission entries with inheritable permission entries from this object*. You can use this checkbox to change the permission levels on all lower level folders to match what you have configured from this screen. It will not affect any higher level folders.

One more thing I want to mention while we are here is the *Effective Access* tab. If you take a look at figure 6.13, I have gone to the Finance folder's security properties and chosen Cindy as the user to check the effective access levels for. As you can see, she has been denied full control and also the ability to create files and folders, but she is able to do things such as execute and read files. (This is not a common combination of access permissions, but I just changed them for my example.)

Chapter 6 - Troubleshooting

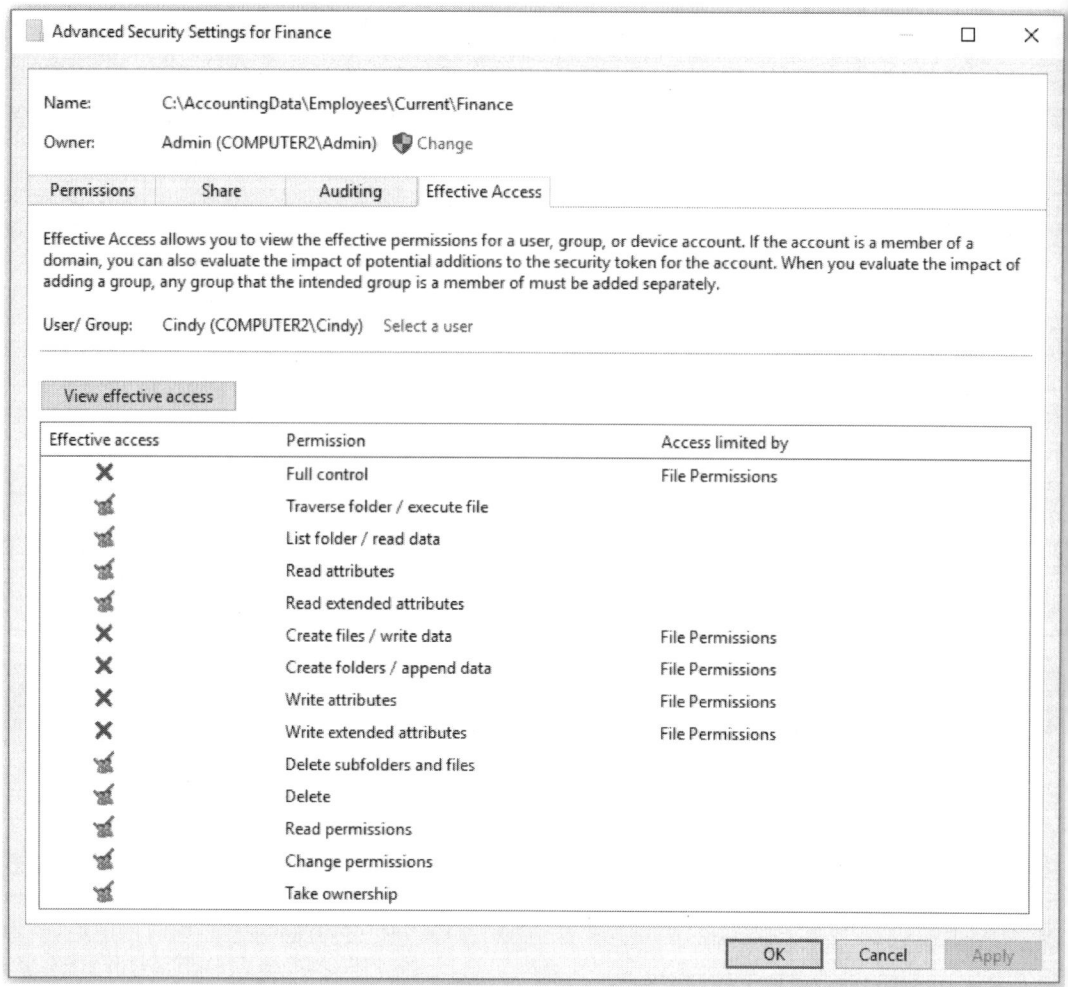

Figure 6.13

Wireless and Internet Troubleshooting
The Internet is one huge network, and when it comes to connectivity problems, wireless Internet connections will be more troublesome than wired connections because there is more involved with making a successful wireless connection compared to a wired connection. There is usually more hardware and software configuration with wireless connections, and that leaves more areas for things to go wrong.

The first step in troubleshooting wireless connections is to see if your computer is connected to your wireless router\access point. The first place you should look is at your wireless connection, and the easiest way to do that is to click on your wireless connection icon in your system tray down by the clock (as shown in figure 6.14). This will tell you if your computer is connected to your access point, and if not, then the

Chapter 6 - Troubleshooting

first thing you need to do is reconnect it. If it doesn't want to connect, then there is an issue with your access point or the wireless device on your computer. You can try to reboot\reset your access point and see if that fixes it, or try to connect to your access point with a different device such as your smartphone or tablet. If other devices connect successfully, then you know it's the computer that has the problem.

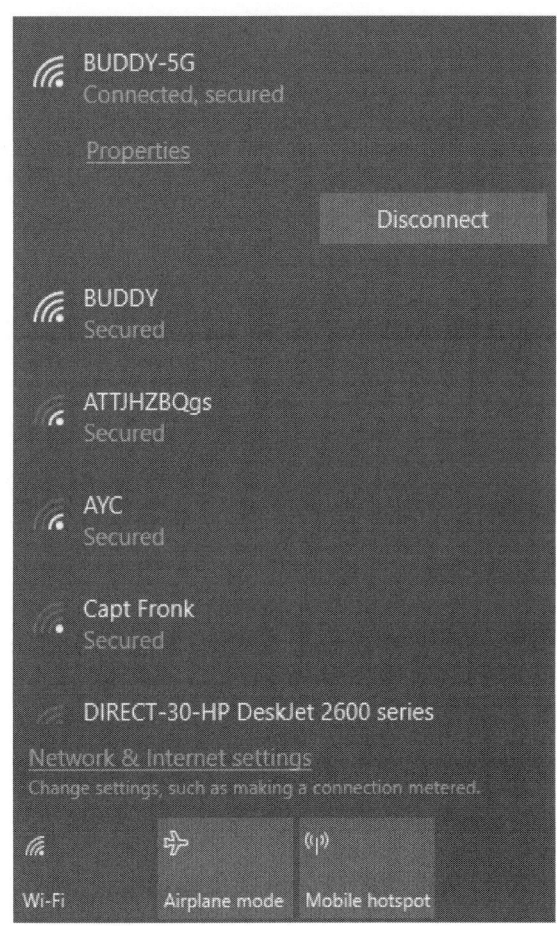

Figure 6.14

Another place you can look to see connectivity status is the Wi-Fi section (figure 6.15). Here you will be able to see what wireless network your computer is connected to and the connection name. Clicking on *Hardware properties* will show you details about your wireless adapter, and also tell you your IP address and what type of security is being used on the connection.

165

Chapter 6 - Troubleshooting

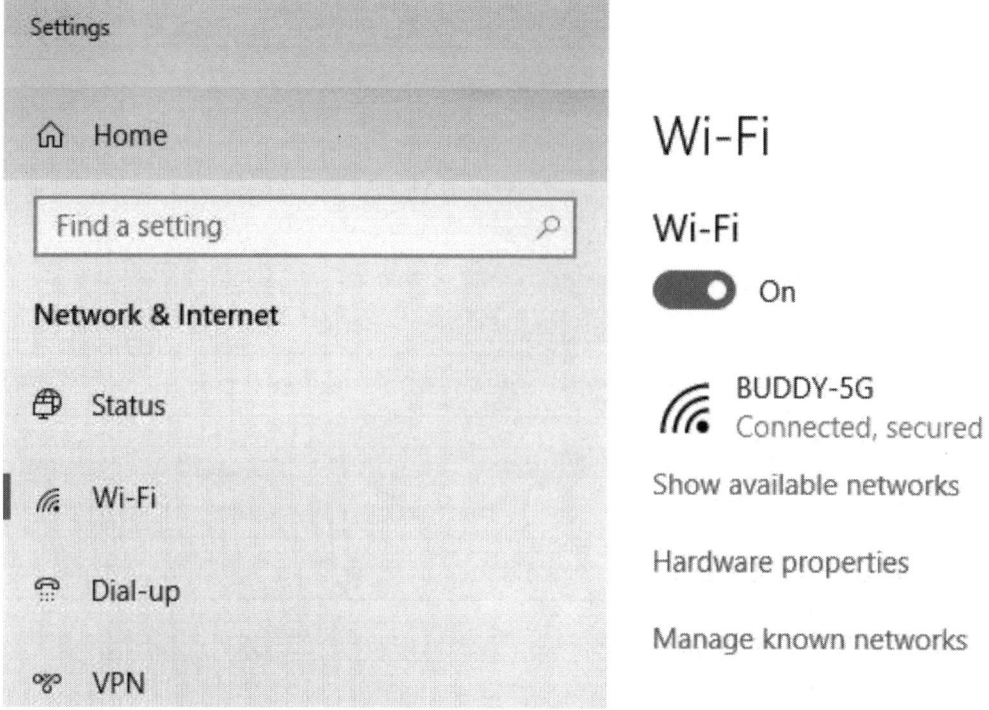

Figure 6.15

There is also some useful information on the Wi-Fi settings screen, such as a link to run the Wi-Fi troubleshooter (figure 6.16). There are also links to open the older Windows network utilities such as the Network and Sharing Center, and a link to check and change your network adapter settings.

> **Tip:** Don't put too much faith in any of the Windows Troubleshooter tools because they tend to not fix any issues way more often than actually helping you figure out the problem.

Chapter 6 - Troubleshooting

Connect to a wireless network

If you can't find the network you want to connect to, select Show available networks to open the list of available networks, select the one you want, select Connect, and then follow the instructions.

Still can't connect? Open the troubleshooter

Related settings

Change adapter options

Change advanced sharing options

Network and Sharing Center

Windows Firewall

Figure 6.16

One important thing to keep in mind with wireless connections is that just because your computer *can* connect to your router\modem\access point, it doesn't mean you will have a connection to the Internet. If your router itself doesn't have an Internet connection, then your computer won't either. The devices that you use to make your wireless connection to the Internet rely on each other for their connection.

Let's say you have your modem from your ISP connected to your wireless router, and then you connect your computer to your router. The modem gets its Internet connection\IP address settings from the ISP, then the router gets its settings from the modem, and finally your computer gets its settings from the router. So, if one of the devices in the chain is not working correctly, then you will not be getting on the Internet. One method you can try is to turn everything off (or unplug the device if there is no power button), and then turn on the modem first and wait until it's fully started. Then turn on the router and wait until it's started, and finally turn your computer back on. For the modem and router, I would wait a few minutes for each one before assuming they are fully booted.

Chapter 6 - Troubleshooting

If your connection to your access point is working, then you will want to see if your computer has an IP address, subnet mask, and default gateway. All of these are needed to make a successful connection to the Internet or any other type of network. You can get this information using the ipconfig command that I discussed earlier. Open a command prompt by typing **cmd** from the run box or Cortana search box, and then type **ipconfig**. Then press enter, and it will show you similar information to figure 6.17.

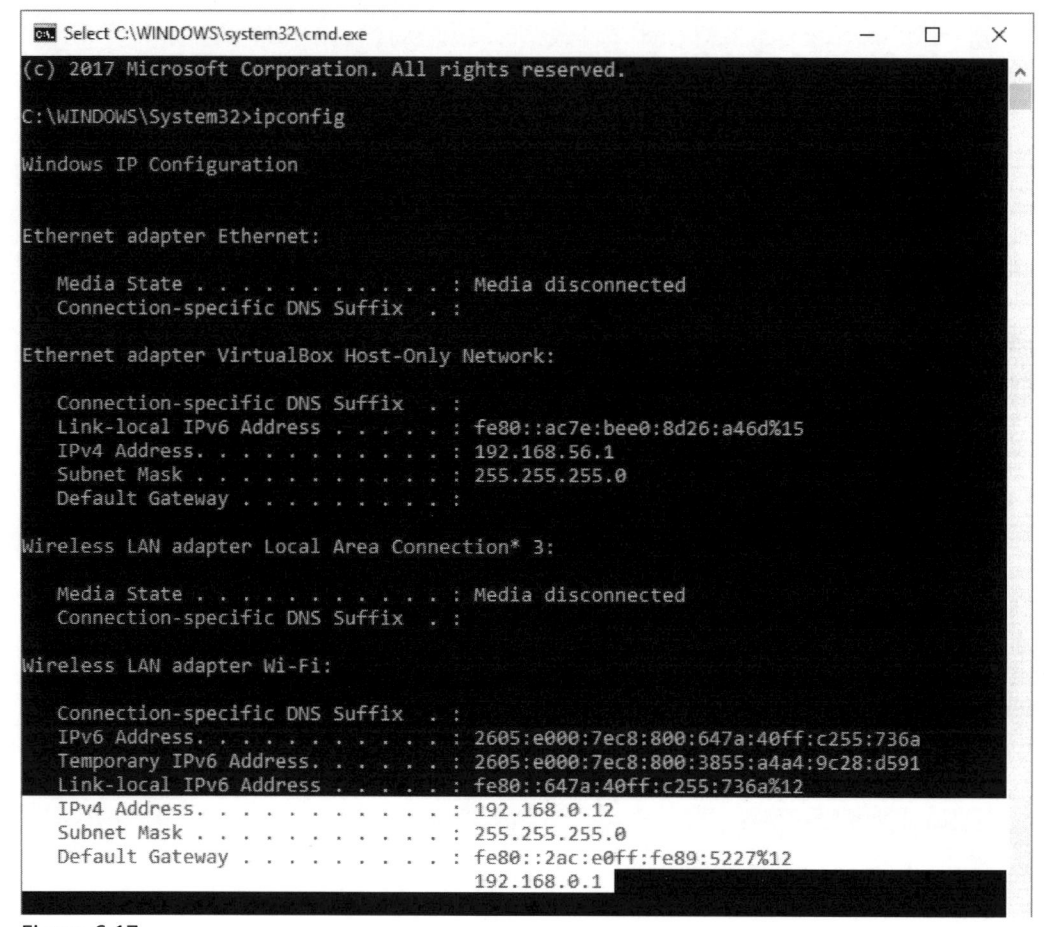

```
Select C:\WINDOWS\system32\cmd.exe

(c) 2017 Microsoft Corporation. All rights reserved.

C:\WINDOWS\System32>ipconfig

Windows IP Configuration

Ethernet adapter Ethernet:

   Media State . . . . . . . . . . . : Media disconnected
   Connection-specific DNS Suffix  . :

Ethernet adapter VirtualBox Host-Only Network:

   Connection-specific DNS Suffix  . :
   Link-local IPv6 Address . . . . . : fe80::ac7e:bee0:8d26:a46d%15
   IPv4 Address. . . . . . . . . . . : 192.168.56.1
   Subnet Mask . . . . . . . . . . . : 255.255.255.0
   Default Gateway . . . . . . . . . :

Wireless LAN adapter Local Area Connection* 3:

   Media State . . . . . . . . . . . : Media disconnected
   Connection-specific DNS Suffix  . :

Wireless LAN adapter Wi-Fi:

   Connection-specific DNS Suffix  . :
   IPv6 Address. . . . . . . . . . . : 2605:e000:7ec8:800:647a:40ff:c255:736a
   Temporary IPv6 Address. . . . . . : 2605:e000:7ec8:800:3855:a4a4:9c28:d591
   Link-local IPv6 Address . . . . . : fe80::647a:40ff:c255:736a%12
   IPv4 Address. . . . . . . . . . . : 192.168.0.12
   Subnet Mask . . . . . . . . . . . : 255.255.255.0
   Default Gateway . . . . . . . . . : fe80::2ac:e0ff:fe89:5227%12
                                       192.168.0.1
```

Figure 6.17

If you are missing any of this information, then you are not getting the correct IP settings from your DHCP server (which will be your modem or router). If you are getting an IP address that starts with 169.254 then that means your computer can't contact a valid DHCP server and is using an APIPA address (which I went over earlier in this chapter). Many times a software or spyware issue can prevent your web browser from accessing web pages properly, so it will look as though your Internet connection is not working when it's really just a browser problem, so run some spyware and virus scans and see if they find anything.

Chapter 6 - Troubleshooting

Another test you can run is to see if your email client is working for sending and receiving emails. If so, then that proves you have an Internet connection and that there is just something wrong with your web browser. This only applies to locally installed email clients and not webmail accounts, since they are accessed via web pages.

If you have more than one web browser, then you should try and use a different one to see if that allows you to access the Internet. If so, then you know the problem lies within your other web browser, and may be a case of a configuration change or spyware infection that has altered its settings. If you only have one web browser, you can try to download another one from a different computer, put it on a flash drive, and then install it on your computer and test it out to see if it works.

What's Next?

Now that you have read through this book and taken your Networking skills to the next level, you might be wondering what you should do next. Well, that depends on where you want to go. Are you happy with what you have learned, or do you want to further your knowledge on networking, or maybe even get into the more advanced Windows networks that use domains?

If you do want to expand your knowledge, or even get certified in Windows networking, then you can look for some more advanced books or ones that cover the specific technology that interests you. Focus on one subject at a time, then apply what you have learned to the next subject.

There are many great video resources as well, such as Pluralsight or CBT Nuggets, which offer online subscriptions to training videos of every type imaginable. YouTube is also a great source for training videos if you know what to search for.

If you are content in being a standalone power user that knows more than your friends, then just keep on reading up on the technologies you want to learn, and you will soon become your friends and families go-to computer person, which may or may not be something you want!

Thanks for reading *Windows Home Networking Made Easy.* If you like this title, please leave a review. Reviews help authors build exposure. Plus, I love hearing from my readers! You can also check out the other books in the Made Easy series for additional computer related information and training.

What's Next?

You should also check out my website at www.onlinecomputertips.com, as well as follow it on Facebook at https://www.facebook.com/OnlineComputerTips/ to find more information on all kinds of computer topics.

About the Author

James Bernstein has been working with various companies in the IT field since 2000, managing technologies such as SAN and NAS storage, VMware, backups, Windows Servers, Active Directory, DNS, DHCP, Networking, Microsoft Office, Exchange, and more.

He has obtained certifications from Microsoft, VMware, CompTIA, ShoreTel, and SNIA, and continues to strive to learn new technologies to further his knowledge on a variety of subjects.

He is also the founder of the website onlinecomputertips.com, which offers its readers valuable information on topics such as Windows, networking, hardware, software, and troubleshooting. James writes much of the content himself, and adds new content on a regular basis. The site was started in 2005 and is still going strong today.

Index

A

Administrative shares 120
APIPA 158

B

BIOS 7
Broadcast 38, 49
Broadcasting 30
Burned-in 30

C

cabling issues 154
Category 5e 35
Client-server 36-38
cmd 17, 41
Control panel 20, 24, 41, 48, 68, 77, 83, 89, 96
Cortana 13
ctrl+alt+delete 92

D

DCHP 23
Default gateway 18, 21, 157, 168
DHCP 19, 20, 22, 23, 156-158, 168
DNS 16, 21, 22, 24
Domain 38, 39
Domain controllers 38, 39
Driver 151, 153
Dynamic 19, 157
Dynamic IP address 16

Index

E

Echo request 82
Electromagnetic interference 155
EMI 155

F

Fiber optic 28
Firewall 76, 77, 79-81

G

Hateway address 19
Groups 68

H

Hardware issues 151
Homegroup 39, 97, 101
Hop 31
Host file 24, 50
Hostname 41, 46, 51, 138
Hosts.txt 52
Hosts file 49, 52
Hub 28

I

ICMP 82
IP addresses 16, 19, 20
ipconfig 17, 18, 21, 157, 168
IP configuration 17, 138
IPsec 77
IPv4 16, 18
IPv6 16, 18, 156

Index

L

LAN 28
Lease 19
lusrmgr 68, 112

M

MAC address 30, 96
Mapping drives 116
Microsoft Account 55
Monitoring 77
mstsc 142

N

NAT 16
NetBIOS 49
netplwiz 89
Network adapter 28
Network discovery 99
Network drive 116
Networked printers 138
NTFS 72, 73, 107

O

Octets 16

P

Packet 31, 82
Peer-to peer 36
Permissions 72, 73, 106, 107
Ping 82

Index

R

RDP 143
Regedit 125
Remote connections 141
RJ45 28, 154
Router 19, 28, 31, 32, 34, 167
Routing protocols 31
Routing tables 31

S

Shares\sharing resources 5, 72, 103, 106, 115, 120, 125, 128, 129
Share permissions 73
Static IP address 19, 140
Switch 30, 38, 154

T

TCP/IP 139, 156
Troubleshooting 151, 164

U

UNC path 74, 75, 99, 117, 120, 137, 159
Universal naming convention 74
User accounts 54

W

WAN 28
Wi-Fi 24-26, 165, 166
Windows firewall 76
Windows update 14, 15
Wireless setup 24
Workgroup 36, 39, 47, 48, 68

176

Printed in Great Britain
by Amazon